UNLEASHING USURY

UNLEASHING USURY

How Finance Opened the Door
for Capitalism Then
Swallowed It
Whole

by
Richard Westra

Clarity Press, Inc

© 2016 Richard Westra
ISBN: 978-0-9860853-3-8
EBOOK ISBN: 978-0-9972870-0-4

In-house editor: Diana G. Collier
Cover: R. Jordan P. Santos

ALL RIGHTS RESERVED: Except for purposes of review, this book may not be copied, or stored in any information retrieval system, in whole or in part, without permission in writing from the publishers.

Library of Congress Cataloging-in-Publication Data
Names: Westra, Richard, 1954- author.
Title: Unleashing usury : how finance opened the door to capitalism then swallowed it whole / Richard Westra.
Description: First Edition. | Atlanta, GA : Clarity Press, Inc., 2016. |
 Includes bibliographical references and index.
Identifiers: LCCN 2016010899 (print) | LCCN 2016016811 (ebook) | ISBN 9780986085338 (alk. paper) | ISBN 9780997287004 ()
 Subjects: LCSH: Loans. | Credit. | Financial institutions. | Capitalism. |
 Economic policy. | Usury--History.
Classification: LCC HG3701 .W47 2016 (print) | LCC HG3701 (ebook) | DDC
 332.7--dc23
LC record available at https://lccn.loc.gov/2016010899

Clarity Press, Inc.
2625 Piedmont Rd. NE, Ste. 56
Atlanta, GA. 30324 , USA
Http://www.claritypress.com

TABLE OF CONTENTS

Acknowledgements / 7

List of Abbreviations / 9

Preface / 11

Chapter One: It's Not *Just* the Inequality Stupid! / 13
    Prolegomenon to the End of Humanity / 18
    "Casino Capital" as a Reincarnation / 23
        of Ancient Usury
    History Shrugged / 26
    Back Out from the Looking-Glass World / 34

Chapter Two: Shylock Unchained / 40
    The Real Feudal World / 43
    Touching the Feudal Bases / 47
    Something Wicked This Way Comes / 53
    Deuteronomy / 60
    Usury against God and Nature / 64

Chapter Three: Shylock Chained / 71
    Making Oliver Twist / 74

Touching the Capitalist Bases / 82
Capital as God, Money as Avatar / 96

Chapter Four: Troubles in Capitalist Paradise / 114
    The Use Value Identity / 120
    The Use Value Ultimatum / 131
    Paradise Lost / 146

Chapter Five: Merchants of Venice on Wall Street / 155
    The Killing / 160
    Money for Nothing / 175

Chapter Six: The Final "Pound of Flesh" / 202
    Money Making Money, Corporate Style / 210
    Usury Without Limit / 215
    "Gilded Tombs do Worms Enfold" / 223

Index / 234

ACKNOWLEDGMENTS

The writing of this book has been influenced by work of numerous scholars. In particular, Robert Albritton, Thomas Sekine, John R. Bell, Makoto Itoh, Martin Hart-Landsberg, Patrick Bond and Seongjin Jeong deserve mention. Thomas Sekine, in particular, has performed an invaluable intellectual service in bringing some of the most important developments in Marxian economics since Marx's *Capital* to light for an English speaking audience. His translation and then brilliant reconstruction and advancement of work by Japanese Marxian economist Kōzō Uno not only reestablishes Marx's economic thinking on a modern footing; it demonstrates that abiding questions in Marxian economics and political economy around which debate in Western academies continues to swirl, unbeknownst to current self-styled Western Marxist gurus, has been answered at levels of logical consistency and conceptual adequacy that their own writings never attain.

In fact, for Japan itself, caught for decades in a deflationary spiral, notwithstanding trillions of yen being pumped onto bank balance sheets, and negative interest rate policy being rolled out in frantic desperation, policymakers would do well to dust off copies of their own masters, such as Uno. That, instead of slavishly swallowing the snake oil peddled in neoliberal dominated Western academies.

As usual, in the process of refining ideas developed in this book I received valuable feedback at select scholarly gatherings. I have had the good fortune over the past decade to be associated at various points with a research collective on capitalism and challenges to it. The home base of this research collective is the Institute for Social Science, Gyeongsang National University, Jinju, South Korea.

Most recently, from December 2013, I have participated as a co-researcher in the activities of that Institute supported by National Research Foundation grant NRF-2013S1A5B8A01055117. Two current conferences where I showcased my work that I would like to mention are: the inaugural conference "From the Thirty Years' Crisis to Multi-polarity: The Evolution of the Geopolitical Economy of the 21st Century World", University of Manitoba, Winnipeg; and the "63 Annual Conference of the Japan Society of Political Economy (JSPE)", Hitotsubashi University, Tokyo.

I have also benefitted from discussions with excellent graduate students here at Nagoya University Graduate School of Law including Wenjia Sun and Volga Can Ozben. Nagoya University is a place where research output is highly valued. The generous time schedule for balancing teaching with research and writing has been a boon to my work. Much appreciated also is the leave I was granted to take up a post as Visiting Professor at the Institute of Political Economy, Carleton University in Ottawa, Canada. Laura Westra offered expertise on Latin terms spicing up the writing in this book. Ayako Fujii provided extremely valuable assistance in preparing the Index and List of Abbreviations. Ann Westra supported me in ways too numerous to itemize.

Whatever faults reside in this book…well, those are my responsibility.

Richard Westra
Ottawa, Canada
2016

LIST OF ABBREVIATIONS

ABS: asset backed security
ARM(s): adjustable rate mortgage(s)
AUM: assets under management
BIS: Bank for International Settlements, the
BOP: balance of payments
BWIMS: Bretton Woods international monetary system
CDO(s): collateralized debt obligation(s)
CDS: credit default swaps
CEO: corporate executive officer
CRA: Community Reinvestment Act
DIDMCA: Depository Institutions Deregulation and Monetary Control Act
DJIA: Dow Jones Industrial Average
EMH: efficient markets hypothesis
EPZ(s): export promotion zone(s)
EU: European Union
FDI: foreign direct investment
FDIC: The Federal Deposit Insurance Corporation
FED: Federal Reserve System
FIRE: finance, insurance and real estate
GDP: gross domestic product
GM: General Motors
GMAC: General Motors Acceptance Corporation
GSE(s): government sponsored enterprise(s)
GVC(s): global value chain(s)
HEL(s): home equity loan(s)
HELOC(s): home equity line(s) of credit
HNWIs: high net worth individuals
ICT: information and computer technology
ILO: International Labor Organization

IMF: International Monetary Fund, the
IPO: initial public offering
ISI: import substitution industrialization
JSPE: Japan Society of Political Economy
M&A: mergers and acquisitions
MBS: mortgage backed security
NASDAQ: National Association of Securities Dealers Automated Quotations
NEM: non-equity mode
NIPA: National Income and Product Accounts
NIRP: negative interest rate policies
OBS: off-balance sheet
OECD: Organization for Economic Cooperation and Development
OPEC: Organization of Petroleum Exporting Countries
OTD: originate to distribute
PFI: private financial intermediary
QE: quantitative easing
R&D: research and development
REPO: repurchase agreement
SEC: Securities and Exchange Commission
SEZ(s): special economic zone(s)
S&L: Savings & Loan
SLABS: student loan asset-backed securitization
SIV: special investment vehicle
TNC: transnational corporation
TINA: there is no alternative
TNB: transnational bank
UHNWIs: ultra-high net worth individuals
US: United States
WB: World Bank, the
WWI: World War I
WWII: World War II
ZIRP: zero interest rate policies

PREFACE

To make the case that changes across the capitalist world at the turn of the 21st century put into play a global financial system which operates as a reincarnation of ancient usury requires several key steps.

Chapter One, using broad brush strokes, introduces the problem.

Chapter Two takes the reader on a fascinating journey back into West European history to see antediluvian "loan capital" or usury in action as it helped to bring then civilization to the brink of collapse.

Chapter Three shows how capitalism chained Shylock as it reset finance and trade with socially redeeming purposes tied to the nexus of capitalist profit making and the social prosperity capitalism initially spreads.

Chapter Four follows the trail capitalism blazes as it increasingly forsakes its market operating principles for a welter of extra-economic, extra-capitalist supports to survive in the 20th century. Yet, notwithstanding these supports, what remains of capitalist substance drives advanced economies into crises.

Chapter Five exposes the big lie of the neoliberal era. It shows clearly why there is no longer any capitalism in the 21st century. Production centered economies are largely disintegrated with the activities which had acted as their engines of growth now disarticulated across the globe. What currently exists is a global network of casino economies with financial systems which operate not like capitalist markets, but like Merchants of Venice expropriating wealth through money games.

Chapter Six concludes with a closer look at how wealth is expropriated upwards to a cabal of über rich. It offers the disturbing prognosis that the current global trend of finance carving "pounds of flesh" from the bones of humanity is leading toward a new Dark Age of world barbarism.

| Chapter One |

IT'S NOT *JUST* THE INEQUALITY, STUPID!

In the world of economics writing 2014 will go down in history as the year of Thomas Piketty. His book *Capital in the Twenty-First Century* became a global best-seller with translations multiplying. Piketty's ability to crunch statistical data has few rivals...the work of Angus Maddison comes to mind, though Maddison, best known amongst economic history buffs, never became a celebrity phenom. Getting back to Piketty, you know you have hit a chord when literally "everyone", from reigning Nobel Laureate liberal economic gurus like Paul Krugman and Joseph Stiglitz to a Who's Who of radical Lefties trip over each other to get critical commentaries on your work into print. Indeed, by now it is probably difficult to find one specialized economics journal which has not devoted a whole issue to Piketty!

Why then after all the brouhaha do I start my own book with a "Johnny comes lately" reference to him? Is this a shameless cry for attention? Hardly! In fact, nothing acts as a better foil for getting at what I want to say in this book than Piketty's title. This is so because in my view it is the most disingenuous title imaginable! Putting the argument of my book in the simplest terms: if we actually had "capital" or capitalism "in the 21st century" – excepting its impacts on climate change and the environment (topics for another book) – we would *not* be witnessing economic goings-on literally devouring humanity, fomenting a more rapid demise of humanity than the three-quarters century or so looming extinction from climate change.

It goes without saying, capitalism spawns inequality. While Piketty's title alludes to Marx and Marx's *Capital*, actually it was Marx's radical contemporaries who first made that case. Capitalists owned and workers did not, *voila*. And while Marx would go on to refine the arguments of his radical contemporaries, pejoratively dubbed "utopian socialists", capitalism was also seen by them as being prone to economic ups and downs, as it was viewed as "alienating" and "exploitative". These latter facets of capital continue to resonate in the 21st century for anyone in the so-called "99 percent" who still has a job to go to. In short, we need not belabor the ills of capitalism. They were and are very well known.

But Marx was no fool! And we need not be made one. So let us briefly deal with what was really at the root of Marx's work up front, now, to avoid being misled by pretenders. Then we can move on to the topic of this book.

For Marx, this thing he dubbed *capital* and the capital*ism* it drove had a method or "logic" to its madness. And this logic, Marx maintained, operated only under particular historical conditions which took hold first in Britain and Western Europe gradually from the 18th century. Further, seemingly lost for much of the academic Left (who should really know better), is Marx's point that the conditions for the operation of capital's logic are historically delimited. This all has nothing to do with Marx's *other* belief that the horror of capitalism as it took shape in his 19th century world would spark heroic working class struggles to overthrow it. Capitalism, Marx understood, like all forms of human societies, is destined to be outpaced by history as the conditions of its existence decompose and become a drag on the human future. And let us be crisply clear on another question. Marx never guaranteed socialism will be the "end of history". Marx recognized that as capitalism putrefies the possibility also existed for the world to enter a dark age of untold barbarism.

We will examine the historical conditions for the existence of capitalism below in as non-technical terms as possible. For now, it is important to think about Marx's reasoning. Over the long sweep of precapitalist history, Marx discerned the existence of major epochs of human society. Each epoch, according to him, was marked by a discrete kind of social system. The earliest societies, Marx referred to as *primitive communistic*, entailing modes of hunter-gathering, people living in extended clans or tribes, and surviving close to subsistence levels. In the following major epoch, a significant leap in human sustenance possibilities occurred based upon sedentary agriculture and the marshaling of vast *slave* labor forces to construct everything from infrastructure to monuments. The Roman Empire is the cardinal example here. Our next historical epoch, is that represented by the social system called *feudalism*. Its best known exemplars persisted for close to a millennium in Britain and Europe. Yet systems sharing a family resemblance with feudalism existed across Asia, with that most closely approximating British feudalism found in Tokugawa Japan.

While historians continue to nitpick at his broad sweep generalizations, what actually struck Marx most in all this was that yes, precapitalist social systems all had "economies". After all, even the proverbial cave man and cave woman had to satisfy their material reproductive or "economic" needs before they chilled, carving cave art into stone walls of their dwellings. But prior to the dawn of the capitalist era, it made no sense to refer to such practices as an "economy". And no one ever considered making such a reference. The reason for this is best explained by economic historian Karl Polanyi. Polanyi, instructively, was not a follower of Marx or "Marxism". His exhaustive historical studies, however, revealed what Marx had surmised a century prior: this being how economic life in precapitalist economies is always bound up with religion, culture, custom, superstition, politics, ideologies, and is indistinguishable from these. And it is only in the capitalist era that economic life appears to "disembed" from these other social practices.[1]

Marx himself approached the question somewhat differently. According to him the interweaving of economic life with the social practices outlined by Polanyi ensnared human beings and their economic livelihoods in *interpersonal* social relations of varying sorts. And in the epochs of *slavery* and *feudalism* these interpersonal social relations which trapped human beings were constituted by interpersonal relations of *domination and subordination.*

What set the capitalist historical epoch apart, for Marx, is the peculiar way *capitalism* as a social system "freed" human beings from precapitalist interpersonal relations of domination and subordination. In his iconic phrase, capital converted these concrete interpersonal social relations into abstract, *impersonal* relations "between things".[2] Quite simply Marx meant that with society "freed" from interpersonal material relations established by "extra-economic" forces like religion – for example, God endowed Kings with "divine right" to rule and mandated peasants to work to feed them – it was the impersonal *cash nexus* of the capitalist market which established connections and order among "freed" individuals. Put differently, rather than being imposed *ex ante* (in advance) by one or more interpersonal social practice, social order was established *ex post* (after), following the "free" transacting by individuals, according to their own interests, in the market. Indeed, one of the early political arguments for capitalism during the period of its gestation was that even authoritarian pretenses of rulers will be brought to heel by expansion within societies of markets and trade.[3]

However, for Marx, the "freeing" of individuals from social relations of domination and subordination to then interact through the cash nexus in capitalist market society came with a catch. This brings us back to what I referred to as the logic of capital. The "catch" here is that capitalist market operations have their own built-in social goal which is profit making. It is impersonal and abstract and measured quantitatively in terms of accumulated mercantile wealth, or money. The point being that it does not matter whether individuals are greedy or altruistic or more or less selfish or even trade fairly or unfairly because, in the end, the capitalist market acts like a Stalinist dictator. That is to say, as we "free" individuals freely pursue our self-seeking proclivities in the capitalist market they are distilled into outcomes beyond *us* as individuals. Outcomes which, at least when capitalist market operations get their way, are true to the social goal of *capital* – profit making or augmenting abstract mercantile wealth. In other words, in capitalist society the economic does not just "disembed" from the social as Polanyi saw things. It wields the social for its own self-aggrandizement according to Marx.

In this fashion, the extra-economic coercions and compulsions of the past are replaced in capitalist society, at least paradigmatically, by impersonal *economic* compulsion. This is the foundation for the "freedoms" human beings in capitalist societies experience in comparison with past historical societies or even Soviet style societies which reinstated extra-economic compulsions. And it is also the condition of possibility for *economic theory*, a point we will return to.

But there is more. For Marx, there exist three dimensions of the capitalist economic compulsion of profit making. The first dimension is that operating in the service of an abstract, quantitative goal beyond the self-seeking interests of any given individual, capitalism produces great social wealth. Capitalist societies have thus yielded human progress far quicker than their historical predecessors. And quicker than their erstwhile 20th century Soviet style competitors. The second dimension, a view Marx shared with some of his more astute contemporaries, and now his self-styled heir Piketty, is that with capitalist mercantile wealth augmentation has come a long list of ills. A gaping inequality is one of these.

Why, however, do I maintain above that by paying careful attention to what Marx actually wrote we need not be made fools by pretenders? This relates to the third dimension. I am not just taking a shot at Piketty here, but also at many supposed Leftist illuminati. The fact of the matter is that while capitalism has been going about its historical business of profit making, simultaneously distributing wealth asymmetrically, alienating and exploiting workers, fostering boom and bust cycles along the way – as a byproduct of its idiosyncratic activities, it must nevertheless necessarily touch some very clear "bases" otherwise it could never exist, or reproduce itself, as a human society in the first place. Indeed, every social system in Marx's historical schema, whatever their foundational principles (slavery, serfdom and so forth), has to meet similar "tests" or touch key bases to materially reproduce a human society. This is another part of what is entailed in the statement that there is a "method" to capitalist madness – though we still need to cover a few more steps before we elaborate upon what precisely is meant by the idea.

But for now, we are at least better positioned to spell out the central argument of this book.

Prolegomenon to the End of Humanity

When I charged Piketty with having the most disingenuous title imaginable for his bestseller, and asserted that if we actually *had* capitalism in the 21st century humanity would not find itself being devoured by its own economy, it was meant in the context of capitalism having a method to its madness. Notwithstanding the significant changes capitalism has undergone from the early 19th century when it firmly took hold in Britain, it has always managed to meet the tests of "viability" necessary for its material reproduction as a human society. We can also say this notwithstanding the different "varieties" of capitalist economies that characterize advanced capitalism as it spread through Western Europe to the United States (US), and across the so-called white settler colonies. Finally, capitalism managed to touch its bases notwithstanding the morphing relation between market operation and government or state support markets. Though there are some caveats to be added on the latter issue which we will get to in a later chapter.

So, what is the central point of this book? And why is this book so vital for getting a handle on the economic morass humanity finds itself mired in that it is compulsory for you to read it? In a nutshell, cumulative economic changes, proving ever so slippery to adequately analyze, set in from the last few decades of the 20th century that proved unparalleled in their impact. Except for quibbles over precise dates and the *causa causante*, there is consensus among critical economists that the most glorious period or "golden age" of capitalism which began in the 1950s (for those living advanced states at least) fell into crisis by the late 1970s.[4] And, it was on the road from there to the 21st century that untoward things started to happen.

First, advanced economies including Britain, the US, major European (EU) states, built prosperity across the 20th century around expansion and sophistication of their industrial production systems and rising real and social wages for the mass workforces that operated them. Yet, by the time the century came to a close, these industrial production systems had been sliced and diced with their components disarticulated across the globe. Parallel to this slicing and dicing of industries the decently paid jobs of the industrial mass workforce vaporized.

In precapitalist feudal societies agriculture employed around 80 percent of the population, basic manufactures about 10 percent and services 10 percent. Capitalist economies were marked by industry and manufacturing which, on average, employed 40 to 50 percent of total labor forces in advanced states. Agriculture employed around 20 percent and services the remainder. At the dawn of the 21st century, manufacturing in the US employed around 20 percent of the workforce, agriculture less, with services reaching over 75 percent of all employment.[5] Other advanced economies maintained somewhat more of their manufacturing employment, though not much more. Capitalism and its logic, however, are attuned to material goods production-centered activities where close to half of working age people are employed in manufacturing related activity. Current employment profiles of advanced economies do not look very capitalist. And these profiles run too much interference on capitalist logic as we will see.

I would not hold my breath waiting for a brave new world of so-called emerging markets to pick up the capitalist slack.

Across the globe as a whole, populations are no longer shifting from agriculture to industrial and manufacturing employment as they did from the dawn of the capitalist era. And when they do move, which is in no way a *fait accompli*, they do so from agriculture direct to services.[6] Bear in mind, countries around the world that had never come close to the sort of employment profile of the advanced capitalist economies are now experiencing the perverse phenomenon of "premature deindustrialization" as their nascent industrial systems disintegrate.[7]

Such glaring trends are precisely what Marx understood by the conditions of possibility for capitalism being outstripped by history. As expressed in his iconic *Preface*, at some point in history the forces of production (existing technologies and related production and energy accouterment) will come into conflict with relations of production (existing social relations of ownership and work) to initiate a period of social and economic tumult until humanity hopefully manages to socioeconomically reconfigure its world.[8] Before the latter lapses into barbarism, that is. What could be more robust evidence of such a conjuncture being reached now than the fact that industrial sectors which had powered employment and prosperity in whole advanced economies through the 20th century can now be operated to satisfy global demand from a single province in China? What is the rest of the world, then, supposed to do?

Second, with the commanding heights industrial and manufacturing of advanced capitalist economies being sliced, diced and disarticulated across the globe, advanced states, foremost and initially the US, commenced an economic restructuring by extensive fixed investment in information and computer technology (ICT). US private business enjoyed a particular bonanza here as government-military investment in ICT during the Cold War had been gargantuan. As the Cold War drew to a close, the releasing of ICT secrets to the public were rapidly coveted and turned into private fortunes.[9] Investment in ICTs from the 1980s into the 21st century exceeded that in every other equipment category including transportation, airplanes, and so forth.[10]

ICT investment initially dazzled economists. It led to triumphal chants by neoliberals that a "new economy", characterized by "brain work", was smoothly replacing the old one, rejuvenating prosperity and employment along the way. Yet the so-called new economy only exacerbated the disinternalizing by business of their production-centered activities. This could occur because ICTs empowered giant transnational corporations (TNCs) to control and monitor global production and sales while outsourcing their each and every facet to multiple tiers of contract suppliers and retailers.

More crucially, widespread deployment of ICTs across society, particularly by the TNC "branded" businesses superintending global production networks, wreaked havoc with capitalist pricing. This in turn undermined the ability of advanced capitalist economies to allocate resources in a way that met a crucial test of their viability for human society. Remember what I described above as the *ex post* "order" arrived at in capitalist market operations? The "objective" or market "rational" pricing that achieves this is predicated upon specific historical conditions – where the goods in social demand are standardized mass produced commodities, largely bringing to bear standardized material inputs, all produced by labor power which itself is standardized or, as Marx understood it, "commodified".[11] Put differently, optimal capitalist market pricing hinges on what capitalist markets largely measure: the *direct costs* of the standardized material goods, standardized material inputs and commodified labor power.

However, widespread application of ICTs in advanced economies rendered production activities more knowledge intensive. The increase in knowledge intensity enlarged the proportion of *indirect costs* over direct costs in the pricing of goods. But capitalist market operations are not attuned to indirect costs. Hence as TNC operations became more knowledge intensive it saddled both individual TNCs and the economy at large with necessarily "subjective" or haphazard pricing of goods. And with the increasing haphazard pricing of goods, including price for labor inputs, the ability of the market to perform its historic role in allocating resources is subverted.

Even TNCs' own internal allocative mechanisms became skewed. Evidence shows that from the 1980s to the years preceding the 2008 meltdown, the US economy experienced a marked trend of disaccumulation. US total stock of fixed capital was 32 percent lower than it would have been had the trajectory of "golden age" accumulation been maintained[12] via investment of TNC earnings in the form of *profit* in production-centered endeavors. Earnings of TNCs were siphoned off by a host of *unproductive* knowledge workers – ICT hardware and software patent owners along with software developers and engineers, advertizing firms, fashion designers, and so forth – in the form of *rent*, technological and otherwise. Think iPhone here where approximately 60 percent of its sales price flows to precisely such rent.[13] It is instructive to discover Citigroup, in its infamous "Plutonomy report", touting precisely this new economy-wide dynamic of rent seeking and opportunistic skewing of social wealth to a pack of über-rich.[14]

Third, it is really from one last momentous change that our story in this book takes off. By the end of the 20th century *capital*, as a factor of production, for the first time since the dawn of the capitalist era, was no longer "scarce"! Vast pools of money in the form of pension funds, insurance funds, mutual funds, money market funds, eventually hedge funds and even so-called vulture funds could be found bloating everywhere in advanced economies. En masse these funds, which actually constituted social saving, were dubbed "institutional investors". By 1995, such funds resident in the 17 major Organization for Economic Cooperation and Development (OECD) economies amassed holdings worth $21.9 trillion equal to 103 percent of OECD 17 GDP. Indeed, in 2007, these so-called institutional investors held what would become known as "assets under management" (AUM) valued at $62.8 trillion: an amount equal to 181.7 percent of OECD GDP.[15] In the US 2007 holdings of institutional investors amounted to a staggering 211.2 percent of GDP.[16]

Ever so prescient internationally-renowned business management guru Peter Drucker had already maintained in the early 1990s, that the exploding of such bloating pools of money heralded the existence of a "post-capitalist society".[17] Drucker's argument was simple. These funds significantly eclipsed *real* capital derived from production-centered activities. The latter could no longer be counted on to provide employment opportunities as we also suggest. For Drucker, given that such pools of money were actually composed of deferred wages and other social savings, they did "not fit any known definition of capital". Drucker then went on to claim that there exists "no social, political, or economic theory that fits what has already become reality". His conclusion was that a peculiar socioeconomic constellation had emerged of "capitalism without capitalists", or a "post-capitalism".[18] The remainder of Drucker's book deals with how new "knowledge" based institutional and organizational forms might be crafted to manage such a post-capitalist society.

Unfortunately for humanity, and this is where our story takes its dark turn, Drucker's progressive, futuristic vision of capitalism without capitalists never came to pass. Rather, as moribund aristocracies during the twilight of feudalism invoked the "divine right of kings" to cling to power, so capitalist ruling class neoliberal ideologues erupted in shrill chants of "there is no alternative" (TINA), so doggedly determined were they not to see power slip from their greasy clutches. Even though right before their eyes, capitalism was being outpaced by history. This is what ruling classes do!

"Casino Capital" as a Reincarnation of Ancient Usury

I dub the bloating pools of funds idle money or simply, "idle M".[19] What this notion captures is the fact that there existed absolutely no possibility for these funds to ever be invested as real capital in production-centered activities. Therefore, from the perspective of the capitalist circuit of investment-production-sales-profit-reinvestment-production and so forth, such funds remain *idle*. Initially, the funds pooled aimlessly. The possibility of their application in endeavors other than "saving" was largely circumscribed by law. But an unholy cabal of TNC capitalists, transnational banking (TNB) capitalists and assorted private financial intermediary (PFI) investment capitalists, along with their bought and paid for government lackeys, had other designs. Their intention was to put these bloating pools of idle M to work in an orgy of money games.

Sweet sounding names given this process are well known... "liberalization", "deregulation", "privatization". Neoliberal public relations imagery portrayed capital as being "freed" from its "big government" tethering. With "the market" thus re-inseminated, so prosperity lost with the golden age demise would be restored. But as already noted, what neoliberal policy freed was *not* real capital but swelling oceans of idle M which had no possibility of ever being invested as capital. Nor was anything that operated like a *capitalist* market reborn. What instead was hatched was a global financial system which operated like a casino. Susan Strange famously referred to this monstrosity as "casino capitalism".[20]

Real capitalism, for all its profit taking, harsh inequalities, exploitation, alienation, boom and bust oscillations, had met the necessary tests to ensure the material economic viability of the human societies in its grip. Even its financial activities had socially redeeming value as we will make clear in a later chapter. And, to the extent they contributed to profit making, they also engendered social wealth and rising living standards as the trajectory of advanced economies from the dawn of the capitalist era to the 1970s show.

Not so with the predatory ravages of newly freed idle M! What this book demonstrates is that the global financial system of "casino capital" constitutes the modern reincarnation of ancient *usury*. Usury, as we will explore in the next chapter, was inveighed against for religious and moral reasons. Yet, like incest, which was subject to social sanctions on similar grounds, usury carried deep-seated and far-reaching deleterious repercussions for humanity. In precapitalist societies usury or money-lending had no socially redeeming value. It corrupted all social classes and fostered widespread indebtedness and expropriation of land in ways that ultimately unraveled staid interpersonal socioeconomic relations through which precapitalist societies reproduced their material lives.

G.W.F. Hegel captured the socially destructive bent of ancient money lending through his notion of "the measureless".[21] That is, money lending or antediluvian "loan capital", as Marx sometimes referred to usury, is *indifferent* to *what* its funds will be used for. And it is *indifferent* to *how* loan plus interest will be repaid. Repayment amounts are arbitrarily set and may be so exorbitant that the debtor is destroyed or must strive to ruin others to meet obligations. Dramatic illustration of such a situation is Shylock's setting of a "pound of flesh" as the "measure" of debt repayment.

Like snake oil administered by desperate parents to cure their offspring's terminal cancer, so the unleashing of vast pools of idle M across the global financial system was touted as the palliative for a putrefying global capitalist economy. By the mid 1980s capital accounts of the major advanced economies in the world had been opened to its unholy flows. This excrescent reincarnation of ancient usury with its casino operations, arcane instruments of financial gamesmanship, and lavish rewards to the croupiers sitting atop the TNBs, PFIs and financial wings of TNCs, appeared to create "profits" without production.[22]

Not capitalism without capitalists as Drucker envisioned the future, but capitalists *without* capitalism!

Yet, you may ask, is it not true that global GDP grew during the last decades of the 20th century and into the 21st? Well…yes. The rub here is that from the 1980s commencement of our neoliberal decades, it was *credit* which actually emerged as "the world's greatest growth market". By end 2005, global "outstanding financial claims" were "3.7 times as high as global GDP"![23] The speculative casino of idle M was set in motion through leveraged play and debt generated money. Each faux GDP growth bang demanded ever more borrowed bucks and greater leverage. The global bubble and bubble burst cycles this dynamic sparked required governments to step in at every burst and sweep under the public rug as many of the bad debts as it could. And so the casino would spring to life once more with increasingly Himalayan levels of debt and out-of-this-world leverage. Think

$10 trillion to $20 trillion of *actual* monies today animating an estimated $1 quadrillion (just try writing out the zeros here!) in notional value of derivatives contracts! [24]

When capitalists *had* capitalism, no matter the extent of borrowing driven by their "animal spirits", as long as rates of profit in their capitalist businesses exceeded rates of interest, loans would be repaid and debtors turn into lenders. However, for our capitalists *without* capitalism, with scant pickings in the way of profit from *real* production-centered economic activity, there is no way to pay off debt except through deductions from current incomes (private or government) and/or more debt.[25]

On the more debt side, each bubble/burst cycle becomes ever more life throttling each time around. Today, with trillions in "quantitative easing" (QE) plus zero interest rate policies (ZIRP) or even negative interest rate policies (NIRP) failing to shock the globe out of its deflationary descent there is literally nowhere to go. In fact from end 2007 to second quarter 2014 global debt spiked by $57 trillion to $199 trillion, an amount constituting 286 percent of global GDP.[26]

On the deductions from current incomes side, what is politely referred to as "austerity" has already befallen much of humanity to service previously incurred debt. That earlier debt was the collateral damage from previous bubbles and bursts. In short, without real profits, besides more debt as above numbers illustrate, our capitalists *without* capitalism are limited to *expropriations* and predatory pillaging of the planet. And, without the logic of capitalism governing global financial activities, their debt exploding and predatory expropriations become "measureless". This makes them reincarnations of usurers of old. They must literally carve what remains in "pounds of flesh" from the bones of humanity to meet debt obligations. Greece is really just the hors d'oeuvre.

History Shrugged

As the global financial meltdown gathered pace in late 2008, no less a personage than Queen Elizabeth II, on a visit to

London School of Economics, asked why economics wizards had not seen the crisis coming?[27] A Who's Who of London School of Economics professors, major UK financial policy makers, and regulatory officials wrote the Queen back a year later. Their letter contained drivel about "psychology" of market participants, the "feel good" aura of wealth effects from the bubble, fallibility of "risk" models, failure to derive proper conclusions from mounting "global imbalances", and so on.[28] But not one word in the letter on what Peter Drucker, quoted above, alludes to:the fact that no economic theory exists to explain what Drucker saw as the new realities of pooling idle M in the US and global financial system.

Drucker, of course, was largely referring to mainstream economic theories, including so-called "heterodox" mainstream theories, in their multiple variants, such as those peddled at the London School of Economics visited by the Queen. I have argued, however, that Marx's work does offer us a foundation for thinking about the world economy and global financial system today. This brings us back to a question we promised above to pursue – the condition required for economic theory to be possible. And why when we truly understand what that is, the reason why economic wizards including those responding to the Queen had little in the way of answers becomes ever so clear. And further, why does being crisply clear on the conditions required for economic theory to be possible arise as such a pressing matter now?

Whenever I think of mainstream neoclassical economics, a film I had seen decades ago always comes to mind. The film is *Victor Victoria* starring Julie Andrews. In it, Andrews, a woman, is cast as a woman playing a man performing as a female impersonator. Why a not particularly good film that by all accounts I should have forgotten is conjured up by my mind when I think of neoclassical economics springs from its motif of subterfuge or dressing-up to be what you are most definitely not.

The historical antecedent of neoclassical economics is what Marx referred to as "classical" political economy. Classical theorists like Adam Smith and David Ricardo were very much mouthpieces for the ascendant bourgeois class. This is not to say that their explorations of the political economy of the day did not produce important knowledge upon which critics like Marx built. After all, it was only *after* Smith and Ricardo that Marx began referring to "vulgar" economics. The problem resided in their bourgeois class blind faith that pursuit of abstract mercantile wealth in impersonal markets was somehow the "natural" way of organizing human material affairs. With bourgeois tinted glasses coloring their vision, so to speak, classical political economy began to read all human history in bourgeois terms.

Anthropologist David Graeber examines the way Adam Smith blithely time travels through history with *Star Trek* like ease.[29] Smith commences with an axiom. We all know it. Every economics textbook starts with it. Human nature has us programmed to "trade". And, further, to be self-aggrandizing in that endeavor. Smith then beams us back to what is purportedly the dawn of time, or "rude society" of "savages". We are told how a division of labor based on barter spawned there. When such "trading" activity met up with a dearth in coincidence of wants, money was invented as the more efficient means for applying our natural propensities. Before we know it, we are transported back to Smith's English village with his butcher, baker and brewer. And, as per the supposed "natural" human propensities, they are found still "trading" to make us all "better off".

Graeber, of course, is at pains to show such rendering of barter is a "myth". Not only as per the central theme of his tome was barter in any form historically preceded by debt or "credit" of sorts. But when it occurred in a fashion even remotely approximating Smith's story, it did so at the boundaries of societies which otherwise would have no contact. Marx had also actually made that point clear over a century prior in *Capital*. As he put it, "exchange... first begins on the boundaries of... communities".[30]

This then brings us to what emerges as a major sub plot in Graeber's book. For purposes of the discussion at hand it is actually this sub plot, rather than Graeber's long winded historical excursus on debt, which is most instructive, given the way it resonates with what also jumps out at us from economic history studies of Polanyi. This is the fact that when activities resembling "trade" or "exchange" did occur in precapitalist economies, they did so enmeshed in, and shaped by, the concrete interpersonal socioeconomic relations giving "order" to the societies in question.

It was through these concrete interpersonal socioeconomic relations that precapitalist societies touched the necessary bases, as we put it, to viably reproduce the material lives of their populations. Impersonal "trade" (with other societies) was always perceived as potentially disruptive to staid precapitalist interpersonal relations and to be imbibed with caution. An example of the practice by which communities sought to ensure their internal interpersonal socioeconomic relations were protected from social impacts of "trading" activity is the creation by the Tokugawa Shogunate in 1634 of *Dejima*. *Dejima* or "protruding island" in the bay of Nagasaki was constructed to accommodate first Portuguese then Dutch merchants. Neither was permitted to cross into Nagasaki. Their wares entered Nagasaki under conditions chosen by local power structures. In effect, Dejima maintained a firewall separating discrete socioeconomic relations of Tokugawa Japan from that of merchant practices of other lands.

Within precapitalist communities, principalities, kingdoms, even nascent states, whether "trade" or "exchange" occurred as direct bartering of goods, barter mediated by forms of money, and so forth, it did so enmeshed in webs of interpersonal social relations. Graeber captures such precapitalist conditions of "exchange" as follows: "When objects of material wealth pass back and forth...the key principle seems to be that the sorts of things given on each side should be considered fundamentally different in quality, their relative value impossible to quantify... Nor did anyone ever consider making such a calculation".[31]

Put differently, the notion of "exchange" has always had two fundamentally different meanings. One meaning captures the exchanging of goods idiosyncratic to precapitalist economies with their interpersonal socioeconomic relations. There, the "value" of something is its value "in use". Value in use, or *use value* as Marx understood it, is a subjective determination rooted in the concrete-particular sensuous, heterogeneous *qualitative* properties of things.

However, in capitalist economies the meaning of "exchange" is entirely different. Socioeconomic relations in capitalist economies are impersonal and abstract. Self-seeking individuals transact impersonally with their "things" in capitalist markets through the cash nexus. Whether it is a good being brought to market in capitalist economies by the capitalist, or even a worker selling their labor power as a commodity, the owner is not interested in its value in use or use value. Rather the owner is interested in its value in "exchange" or simply its *value* as a value object for sale or "trade". Value in this sense is a quantitative determination. Of course this fits with the social goal of capitalist market operations: profit making or augmenting of abstract-general mercantile wealth, itself quantitative. Mercantile activities across capitalist markets are thus carried out with studied indifference to use value.

This is why Marx maintained capitalism is a historically delimited society. Capitalism arises in human history when the constellation of goods in social demand along with appropriate technologies to produce these lend themselves to suppression of qualitative considerations in material life in favor of quantitative ones. Predominately agricultural societies of the past, where human material life was dependent in so many ways on the vagaries of nature, are ill suited to capital. Similarly, future potentially eco-sustainable societies would also be ill suited to capital as the nimbleness required for managing human material affairs will necessitate bringing qualitative use value considerations back into economic life while suppressing quantitative value ones.

This takes us back to *Victor Victoria*! Neoclassical economics refers to its field as "economics". Implicit in this designation is that something timeless or transhistorical is being studied. After all, is it not the case that every human society necessarily engages in "economic" practices? This, of course, is true, as we have already noted. The problem for theory begins with the fact that prior to the dawn of capitalism the "economy" is bound together with other social practices – religion, culture, custom, politics, and so on. It is thus indistinguishable from these, making it nonsensical under such historical conditions to even begin to talk about something called "the economy" or "economic" practices. And no one ever did. It is only in the capitalist era that the economy appears "transparently" for theory to explore, disentangled or dis-embedded from the interpersonal social relations brought to bear by the above social practices.

Bracketing for the moment questions of the veracity of classical or neoclassical bourgeois theories, despite their self-identification as theories of "economics", the truth of the matter is they could *only* begin their work as theories of the *capitalist* economy. This is the case, as we emphasize, because prior to the capitalist era the "economy" never appears transparently for theory to study. It is inseparable from other precapitalist social practices. Hence to understand how economic life operated in precapitalist feudal Europe, for example, we would need to examine the web of hierarchical interpersonal relationships constructed around religion, custom, politics and ideology of the period.

But, like Popes, Princes and Kings of old, who justified their rule as "natural" through the doctrine of the divine right of kings, so the new apostolate of bourgeois ideologues sought to justify the rule of capital as a natural order. However, if it was recognized that human economic life had been successfully operated across millennia by principles other than those of capital, then this would directly contradict the professing by bourgeois ideologues of their society as a natural order. It would also lead to questions about the future. That is, if it is determined that capitalism is only one way of organizing human material affairs, then the intellectual door is opened to thinking about its limitations. And also to thinking creatively about how human economic life might be better organized to satisfy human economic needs and promote human flourishing.[32]

Further, the recognition that other principles of economic life preceded those of capital complicates the job of theory. Let us think about it this way. Economic life is a necessary part of every human society. It consists fundamentally of the metabolic interchange between human beings and nature which furnishes the useful goods or use values of human reproduction. This is the "hardware" of human material existence. However, the hardware requires a particular operating system or "software" to set the reproduction process in motion. The different social systems such as slavery, feudalism and capitalism each work with their own software, so to speak. Yet, because it is only in the study of capitalism that we become aware of the existence of "the economy" disentangled from other social practices, theory must first elaborate the logic or method of capital. This elaboration necessarily must expose all the deep secrets of its operating system. This is to say it has to demonstrate how capital meets its social goal of profit making while simultaneously ensuring it touches all the bases to cement its viability as a human society. And, because the study of capitalism provides the first window of opportunity for examining economic life as such, the study of economies of other historical social systems can only proceed in the comparative light of in-depth study of capital. But they cannot be studied using the same methodology as applied to the study of capital given the unique historical features of the latter.[33]

For classical political economy and its progeny, neoclassical economics, the aforementioned truth is anathema. Rather, true to its ideological mission of proffering capitalism as a natural order it must pretend, like *Victor Victoria*, to be something that it is not. Not a woman pretending to be a man pretending to be a woman, of course. But a story that begins with ideologically cherry picked ad hoc attributes of capitalism. Then it claims these as transhistorical principles of a field it self-refers to as "economics". This field designed to reinforce TINA is dressed up as universal science through its mesmerizing application of high calculus of physics. That is, neoclassical economics starts as ideology pretending to be an economic theory masquerading as a science. But, when this ideology masquerading as a science is discovered to be a theory of a nonexistent society (even its one-sided views of capitalism tell us little about how the capital actually operates), and is stripped bare, well... only ideology remains.

However, to pull off such subterfuge the classical theorists and neoclassical economics need a sleight of hand of Biblical proportions. They found this in the conflation, commencing with Smith, of two very different meanings and kinds of "exchange": value in use or use value, and value "in exchange" or simply *value* as a mercantile quantity indifferent to use value. As we have noted, in precapitalist economies "exchange" in only the rarest of circumstances occurs outside webs of interpersonal relationships. And whether it involves direct face-to-face barter or is mediated by money its considerations are always the heterogeneous qualities of goods. And its purpose is always use value in consumption. Such "exchanges" are then but one-off affairs. They also contain no dynamic for making society "better off". as the perceived gain of one barterer today, which is in any case subjective based on the differing quality of the goods bartered, would nevertheless be lost tomorrow.

Further, it is nonsense to believe that the operating system of capitalism can be grasped from the perspective or "preferences" of the consumer. To understand capitalism theory must begin from the perspective of the *seller*, or the capitalist. This is the case not just because profit making is the fulcrum upon which capitalist order revolves but because the capitalist market software is oriented to processing the quantitative price signals of society-wide mercantile exchange of "things", with *indifference* to their use value, in the service of that abstract social goal.

However, by conflating two different meanings of exchange and building its theory on "exchange" of use values directed toward consumption, classical political economy furnished groundwork for a transhistorical theory of "economics". It also set the stage for the phantasmagoric model building of neoclassical economics. And while the mathematical prowess of the model builders is admirable, the models purporting to teach transhistorical "economics" in the end do not depict an "economy" of any society that has actually ever existed in human history. Not precapitalist societies as careful excavations of the historical record show. And not capitalism as Marx makes clear.

As Japanese economist Thomas Sekine argues, at least the classical political economists attempted to keep it real by maintaining a central role for merchant arbitrage in their conceptualizing of "exchange". Neoclassical economics textbooks, on the other hand, suppress even that aspect of market operations with their notion of "substitution" (choosing to consume one thing instead of another). As Sekine parodies it, when little Adam and little David play in their sandbox, they are certainly preoccupied with the "sacrifice" each would have to make to maximize units of their individual satisfaction in the time they could play with a particular toy. Being well behaved mini-bourgeois they negotiate until their "offer curves" intersect optimally. However, such sandbox play is a clear example of interpersonal, face-to-face "exchange" of use values where qualitative considerations are paramount. In fact, "exchange" in this context is more akin to "sharing" than "trading". And so, the subterfuge and *Victor Victoria* carry on.[34]

We will have occasion in a later chapter to peruse recent shifts in neoclassical economics theorizing. In particular, those shifts to which sophisticated high calculus is being applied with great scientific pretense to maintain the ideological masquerade in the face of difficult to ignore real economic change. Our constant here, however, is always the phantasmagoria of the whole "economics" enterprise. And this brings us back to our questions at the beginning of the chapter and why they matter.

Back Out from the Looking-Glass World

"Economics," like the earlier doctrine of divine right of kings, with the latter's supporting view of a cosmos where the world is flat, constitutes the historical battleground. Instead of divine inquisitions, neoclassical economics is defended by its apostolate through thought patrolling of "economics" departments in elite universities, the control of tenure and publication in "prestigious" outlets; even the awarding of the prestigious Nobel Prize for "science". Corporate media, as well, endlessly parrots its spurious claims. On its basis, only platitudes can be offered in efforts to explain forces that are effectively devouring humanity. In fact even the question asked by Queen Elizabeth – why the 2008 meltdown was not "predicted" – is an expression of the wrong-headed hold neoclassical economics has on our thinking. Questions about "prediction" should be asked to meteorologists about why a thunderstorm today when the weather report promised sun for our picnic? Or, why did an earthquake of such magnitude occur so unexpectedly and foment a tsunami? In short, when dealing with forces of nature humans must rely on prediction.

But, notwithstanding the shrill ideological chants of bourgeois economists which uphold capitalism as a natural order, the reproduction of human economic life across its historical forms is *not* a force of nature. It is not like natural powers that we must learn how to better conform to by predicting their ups and downs in order to protect or shelter ourselves. Human economic life is a social construct. It is set in motion by purposive actions of real flesh and blood human beings. And it can be changed by purposive social action of those same human beings accordingly.

What Marx's work teaches us is that to fully grasp the economic predicament humanity faces the last thing we need is to *predict*. Rather, we need to *"post-dict"*, to enter a new word into the lexicon of economic studies.[35] In the framework of this book, "post-dicting" means that in order to explain why the global financial system works as a reincarnation of ancient usury, we need to understand the method of capitalist madness. That is to say, we need to be clear on how capital touched all the bases to viably reproduce economic life of a human society as a byproduct of its fundamental goal of profit making or augmenting abstract mercantile wealth. And what the specific historical conditions are which enable the operations of capital as such. And finally, what forces contributed to the historical undoing of capitalism, giving rise to the bloating oceans of idle M that would turn to feed on remnants of capitalism and ultimately on humanity itself.

Concomitant with the foregoing, we need to reexamine how capitalism brought society back from the abyss it stared into as the feudal carapace began to crumble. This draws us back, in turn, into probing the matrix of interpersonal socioeconomic relations and extra-economic practices which held the precapitalist feudal social system together, and that reproduced the material life of feudal populations. Only on that basis can we make sense of why the money economy of merchant trade and money lending proved so destructive to feudal civilization. And why usury was so universally inveighed against by the precapitalist power order.

Putting this all in the simplest terms, to make the right economic decisions for the human future we have to understand how we got to where we are. Neoclassical economics can tell us nothing about our past or our present. It offers a monotonic perspective from which it is impossible to even begin to differentiate among kinds of economy existing across the sweep of history as demanded by this study. Its pretentious mimicking of high physics advances so-called "policies" which essentially have us scurrying around blindly as global financial trends unleashed by reincarnated usury have not only swallowed capitalism whole but are threatening to carve the final "pounds of flesh" from the bones of humanity and destroy civilization itself.

Endnotes

1   See Karl Polanyi, *The Livelihood of Man* (London: Academic Press, 1977).
2   Karl Marx, *Capital Volume I*, Chapter 1 Section 4 "The Fetishism of Commodities and the Secret Thereof", https://www.marxists.org/archive/marx/works/download/pdf/Capital-Volume-I.pdf, p. 48.
3   Albert O. Hirschman, *The Passions and the Interests: Political arguments for Capitalism before Its Triumph* (Princeton, NJ: Princeton University Press, 1997).
4   See Michael J. Webber and David L. Rigby, "Growth and Change in the World Economy Since 1950", in Robert Albritton, Makoto Itoh, Richard Westra and Alan Zuege (eds.) *Phases of Capitalist Development: Booms, Crises and Globalizations* (Basingstoke: Palgrave/Macmillan, 2001).
5   Richard Westra, *Political Economy and Globalization* (London:

Routledge, 2009) p. 141.
6   International Labor Organization (ILO), *Global Employment Trends* (Geneva: International Labor Office, 2008).
7   Sukti Dasgupta and Ajit Singh, "Manufacturing, Services and Premature De-industrialization in Developing Countries: A Kaldorian Empirical Analysis", Center for Business Research, University of Cambridge Working Paper no. 327, http://www.cbr.cam.ac.uk/pdf/WP327.pdf.
8   Karl Marx, *Preface* to *A Contribution to the Critique of Political Economy*, https://www.marxists.org/archive/marx/works/1859/critique-pol-economy/preface.htm.
9   See the discussion in Linda Weiss, *America Inc.? Innovation and Enterprise in the National Security State* (Ithaca: NY: Cornell University Press, 2014).
10 Gérard *Duménil* and Dominique *Lévy*, *Capital Resurgent: The Roots of the Neoliberal Revolution* (Cambridge, MA: Harvard University Press, 2004) pp. 152-3.
11 The commodification of labor power for Marx is central to the operation of capitalist logic. Its historical conditions are the destruction of precapitalist peasantries and separation of workers from the land and direct access to their conditions of material sustenance. Also, workers whose lives were tied to a given craft must also be separated from direct access to their conditions of material sustenance and wherewithal of the trade they plied. Paradigmatically, capitalism begins its operations as a social system when all forms of production are coveted in the hands of the capitalist, bourgeois class. And workers find themselves with one good or "property" to "trade", which is their power to labor. Or labor power. But this is not *just* about class division. The efficiency of capitalism is bound to the fact the labor power of the working class is made available in the market like any other input into production. Capital must be able to purchase this labor power and apply it to producing *any* good according to supply and demand conditions and opportunities for profit making. This does not mean that workers have no "skills". It is simply the case that capitalism necessitates a class of working people who have rudimentary skills that can be applied to different production tasks as required by capitalist market forces.
12 Gérard Duménil and Dominique Lévy, *The Crisis of Neoliberalism* (Cambridge, MA: Harvard University Press, 2011) pp. 151-2.
13 *The Economist*, "Slicing an Apple", August 10 2011, http://www.economist.com/blogs/dailychart/2011/08/apple-and-samsungs-symbiotic-relationship.
14 Citigroup, "Plutonomy: Buying Luxury, Explaining Global

15   Imbalances", October 16 2005, http://pissedoffwoman.wordpress.com/2012/04/12/the-plutonomy-reports-download/ (accessed August 10 2015).

15   International Monetary Fund, *Global Financial Stability Report: Grappling with Crisis Legacies*, September 2011, http://www.imf.org/external/pubs/ft/gfsr/2011/02/pdf/text.pdf accessed August 11 2015.

16   Eric Gonnard, Eun Jung Kim and Isabelle Ynesta, "Recent Trends in Institutional Investor Statistics", *Financial Market Trends* (Paris: OECD, 2008).

17   Peter F. Drucker, *Post-Capitalist Society* (New York: Harper Business, 1994).

18   Drucker, *Post-Capitalist Society*, pp. 69-70, 77-8.

19   See Richard Westra, *The Evil Axis of Finance: The US-Japan-China Stranglehold on the Global Future* (Atlanta, GA: Clarity Press, 2012) Chapter 4.

20   Susan Strange, *Casino Capitalism* (Manchester: Manchester University Press, 1997)

21   *Hegel's Science of Logic*, Translated by A.V. Miller and Edited by H.D. Lewis (Atlantic Highlands, NJ: Humanities Press International, 1989) p. 371.

22   My terminological usage here, along with the theoretical antecedents upon which I develop this notion, are similar to that of Costas Lapavitsas, *Profiting Without Production: How Finance Exploits Us All* (London: Verso, 2013). We will have the opportunity to engage further with his excellent book in later chapters.

23   Charles R. Morris, *The Two Trillion Dollar Meltdown* (New York: Public Affairs, 2008) p. 140.

24   Michael Sivy, *Time*, March 27 2013, http://business.time.com/2013/03/27/why-derivatives-may-be-the-biggest-risk-for-the-global-economy/.

25   Such debt dynamics were already detected in the early global economic bubble/burst cycle. See, for example, Elmar Altvater and Kurt Hubner, "The End of The U.S. American Empire?" in Werner Väth (ed.) *Political Regulation in the "Great Crisis"* (Berlin: Sigma, 1989) pp. 61-2.

26   McKinsey Global Institute, *Debt and (not much) deleveraging*, February 2015, http://www.mckinsey.com/insights/economic_studies/debt_and_not_much_deleveraging.

27   Andrew Pierce, "The Queen asks why no one saw the credit crunch coming", *The Telegraph*, November 5 2008, http://www.telegraph.co.uk/news/uknews/theroyalfamily/3386353/The-Queen-asks-why-no-one-saw-the-credit-crunch-coming.html.

28 British Academy Forum, "The Global Financial Crisis – Why Didn't Anybody Notice?" http://www.britac.ac.uk/events/archive/forum-economy.cfm.
29 David Graeber, *Debt: The First 5,000 Years* (Brooklyn, NY: Melville House, 2012) pp. 24ff.
30 Marx, *Capital Volume I*, Chapter 2, p. 60.
31 Graeber, *Debt*, p. 112.
32 For those interested in pursuing this point see Richard Westra, *Exit from Globalization* (London: Routledge, 2014).
33 On how such a theory may be formulated see Westra, *Political Economy and Globalization*, pp 13-42.
34 Thomas T. Sekine, "General Equilibrium and the Dialectic of Capital", in John R. Bell (ed.) *Towards a Critique of Bourgeois Economics: Essays of Thomas T. Sekine* (Berlin: Owl of Minerva Press, 2013) p. 198.
35 See Thomas T. Sekine, "Uno's Method of Marxian Economics", in Bell (ed.) *Towards a Critique of Bourgeois Economics*, p. 10.

| Chapter Two |

SHYLOCK UNCHAINED

In a fascinating little book, *The Passions and the Interests: Political arguments for Capitalism before Its Triumph*, adverted to briefly in Chapter One, economic historian A. O. Hirschman summarizes what has been the most widely accepted narrative on the rise of capitalism.[1] That narrative, propounded by Max Weber, best fits with the ideas of neoclassical economics which were gestating as Weber wrote. Weber was clearly smitten by neoclassical economics' foundation in the "rational" calculating individual supposedly animating capitalist market operations. Indeed, Weber grounds his sociology on a notion of archetypical human action exemplified by "economics'" so-called rational individual. This became Weber's key "ideal type" of action against which other forms of "less" rational or irrational action is assessed.[2]

For Hirschman, Weber's book *The Protestant Ethic and the Spirit of Capitalism* has been particularly influential through the case it makes for the symmetry between capitalist "rationality" and that of Protestantism which emerged historically just preceding the rise of capitalism. Of course, if we follow Adam Smith, our human nature to "truck and barter" is already cemented from our days as "savages" in "rude society". However, in Weber's argument, there must have been some psychological impetus just prior to the rise of capitalism which drove individuals, particularly those that became capitalists, to get down with the rational benefit-maximizing individual program in a big way.

Hirschman, however, questions the extent to which capitalism is kick-started by the psycho-social rejuvenating power resident in the Protestant search for individual salvation. Rather, what he proposes is "that the diffusion of capitalist forms owed much to [a]... desperate search for a way of *avoiding society's ruin*".[3] In his own narrative of struggle between the "passions" and the "interests" Hirschman does touch on the lure provided to "passions" by the spreading money economy. In this chapter I want to make a stronger case not necessarily about the "passions" of destructive elements in society inflamed by new potentialities of abstract wealth but of how the money economy of merchant arbitrage and the predatory ravages of antediluvian "loan capital" acted as a corrosive acid of sorts which dissolved staid precapitalist social relations of material reproduction. And, that at a certain point, with no way back, human material existence had to be reset on a new basis to avert the ruin of what civilization theretofore bequeathed.

Again, notwithstanding continuous nitpicking at his broad-sweep framework by historians, anthropologists and others, Karl Marx's pithy theory of "historical materialism" sketched in the famous *Preface* offers an unrivalled way of thinking about macro historical change. To be sure, and this is unfortunate, Marx's iconic words in the *Preface* have led both some "Marxist" fellow travelers and certainly Marx's raft of detractors to fault him as the arch determinist. In the *Preface*, for example, Marx states:[4]

> At a certain stage of development, the material productive forces of society come into conflict with the existing relations of production or – this merely expresses the same thing in legal terms – with the property relations within the framework of which they have operated hitherto. From forms of development of the productive

> forces these relations turn into their fetters. Then begins an era of social revolution. The changes in the economic foundation lead sooner or later to the transformation of the whole immense superstructure.

Or, elsewhere, in his early, *The Poverty of Philosophy*, Marx observes:[5]

> In acquiring new productive forces men change their mode of production; and in changing their mode of production, in changing the way of earning their living, they change all their social relations. The hand-mill gives you society with the feudal lord; the steam-mill, society with the industrial capitalist.

In this book I do not want to get sidetracked in abstruse debate with today's Marxist illuminati. In other work I make the case that Marx's economic studies of the capitalist economy in *Capital* meet the test of science. His formulations on precapitalist economies and related historical trends, which Marx could *only* have developed in the comparative light of the study of capitalism, constitute an *approach* to human economic history in toto. It is a comprehensive approach which, arguably, has few rivals, as declared above, but an "approach" nevertheless rather than *theory* in the strong sense of scientificity.[6]

This brief segue is intended simply to underscore that, while Marx offered up structural principles upon which he believed systemic social change in major historical epochs would be impelled, he never claimed that the process would emerge automatically, without human agency. Indeed, though it appeared from his 19th century perch that working class revolution and socialism was nigh, Marx's "post-dicting" cautioned him to acknowledge that untold barbarism might well follow capitalist breakdown. The early historical model for such a prognosis was the transition from *slavery* to *feudalism* in Europe. So catastrophic was the social dislocation following the collapse of the Roman Empire that there exists little in the way of written historical record for goings on during the first few centuries of the Dark Ages!

Let us however turn to the socioeconomic constituents of the feudal order and then look at the disorder of its crumbling. Britain and Europe constitute the geospatial laboratory because it is there that precapitalist social systems around the world first unraveled leading to the rise of capitalism. Our eye here is on how feudalism meets the tests of viability as an historical society for it is on that basis we can then explain why the activities of antediluvian merchant and money lending capital proved so disruptive. This discussion ultimately foregrounds what is the main argument of this book.

The Real Feudal World

To set the stage for the discussion let us deal with some issues of historiography. The above reference to a "Dark Age" captures the half millennium period in Western Europe from the year 500 AD to around the year 1000. But while bits and pieces of *feudalism* – as a world historic social system and mode of organizing human material affairs – are discernible at the close of the Dark Ages, the system evolved in its paradigmatic form in Britain and Western Europe from 1000 onwards.

Why these few points of historiography are important relates most specifically to the fact that in Western Europe, the great *slavery* based "classical" civilizations of ancient Greece and Rome collapsed precipitously. Not only that, relentless, successive barbarian invasions wracking Western Europe virtually extirpated every last vestige of their high elite culture, not to mention their transportation infrastructure, aqueducts, irrigation systems, trade networks and centralized luxury craft production facilities. It is true that during the 768-814 reign of Charlemagne efforts were made to resurrect the imperial political structure of classical civilization in its Roman variant. This was the Carolingian Empire backed by Christianity and the Pope. Yet it was soon torn asunder as new hordes of barbarians swarmed across the continent. The residuum of high culture that did survive was squirreled away by Christian monks in isolated monasteries.[7]

It was in the context of such a thoroughgoing devastation of the old "classical" order that the new feudal socioeconomic arrangements gestated. Given the vanishing of long distance trading networks and the destruction of the large scale centralized management of economic affairs characteristic of the Roman and short-lived empire of Charlemagne, human material reproduction settled into a new "localized" community framework. This was the manorial or seigniorial system.

The "seignior" is the lord. Historical accounts are certainly sketchy here. However, best evidence is that the social class of lords descended from either the great Roman magnates who managed to flee with their retinues to far-flung estates as barbarians swooped in. Or the vassals of Germanic kings who had attempted to usurp the imperial authority of Rome after the fall of the empire. Feudatories or "fiefs" were the forms of political organization which arose in the absence of the centralized politics of empire. The manor was the economic unit.[8]

Every manor had its lord of the manor. Some lords controlled multiple manors. Spatially, manors encompassed at least one village and adjoining lands. The manor itself was divided into the "demesne" or lords domain. Then there were the peasant holdings. Early in the feudal era lords did engage slaves or serfs who "owed" labor services to cultivate the demesne. By the 12th century, however, agricultural cultivation of both the demesne and manorial land was performed by peasants. The largest part of the manor was subdivided into tenements where peasants were domiciled.

Like slavery as a social system feudalism enmeshed peasant cultivators in interpersonal relations of domination and subordination. But peasants were *not* slaves. The webs of interpersonal relations of domination and subordination which ensnared the peasantry entailed very clear sets of *reciprocal obligations* between peasants and lords. These obligations bound the lords to courses of action as firmly as the peasants. Slaves were like chattel, with no "rights". Peasants had rights which were nested in customs and law and adjudicated in courts. It is true that seigniorial courts were predisposed to side with lords and the lord could back the decision with potential armed force. But village communities maintained their own litany of customary rights which offered peasants an important collective organizational mechanism for negotiating with the lords.[9] One writer of the period put the issue of peasant power this way: "United they could confound Charlemagne. When they are by themselves, they aren't worth so many chickens".[10]

In fact there is evidence that even seigniorial courts were staffed by well-off village community elites. They constituted the service stratum of intermediaries without which the manor would have been unmanageable. True, the lord had his bailiffs and the like. However it was the day-to-day operation of the courts staffed by villagers that made the decisions over customs, communal affairs, and law-making that smoothed manorial life. Even the essential services provided for running the demesne by the ploughmen, herdsmen, dairymaids, harvesters, smiths, construction workers and so forth, involved labor transfers to the lord directly from the extended family or household economy of peasant agriculture which was the bedrock of the feudal era. We will indeed return to this point.

It is not just a question of services. The furnishing of those basic goods and food stuffs without which the material reproduction of feudal society would have been impossible, all depended on the transfer of surplus labor and the products of such from the social class of peasants. Political and military power was certainly vested in the hands of the lord. But the class of lords and other emergent members of the aristocracy including its ecclesiastical branch all were dependent upon the work rhythms of the class of peasants. Lords fulfilled "no entrepreneurial function". The sources of extra-economic compulsion for peasant labor were religion, ideology and custom.[11] As late as the 16th century, historian Christopher Hill reminds us, the predominating view "assumed that religion was the cement of society, and that the crucial questions of politics were internal subordination and external sovereignty".[12]

The ground of this edifice was the feudal era's regime of *land*. In legal terms land was an "immovable".[13] Not just in the obvious sense that you cannot pick it up and walk away with it. Land included all those things that came with it. Again, we do not mean solely the built infrastructure on land. We mean: the people who worked it, the social classes dependent upon the surplus labor of those working the land, and the products the land yielded. Added to this was the web of interpersonal relations, mutual obligations and rights that attended to the social classes that reproduced their livelihoods through it. Land, as medieval historian Martha Howell emphasizes, "could not be fully possessed by a single individual". As late as "the centuries that began the modern era, statute, contract, and custom alike joined to restrict land's alienability and preserve its power for the generations to come".[14]

Was land in the feudal era ever "exchanged"? Records show it was. Did this "exchange" involve a "price"? Again, yes. However, the process of "exchange" and the pricing of land bore scant resemblance to the working of a *capitalist* market. Rather, "exchange" unfolded under constraints of the gamut of interpersonal relations and extra-economic social practices which governed social life in feudal society. Even prices were set depending on the party to whom land rights were being transferred. Or they were set by custom or order of the lord of the manor. Such interpersonal structures complicated land law and provided fertile ground for struggles over it. Just because this or that primary source tells historians that land was alienable in theory, that does not mean that land rights were *actually* transferred to any great degree even in commercial hubs during the feudal period.[15]

Touching the Feudal Bases

Economic life in human societies across the sweep of precapitalist history *cannot* be studied directly, as argued in

Chapter One. Again, simply put, this is the case because economic life in precapitalist societies is always found intertwined with non-economic practices and indistinguishable from them. Economic theory originates with the rise of capitalism. This is not because human beings' perspicacity suddenly multiplied then. It is because the possibility for studying this thing we call "the economy" is based in socio-material reality. That "reality" is the fact of "economic" goings on first appearing "transparently" in the capitalist era as they "disembed" from other social practices, as Polanyi states. What this effectively means is that to the extent that "economics" as a field of study is possible it must necessarily be an economic theory of capitalism or *capital*. And theory must come clean or, put into other words, tell the *truth* about what is being attempted. After all, it is the search for capital-T truth that is the hallmark of modern science. Not the adoption of this or that "method" which is just a tool in the service of science.[16]

In the precapitalist social milieu there simply exists no foundation for anything remotely resembling a "scientific" approach to the organization of human material existence. David Hawkes puts it thus: "In what we call 'economics,' theories and practices that were once the preserve of the sorcerer and the alchemist achieve respectability".[17]

When we take up questions of the rise of capitalism in the following chapter, the question of why the study of *capital* can be conducted in terms of economic theory will be addressed to a fuller extent. For now, it is important to reiterate the fact that our study of economic life in the precapitalist social system of feudalism is possible *only* in the comparative light of the later study of capitalism. The proposition that there exist "general norms of economic life" that all human societies must meet or, as we put it, that the viability of an historical society hinges on key economic bases being touched, derives from in depth study of capitalism.[18] Without being clear on what these economic "bases" or "norms" are, and how they are "touched" or met in feudal society, it would not be possible to show precisely why the money economy of merchant trade and usurious "loan capital" proved so toxic to the feudal order – and, for that matter, then to civilization.

The first "base" that any economy must touch to reproduce material life of a human society is this: No human society can survive for long if the direct producers do not at minimum receive the product of their *necessary labor*.

What is "necessary labor"? Let us imagine Robinson Crusoe working alone on his island. Robinson is compelled by *necessity* to organize his time around various life sustenance production activities. Robinson may even decide once his immediate needs are satisfied to prolong his work (before he relaxes with a book) in order to put things away for a rainy day or upgrade his living facilities. The time each day Robinson spends in these activities constitute his *necessary labor*.

Only if a few armed pirates encountered Robinson on his island, and liking his set up but not wanting to work themselves, and so coercing Robinson to *extend* his work time each day to support them, would Robinson end up performing our aforementioned *surplus labor*. Whatever the apportioning of the total product of Robinson's work, if the pirates did not allot Robinson the equivalent of his necessary labor that sustains Robinson's life, Robinson would soon expire, forcing the pirates to do the work they disdain. Indeed, even slaves must receive the product of their necessary labor. If they are not housed and fed, slaves will die. Then the master will be forced to work for his/her own provisioning. Or find more slaves. That path, however, is certain to end badly for both slaves and eventually masters.

Peasants receive the product of their necessary labor through the central regime of land in feudal society. That regime is grounded in peasant tenements and webs of interpersonal relations of production ensnaring lord and peasant. That is to say, the peasants in the feudal economy are the *direct producers*. The peasant tenement is the bedrock unit of agricultural production in the society as a whole. Occupancy of peasant tenements included the nuclear family, often surviving in-laws, even migrant workers and possibly servants. Tenements themselves sported a family dwelling with yard, outbuildings, fruit and vegetable gardens and the cropland where feudal staples were produced. Peasants of the manor also enjoyed access to a "commons" of pasture, forest, waterways to fish and wastes for fertilizer. Tenements entitled peasants to graze the livestock from which other essential products such as dairy, wool, leather, and so on emanated.

To be sure, across Britain and Western Europe the variation among peasantries and tenements was quite large depending foremost on geospatial conditions. As well, even in a given region, the peasantry and its tenements were hardly homogeneous. This certainly was not an egalitarian society! Lords of the manor also initially enforced restrictions on peasant access to commons resources. Hence, poaching a la Robin Hood was rampant. Ultimately, however, the task of commons access management fell to the village community and community assemblies (composed generally of male heads of households).

Peasant labor was largely preoccupied with production of basic goods – wheat, rye, along with barley and oats in some regions. Agriculture productivity on average was low, one tenth, approximately, of what farming yields today. Therefore, besides ensuring basic needs of the household working the land, the average tenement could only feed a few more people. Hence most of the population in Britain and Western Europe necessarily worked the land.[19]

To sum up, given the regime of land in feudal economies, there existed no separation between the direct producers and *all* the major means of production available to the society as a whole. The peasantry, in other words, were ensured the product of their necessary labor through the fact that the major means of production – land – along with implements to work it, *was in their hands*.

The second "base" or "norm" that any economy must touch to reproduce material life of a human society is this: No human society can survive for long unless social demand for basic goods is satisfied with minimal waste or chronic misallocation of social resources. The key "social resource" upon which material economic life of all human societies pivot is, of course, human labor. And the allocation of available labor to production of basic goods in the feudal economy was vital for its viable material reproduction.

Remember, feudalism was a social-class-divided society. Lords, their household and manorial retainers, manorial bailiffs and sheriffs, the Christian clergy, and so forth, did not perform productive labor. That was engaged in by the feudal peasantry. But, under direct interpersonal compulsion through the political and military power of the lords, the ideology of divine right of kings, religion as the law of God sanctioning the feudal order, and village custom, the peasants supplied *surplus labor* to meet the basic needs and more of those social classes that did not produce.

Estimates by scholars are that, in the later feudal period, peasants handed over between one quarter and one third of their total yield to the various categories of ruling classes. Again, lords performed *no* entrepreneurial functions here. The interest of lords, similarly embedded in ideology, custom and religion, was in power and prestige and engaging in forms of conspicuous consumption to elevate their social status. Peasants did make agricultural improvements. However, even here, social custom and ideology bound peasants to maintaining their rights to the commons as well as "time-tested" farming practices which ensured both their material reproduction and meeting the interpersonal obligations to the ruling class.[20]

David Graeber, in his opus, comments: "Historically... market economies...are a relative newcomer. For most of human history, human economies predominated".[21] Feudalism is one such "human economy". It is "human" because the material reproduction of feudal society unfolds through face-to-face *interpersonal* socioeconomic relations. Put differently, private labor is never *directly* social. In capitalist society, as we will see, private labor is rendered social *ex-post*, or *behind* the backs of the direct producers through its *impersonal* ("extra-human") market cash nexus. In feudal economies it is rendered social through two economic principles.

The first principle is what economic historian Karl Polanyi dubs *redistribution*.[22] Redistribution operates *on top* of the backs of direct producers through interpersonal socioeconomic relations of domination and subordination. Redistribution is the principle by which "private" labor of peasant tenements is allocated to ensure the viability of feudal society as a whole. Within the context of feudal social class relations of domination and subordination goods, tribute, taxes, tithes and so forth, move, or are "redistributed", from the direct producers, toward the "center". This latter being initially the class of lords, their retainers, priests and myriad "service" providers, ultimately princes and kings that increased their sway in the later feudal era. In other words, redistribution takes place according to the "status" of layered social sectors. The peasants, of course, are at the "bottom" of the order. But whatever the configuring of redistribution the peasant class of direct producers *must* receive the product of their necessary labor. If they do not, at minimum, receive this, feudal society would ultimately die out.

The second principle of sociality in feudal society is what Polanyi dubs *reciprocity*. Reciprocity captures the wide gamut of activities engaged in from the earliest human times involving some variant or degree of *sharing* or *cooperation*, including things like "gift" giving, mutual aid, "give-and-take" in the context of kinship or customary relations. Reciprocity also encompasses activities of one-off "exchanges" of goods according to their qualitative properties. Reciprocity as an economic principle helps us understand things like the sharing of the commons in feudal society and early "market" activities. In fact, two of the key clauses in the 1215 Magna Carta (47, 48), cut from "modern" renditions of the document, treat precisely the crucial question of the centrality of common forest resources to feudal material reproduction.[23]

And, as Martha Howell explains, well into the later feudal period even as mercantile commerce was expanding, "gift" giving whether as a material good or coined money occupied a significant part of what is recorded as "exchange" in feudal society. Gifts brought to bear the "personal" attributes of those engaged in "exchange". It further drew to the fore the nature of the interpersonal relationships marking "exchanges". To quote Howell: "By abstracting and depersonalizing things and people, commerce enabled secrecy, thereby opening the door to fraud, cheating, and illicit gain".[24] The "gift" emerged as counterbalance to the socially deleterious impacts of spreading impersonal market activity.

It is worth summarizing a recent debate to close this section. David Graeber takes issue with Polanyi's adoption of *reciprocity* as the most basic principle of human material economic intercourse.[25] Rather, Graeber introduces the notion of "baseline communism" to explain foundational activities of human sociality. His preference for the latter derives from what he sees as a timeless human propensity to *give* under adverse conditions without expecting anything in return. For example, as is the case where strangers rush to give aid when a natural disaster befalls another community. However, my view is that *reciprocity* in its broadest usage, as Polanyi intended, includes the sorts of "communal" activities Graeber defines as "baseline communism". After all, when our community helps yours rebuild following a tornado which missed us this time, we do not need to ask or utter possible future expectations in any way. We know your community will reciprocate under changed circumstances because that is the human, "communistic" thing to do.

Where there *is* agreement between the two is that *no* human society, including capitalism, or even socialism, could dispense with such kinds of economic activity. Though it is the case that only in the very earliest human societies, in which *no* social class division existed, could human material life be viably reproduced solely according to modes of *reciprocity*.

In precapitalist societies with social class division, *redistribution* is required as their central organizing economic principle. And to guarantee the economic viability of precapitalist *feudal* society, redistribution demanded forms of extra-economic compulsion in direct interpersonal relations of domination and subordination to ensure peasants engaged in surplus labor on their tenements.

Put in terms we introduced in Chapter One, *redistribution* and *reciprocity* within the context of the feudal regime of land, along with its staid interpersonal relations, constitute the software of feudal economic life. It is that software which manages the metabolic interchange between human beings and nature common to all human societies.

Something Wicked This Way Comes

We already noted the fact of low agricultural productivity in the peasant tenement based economy. Much of the produce of basic grains thus ended up being consumed within the peasant family household. As well, a good portion of the produce of the lord's demesne was either consumed or stored for future consumption. And, peasant transfers of produce to the lord were also largely in kind. Nevertheless, the feudal economy was not cashless.

The peasant household that grew its own food, processed it, made clothes in-house, did its own construction and repair of dwellings, would often need cash to purchase salt or iron, for example, which its tenement could not supply. To obtain cash it either had to market some of its produce or family members had to render services for cash.[26] Peasant labor on the demesne, even agricultural labor, for example, was sometimes remunerated in cash, increasingly in the later feudal era. But even here, little in the way of cash remained in peasant hands after purchases or obligations such as tithes to the church.

Cash circulation in the early feudal era did little to change the dependence of the feudal peasantry on the vagaries of nature, however. Food consumption in particular was closely linked to the latter. The prospect of famine always lurked in the background of the feudal economy. Notwithstanding the use of money, therefore, prices were "strictly controlled" by the village administration in attempts to forestall that.[27]

Certainly some surplus produce of the seigniorial demesne was marketed. Lords required cash to support the requisite ostentatious displays of wealth and power befitting their station. As well, cash was necessary for prosecution of military campaigns of various sorts. But, given the circumscribed income flow from the peasant tenement agrarian base of the feudal economy, lords and ultimately princes and kings were driven into the predatory clutches of usurious money lenders.[28] Many a story is told of knights vying for prize money at tournaments going into hock to equip in high style. If they ended up the vanquisher they would settle their debts and depart after impressing a fair damsel and/or engaging in the standard whoring, gambling, drinking and so forth. If they ended up the vanquished, merchants and usurers profited from liquidating knightly assets. This loss would then be recouped on the backs of peasant labor on the knight's land. Or, if they lacked land, knights might turn to highway robbery.[29]

The official affairs of lords, services of knights who defended castles and lands, and duties of varying categories of high officials, had largely been recompensed in land in the early feudal period. Eventually, these affairs would be settled completely in cash. That, however, demanded availability of money coin on a radically altered scale.

Where, then, did the cash come from? During what has been dubbed the "long thirteenth century", beginning in the 1160s and ending in the 1330s, a wave of new silver mines opened across Europe. These yielded abundant supplies of precious metal to be used in coining. Gold mining in Eastern Europe added to the expanding money supply, though gold was used mostly for settling long distance trading accounts.[30] Existing records show, for example, that minting in London and Canterbury during the years 1247-50 produced 70 million new pennies worth £300,000. Estimates are that by the mid-13th century £400,000 in pennies were in circulation in Britain. In 1279-81 120 million new pennies were minted there, worth £500,000. The first new gold coins to be struck in Europe (other than relics of the Roman Empire which circulated during the Dark Ages), to take another example, appeared in 1252 Genoa and Florence.[31]

What were the initial corruptive impacts of this money

inflow into feudal society? We have to remember that feudalism as a social system took shape under very specific historical conditions: the breakdown of centralized forms of authority. This saw the devolution of power to a patchwork of feudatories or fiefs across the West European continent. Economically, long distance trade and its transportation infrastructure were eradicated. Supportive infrastructure for larger scale agriculture and craft production was also destroyed. While the expanded supply of precious metal was not in itself a *cause* of feudal unraveling, it exacerbated tensions within the society.

Movement of lords, barons and sundry nobles along with the retinues accompanying them, for example, was restricted to where the produce of their estates could be physically transported for their own consumption or used to pay in kind for lodgings. When the produce of estates was more readily and in greater quantity convertible into coin money, nobilities were liberated from residing in their rural manors. They then gravitated to urban areas.

The availability of large quantities of coin enabled princes, barons, and lords to settle obligations with knights and various categories of high officials with money. Previously, when officials were paid in land, they soon came to see its inalienability as the basis for acting in their own interests rather than that of their higher up patron. When rulers had abundant money in hand this empowered them to hire and fire officials. The fact of money payment of salaries fomented a "revolution" in governing. It allowed for the centralizing of power within feudal society. The 13th century thus witnessed the rise of great capital cities in Western Europe for the first time since the fall of the Roman Empire. To these great cities flocked many of the landed nobility who formed "courts" surrounding kings and princes.[32]

With the cities reemerged centralized facilities of luxury craft production. This included everything from goldsmiths and jewelers to leatherworkers, sculptors, stonemasons, painters and carpenters. Multiplex retail establishments also proliferated to cater to the new urbanized nobility. Universities to educate and train the necessary functionaries to administer centralized authority along with the requisite lawyers and notaries date from the 13th century. Of course, as cities expanded so did their underclass populations. Prostitutes were ubiquitous. Legions of workers made themselves available to carry out menial jobs such as rat catching, cleaning cesspits and removing "night soil" by cart to city outskirts. Brigands, beggars and rag pickers abounded. It is estimated that 30 percent of urban inhabitants were destitute. As today in the non-developed world, they dwelled in shantytowns encircling the new capitals.[33]

Lest we are lulled into an idyllic vision of these changes as the simple march of civilization it is important to turn our gaze onto the human costs. Let us recall points from the previous section on meeting the economic "norms" in the feudal system to viably reproduce its material existence. While it is true that new court capital cities sprouted urban gardens and were serviced by merchant trade, the vast requisite supply of basic grains and other like foodstuffs depended on surplus production of the agricultural base of feudal society. This was the peasant tenement. Agricultural productivity of peasant tenements was low; lords contributed no entrepreneurial functions. The potential agricultural surplus produce was thus subject to peasant surplus labor and farming yield. That, in turn was subject to the rhythms of tenement and manorial life which certainly were bound to the seasons. Indeed, it has been estimated that a peasant laborer in Britain could provide all the necessities for his family with an annual work schedule of just 14 weeks![34]

As the flood of money and lure of transacting in it permeated the upper echelons of feudal society, one thing stood in the way of even greater social change: the vast majority of the population, the peasant class of tenement proprietors and the direct producers. And they had good reason to resist. The best historical evidence reveals that when lords and other landed nobility commuted payment or rent in kind into coin the burden upon all but the wealthiest peasants was dramatically increased. Being forced to sell on the market a significant portion of what the peasant family household previously consumed resulted in radically diminished peasant living standards. To be sure, not *all* lords benefitted from this shift. But the greater lords and certainly kings and princes gained handsomely. In fact, it was only when money made it into the hands of the vast peasant population that rulers were able to impose large scale direct taxation on feudal populations.[35]

Evidence shows that the Black Death which wracked Europe in the second half of the 14th century slowed this process. But, as the plague subsided by the early 15th century, the concatenating impacts of the money economy picked up their own plague-like spread. Between 500 and 1000, what "trade" took place in Western Europe was largely based on barter and confined to local "fairs". But, for a feudal economy predicated upon staid landed obligations settled in kind and limited barter for essentials to morph into an economy where obligations are met in cash, venues for marketing produce and trade and transportation networks providing goods had to multiply.

The 13th century was not only a time when the growth of court capital cities furnished a weighty source of monetary demand for peasant produce. It was also a period where networks of weekly markets and enlarged versions of early medieval "fairs", sprang up across Europe. The great fairs of Champagne, which followed one another throughout the year, were the focal points for long distance trade in European Christendom. From the closing decades of the 13th century their financial operations and merchant activities were monitored by the kings of France.[36] By 1450 Germany was home to around 4,000 market towns and villages which enabled the money economy to penetrate deep into rural feudal society.[37] But whatever money from this surge fell into peasant hands never remained there long as before. It was siphoned out of them for rents, taxes, and to pay urban merchants. Moreover, the 13th century brought to the fore an unholy cabal of urban moneylenders – Jews and Lombards – who descended upon the key countryside fairs at seasonal junctures when manufactured farm implements were required and harvests readied for sale.

While the use of coin was a seasonal thing in the countryside, for the urban areas where monies ultimately made their way into the pockets of merchants and usurers, the use of transactions money was a daily norm of life.[38]

If there was any silver lining to the Black Death it resided in two trends. First there was a temporary respite in cash rent burdens on the peasantry and retrenchment of traditional feudal obligations. Second, depopulation contributed to agricultural rationalization. During the late 14th century evidence indicates a diminution of small manorial tenements. The increased size of farms opened the door to expanding animal husbandry. That in turn meant more meat and wool production geared to the urban market. And greater quantities of manure were made available for agricultural fertilizer.[39] Such agricultural rationalization in fact accelerated processes that had commenced by the end of the 12th century. Then, only about half the land in France, a third of that in Germany, and one fifth of the land in Britain was being cultivated. Surrounding small manorial tenements were large untilled areas of swamp, forest and so on. The utilization and eventual rationalization of agriculture on this land made for both population growth and urban expansion.[40]

Of course, decimation of smallholder tenements did not simply stem from depopulation. It followed from dislocations of the feudal social system by the money economy of merchant trade and the ravages of usury. In fact, without the spreading money economy and commutation of rents in kind to cash, usurers would have little incentive to lend to peasants as peasants had little need to borrow. The converting of "tillage into pastures" that the desire of landowners for cash fueled was decried in feudal society as pamphleteers of the day made abundantly clear. It also provided a direct evidential link between usury and the expropriating of peasants from land, a process accelerating into the 16th and 17th centuries.[41]

But we are not just talking here about direct expropriation of land in lieu of payment to merchants and usurers. Urbanization with its money economy exerted a centripetal pull on the rural economy of staid interpersonal relations of domination and subordination. Peasants realized that freedom from feudal obligations could be gained by fleeing to the new cities and acquiring monetary incomes. This lure proved ever more attractive for smallholders in direct relation to demands of lords qua landlords for payment of rent and dues in coin.[42]

The movement of peasant populations or "master-less men" roaming the countryside proved extremely disconcerting to the ruling classes. In Britain, where this process was proceeding apace, it was met by harsh legislation in the 1500s. The Poor Law and later Settlement Acts "shaped the fate of a whole civilization" as Polanyi puts it.[43] For two centuries as rot set in, and feudal economies putrefied, no question was more pressing than: "Where do the poor come from"? This sampling of answers is as astounding as revealing. Was it too high rural incomes leading to high food prices? Were urban wages too high? Was it agricultural livestock crowding out the peasantry? Were there too many dogs in villages? Maybe it was the peasant diet. If peasants were eating too much bread this should be restricted. Even Britain's penchant for tea stood accused! One writer suggested tea should be banned for the poor. Better for them to drink "home-brewed beer" to remain on their tenements! In the end, commentators were oblivious to the momentous transformations underfoot which ultimately unraveled the feudal order. So they continued to grope for medieval "policy" solutions.[44]

The money economy also undermined craft guilds which theretofore had produced rudimentary manufactures of feudal life. Guilds strictly regulated quality control over craftsmanship. They also regulated trading practices. Guilds were thus committed to the notion of a "just price".[45] This notion of "just price" in the feudal era always implied the kinds of interpersonal face-to-face "exchanges" of goods for their *use* value; something that, in Chapter One, we suggest is akin to sharing.[46] It was such face-to-face interpersonal "exchange" of use values marked by qualitative considerations in economic life through which "trading" activities at early local fairs unfolded. This remained the case even if the "exchange" was mediated by coin in certain instances. Indeed, not only "just price", but "just wage" was a central theme of feudal "exchange" and material intercourse. Feudal monarchies, as exemplified by the 13th century reign of St. Louis of France, portrayed themselves as embodiments of *justice*, particularly when it came to "economic" goings on.[47]

Merchant activity, however, was another story altogether. When merchants intervened between producers and consumers, pricing became increasingly "irrational" from the perspective of feudal interpersonal socioeconomic relations. The "measure" of costs in feudal society was always "geared...to preserving a traditional way of life".[48] But merchants sought to buy cheap and sell dear. What drove their trading had little to do with "traditional" life. Rather their pursuit was abstract mercantile wealth. Hence, they strived to circumvent guild production wherever possible to garner the greatest profits. It is precisely this kind of deviation from expectations that everything in feudal society should have a "just price" that factored into Christian inveighing against usury as the money economy of trade and abstract exchange struck hard at peasant life.[49]

Deuteronomy

Etymologically, usury originates in the Latin word *usura*. In the Middle Ages it became known as *usuria*. Its modern spelling derives from that usage. The bedrock source of ancient condemnations of usury is Deuteronomy in the Old Testament of the Christian Bible. Bracketing here translation disputes, Deuteronomy holds: "Thou shalt not lend upon usury to thy brother; usury of money, usury of victuals, usury of anything that is lent upon usury". Yet, it continues, "Unto a stranger thou mayest lend upon usury; but unto thy brother thou shalt not". This so-called "Deuteronomic double standard" became a contentious point in the feudal era. It was used to justify lending practices of particular ethnic and social groups such as the Jews and Lombards. A second point of dispute also arose. This was the differentiation between usury and interest.[50]

For Christian purists, of course, humanity is all one. To justify charging interest to Christians or others amounts to turning the world's population into "strangers" which is tantamount to endorsing Thomas Hobbes "war of all against all" as the human condition. Similarly, *usura* in its formative incantation is simply paying for the use of money. There is thus no difference between usury and interest.[51]

During what we refer to as the Dark Ages, where barter economies largely predominated, the fever pitch attending discussions of usury receded in the Christian world.[52] In the attempted resurrecting of Roman imperial rule by Charlemagne, trade and centralized coinage returned briefly to Europe. Thus, backed by Pope Leo III who crowned him, Charlemagne promulgated prohibitions on usury in his system of civil laws. Usurers suffered severe punishment under the Carolingian order given its melding of church and state. However, as we note, the Carolingian order was short lived. Europe again retreated into its patchwork of feudatories. It would take the Crusades and the drawing of a line between Christian Europe and Islam that would once more nudge Europe toward a more unified political order with religion and the church at the helm.[53]

A major effect of the 1096 Crusade called by Pope Urban II was its reconnecting of Western Europe with what had been the eastern part of the Roman Empire. It further cultivated contacts with the Arab world. Jews came to play an important role in commercial relations between the two cultures. Given their itinerant history, Jews embodied what amounted to an international outlook for the times. Their forte was money lending. Yet they were not the only lenders of the Crusades, though lending and usury became synonymous with Jews. Lombards from northern Italy and Visigoths or Cahors from southwest France were descendants of barbarian tribes and only converted to Catholicism belatedly. Their tribal codes offered no restrictions on lending. They were the competitors of the Jews in the 1000s and 1100s.[54]

And, when God needed "loan capital", loopholes could be found. The ascendance of the militant monastic order, the

Knights Templar, is a case in point. The Templars eclipsed Jews as Europe's lender during the Crusades. They began their days as celibate mendicants. Ultimately they established an elaborate fundraising network through their temples in England, Spain, France and even Germany. The church formally recognized them in 1128. Templars were also a military organization which owed no secular allegiance. The order dedicated itself to recovering Jerusalem in the Fourth Crusade. Templar nascent international banking operations entailed efficient movement of funds throughout Europe, specializing in bills of exchange and foreign currency transactions. In this way, Templars never loaned funds directly. They made their profits on the foreign exchange transactions involved in tendering a bill of exchange denominated in one currency, to be paid in another. Even when the order was brought down and their wealth confiscated by greedy monarchs across Europe, Templars avoided the charge of usury.[55]

In fact, to truly grasp how the scourge of usury so corrupted feudal society it is to monarchs we must look. Charles Geisst puts it thus: "While Jews and the Templars often were the bogeymen in the history of medieval usury and banking, monarchs were usually the instigating force behind most monetary problems".[56] Remember, kings and princes of the feudal era were dependent for their incomes, as lords and other nobility, upon their private estates. They also had no standing armies. War was costly. More so as costs of paying and billeting soldiers, building fortifications and so on leaped. King John borrowed 40,000 silver marks to equip his allies at the battle for Bouvines in 1214. The Franco-English war in Gascony cost Edward I £750,000, an enormous sum when we think back to the total amount of pennies minted at that time.[57]

So rapacious were the monarchs that they recruited Jews to engage in usurious practices under monarchical protection for a share of the booty. In Britain it was said: "The Jews fleeced the subjects of the realm as the king fleeced them".[58] Monarchs easily turned on "their Jews". To pay for wars in France and Ireland King John ordered a special levy in 1210 which rounded up Jews across the realm. They were tortured and imprisoned to ensure that their wealth was commandeered for the king.[59] French king Philippe IV, with his record of chronically poor administration and finance, set in motion the expropriation of the Templars beginning in 1307. He also pressured Pope Clement V to persuade other monarchs to follow suit. Britain's Edward II temporarily held back given the fact of the traditionally close relation between Templars and the Crown; Crown jewels and other wealth had often been deposited with them. And, given that Edward I had expelled the Jews from Britain, Edward II was himself dependent upon the Templars for his own financing. Ultimately he succumbed and the order was dissolved in 1308.[60]

No sooner did the Templars leave the European financial stage than the vacuum was filled by the great Italian Florentine financial oligarchies, the Bardi and Peruzzi. Again, however, these met their demise in default by Edward III of Britain during course of the Hundred Years' War with France – though to be sure, the precipitous collapse of the Florentine financial oligarchs during the war has spawned conspiracy theories which rival those of "9/11"![61] On the other side, to rebuild France following the Hundred Years' War, Charles VII borrowed from financier Jacques Coeur. But he then imprisoned him to avoid repayment. Given the ravages of the Hundred Years' War, taxation was not a viable means of conflict finance. Hence, the resort to borrowing, as averred by historian Jacques Le Goff, "doomed Christendom to a state of almost perpetual crisis".[62]

Finally, the Florentine Medici bank persevered somewhat longer than its great Italian forerunners but collapsed at the close of the 15th century. To do a post mortem on this era, the fortunes of antediluvian money lending shifted with political winds. Evading charges of usury, Italian financial oligarchs sought high profits in alliances with monarchs. The latter were poor credit risks but able to pay high rates of interest if their affairs succeeded. Under conditions of political quiescence, there would be no basis for high interest rates. Usury thrived, however, in times of tumult.[63]

Usury against God and Nature

Besides the opaque words of the Old Testament, on what epistemic basis was the condemnation of usury pursued? Grasping what is at stake here is vital for understanding what really changes at the most fundamental level regarding money with the rise of capitalism. It also sheds light on current financialization where finance comes unhinged from capitalism which as we will see played an important historical role in taming it for socially redeeming purposes.

It is worth reemphasizing that the feudal system which crystallized post 1000 A.D., in touching the necessary economic bases, as we put it, delivered a modicum of security and prosperity to the masses. The Church played a crucial ideologically stabilizing role in the feudal order. In this role, its treatment of important matters of religion led it to address questions that fall within the ambit of what today is referred to as "economics". But the Church never conceived of its intellectual forays as treating such a thing, per se. As put by Le Goff: "By failing to recognize the specific character of medieval behavior and thought, economic theories... have closed their eyes to a genuine understanding of the past... and have therefore also deprived us of any light that the past can shed on the present".[64]

To summarize: from mining discoveries, possibilities were opened for the spread of coin and its subsequent intervention in staid feudal interpersonal socioeconomic relations. The availability of money and the expansion of uses for it led to increased demand for money and hence spiraling rates for loans. Rates rose for every category of borrower from princes and kings to businesses and individuals for private consumption. Inquiry by Philip IV in 1284 revealed usurers demanding interest payments up to 266 percent.[65] Personal loan rates in Britain, for example, ranged from 40 to 120 percent. Business loans in Italy, 20 percent and up. Money lending was getting out of hand. The church sprang into action through a series of "Councils" which condemned it unequivocally.[66]

Church efforts unfolded with great fervor as expulsions

and pogroms visited upon Jews ran their course and Christians emerged as the main usurers in late feudal society. Church pronouncements made it clear that the Christian usurer was the most egregious of sinners. As a 12th century Code of Canon Law mandated, ""[o]f all merchants the most accursed is the usurer, for...he sells something given by God...and, after usury, he takes the thing back, along with the other person's property, which the merchant does not do".[67] Usurers are sinners then because usury is theft. But the usurer is not an ordinary thief. Usury is stealing from God as stated above. This is specifically the case because usury is payment for the *time* elapsing between when money is lent and the time of repayment with interest. Therefore it is *time* that is stolen. But, because *time* is the prerogative of God, it is God's prerogative that is being stolen![68]

Time was a very sensitive issue for the church as its monopoly on allocating social values weakened in the years leading up to the Renaissance. The ultimate sanction for usury was the "time" usurers repaid during their eternal stay in Hell where they would have no rest. Dante, in *The Inferno*, "places usurers in the third ring of the seventh circle, a place worse than the one reserved for blasphemers and sodomites".[69] Worldly repayment possibilities for "time" also existed, however. The cathedral of Notre Dame in Paris was built by funds donated to the church by a wealthy usurer who was urged to do so by the bishop of Paris as a means of saving his soul.[70]

But there exists a dimension of the time-usury nexus more instructive for later discussion of capitalism and reincarnation of antediluvian usury as "casino capital". In his critical survey of Renaissance Britain anti-usury pamphlets David Hawkes elaborates upon their depicting of usury as Satanic and the usurer as possessed by the Devil.[71] It was seen as Satanic because the essence of life is the soul. In selling time usury in effect sold life. And in selling life the usurer sold his own soul. Hawkes refers to Shakespeare's *Merchant of Venice* and Shylock's utterance that "Antonio is a good man" where "good" alludes to creditworthiness of Antonio. But reduction of morality in feudal society to such a narrow principle was taken to be a degradation or "commodification" of the human essence or soul and Satanic. The idea of the usurer possessed by the Devil, on the other hand, emerged from the fact that in harnessing *time* for ends not ordained by God, the usurer was grasped as being impelled by an objective, "extra-human" force. This force was then projected onto money as the evil Satanic determinant of the usurer's very nature.

Money, as such, in the hands of the usurer, was further apprehended as playing the "dual Satanic roles" of tempter and accuser. Usury in this way spread terror throughout late feudal society. It did so because, as adverted to above, no *economic* (as in capitalist "rational") measure of "debt" existed as a discrete separate strand of the Christian ideological web. Rather, finding an equivalent to debt owed the usurer "involved the infliction of a quantifiable degree of pain on the debtors body". The demand by Shylock in Shakespeare's *Merchant of Venice* that money debt be serviced by a particular part of the human body – a pound of flesh – is testament to this view. Somewhat less extreme was the power exerted over the body of a debtor through committing them to a debtors prison. Though, in the 16th and 17th centuries, the effective outcome here was also death.[72]

Finally, critiques of usury as elaborated by Hawkes, grafted Aristotle's conceptualization of *tokos* or "bringing forth", "breeding"onto views espoused in religious edicts. This condemned usury in terms of "unnatural birth". As he explains, "exchanges" of goods, or "exchange" of goods for money were seen as "agreeable to nature". This is the case because "exchange" in precapitalist economies revolved around use value in consumption. The use value of goods is predicated upon their substantive, qualitative properties. These qualities are the "essence" of goods. That ceases to exist when they are consumed. The "essence" of money on the other hand was viewed as its exchange value.

Differing from use value, in Aristotelian understanding, exchange value or "moneyness" is not something inhering in objects. Rather, it constitutes a human imposition upon them. And it is "relational", being realized only in their "exchange". As late 16th and 17th century writings reveal, money as *capital* was a completely alien or irrational concept. To hoard money is to waste it. Rather, the "telos of money is to be spent" or "exchanged" for use value in consumption.[73]

The rationality of "lending" in the precapitalist, pre-financial feudal era was forged around what was the most pressing issue of the times – "fungibles" such as food. It is not the same food that is repaid, of course, as the original is consumed. Usury of food or "victuals", as held by Deuteronomy, is certainly possible. Its irrationality stemmed from the fact that the usurer demanded more than the equivalent of the "victual" consumed.

In the case of money, the cognitive dissonance derived from the fact that that money is not like other objects even though its perceived telos was that it should be "exchanged" for use value in consumption as good for good. Money was the standard for "measuring" the "value" of all goods. Thus, in seeking a greater quantity of money than loaned, the usurer was in effect demanding something both quantitatively *and* qualitatively different from that loaned. This was the unnatural breeding or "re-creation" engendered by usury. And it is the reason its social effects were viewed as so infectious. Hawkes declares: "Not only was usury of money irrational, it was guaranteed to spread irrationality through every area of economic, social and sexual intercourse. It threatened to impose on people a purely quantitative, abstract, objectified, and above all unnatural view of the world".[74]

To sum up, our extended elaboration upon antediluvian "loan capital" or usury serves our later purpose of exploring the "rationality" capital imposes upon the modes of socioeconomic intercourse which were viewed in precapitalist society as irrational and "unnatural". It also grounds the later discussion of the historical reincarnation of ancient usury as modern "casino capital".

But what ultimately underlies our narrative on the ravages of the money economy of merchant trade and "loan capital" was the unfolding of substantive changes in the economic substructure of feudal society. In this fashion, the feudal software or operating system became increasingly corrupted. We have touched upon some of these changes in agriculture and social infrastructure as reflected in the growth of urban agglomerations and trading networks. In the following chapter we will look at changes in material production techniques and emergence of new technologies. It is this revolutionizing of the "forces of production" in Marx's language, set forth in the beginning of the chapter, which gave rise to the sweeping socioeconomic transformation bringing capitalism into being. Such transformation of the economic substructure then reverberated throughout the world of ideas as the new ruling class fought to create a new common sense or rationality justifying its domination.

Endnotes

1   See Hirschman, *The Passions and the Interests*, pp. 128ff for what follows.
2   Robert Albritton, *A Japanese Approach to Stages of Capitalist Development* (Basingstoke: Macmillan, 1991) pp. 203-6.
3   Hirschman, *Passions and the Interests*, p. 130.
4   Marx, *Preface* to *A Contribution to the Critique of Political Economy*.
5   Karl Marx, *The Poverty of Philosophy*, 1847, https://www.marxists.org/archive/marx/works/download/pdf/Poverty-Philosophy.pdf.
6   Westra, *Political Economy and Globalization*, pp. 38-42.
7   See, for example L. S. Stavrianos, *A Global History: From Prehistory to the 21st Century*, Seventh Edition (Upper Saddle River, NJ: Prentice Hall, 1999) Chapters 5, 8 and 14.
8   Stavrianos, *Global History*, p. 229.
9   See Robert S. Duplessis, *Transitions to Capitalism in Early Modern Europe* (Cambridge, UK: Cambridge University Press, 1997) pp. 14-16.
10 R. H. Hilton, "A Crisis of Feudalism", in T. H. Aston and C.H.E. Philpin eds. *The Brenner Debate: Agrarian Class Structure and Economic Development in Pre-Industrial Europe* (Cambridge, UK, Cambridge University Press, 1987) p. 125.
11 Hilton, "A Crisis of Feudalism", pp. 126-7.
12 Christopher Hill, *Reformation to Industrial Revolution* (Middlesex:

Penguin Books, 1969) p. 18.
13 Martha C. Howell, *Commerce Before Capitalism in Europe, 1300-1600* (Cambridge, UK: Cambridge University Press, 2010) pp.49ff.
14 Howell, *Commerce Before Capitalism*, p. 35.
15 Howell, *Commerce Before Capitalism*, pp. 36ff.
16 Paul Feyerabend, *Against Method* (London: Verso, 2010) is the signal work here. Feyerabend examines the processes of great scientific discoveries in history to show that in the real business of science, as the search for truth, there was and is *no* one "method" to which science is beholden. And which stamps science as science!
17 David Hawkes, *The Culture of Usury in Renaissance England* (Basingstoke: Palgrave, 2010) p. 9.
18 The conceptualizing of "general norms of economic life" in Marxian political economy originates with Kozo Uno, Principles *of Political Economy* (Sussex: Harvester Press, 1980).
19 Duplessis, *Transitions to Capitalism in Early Modern Europe*, pp. 16-20.
20 Duplessis, *Transitions to Capitalism in Early Modern Europe*, pp. 22-3.
21 Graeber, *Debt*, p. 130.
22 On what follows, see Karl Polanyi, *The Great Transformation* (Boston: Beacon Press 1957), Chapter 4.
23 See Peter Linebaugh, "The Secret History of the Magna Carta", *Boston Review*, http://bostonreview.net/archives/BR28.3/linebaugh.html.
24 Howell, *Commerce Before Capitalism*, pp. 146ff, 206.
25 Graeber, *Debt*, pp. 89ff.
26 Duplessis, *Transitions to Capitalism in Early Modern Europe*, pp. 23-4.
27 Jacques Le Goff, *Money and the Middle Ages* (Cambridge: Polity Press, 2012) pp. 77-8.
28 Hilton, "A Crisis of Feudalism", pp. 129, 131.
29 Graeber, *Debt*, pp. 294-95.
30 See, for example, Peter Spufford, *Power and Profit: The Merchant in Medieval Europe* (London: Thames & Hudson, 2006) pp. 354ff.
31 Le Goff, *Money and the Middle Ages*, pp. 42, 45.
32 Spufford, *Power and Profit*, pp. 60-5.
33 Spufford, *Power and Profit*, pp. 84-8.
34 Michael Hoffman, *Usury in Christendom: The Mortal Sin that Was and Now is Not* (Idaho: Independent History and Research, 2013) p. 43.
35 Spufford, *Power and Profit*, pp. 64-5.
36 Le Goff, *Money and the Middle Ages*, p. 15.

37	Duplessis, *Transitions to Capitalism in Early Modern Europe*, p. 24.
38	Spufford, *Power and Profit*, pp. 96-8.
39	Hilton, "A Crisis of Feudalism", pp. 133-4.
40	Stavrianos, *A Global History*, p. 321.
41	Hawkes, *The Culture of Usury*, pp. 106-8.
42	Stavrianos, *A Global History*, p. 324.
43	Polanyi, *The Great Transformation*, p. 86.
44	Polanyi, *The Great Transformation*, pp. 90-1.
45	Stavrianos, *A Global History*, p. 324.
46	Howell, *Commerce Before Capitalism*, pp. 277-78.
47	Jacques Le Goff, *Your Money or Your Life: Economy and Religion in the Middle Ages* (New York: Zone Books, 1990) p. 28.
48	Stavrianos, *A Global History*, p. 324.
49	Hoffman, *Usury in Christendom*, p. 43-4.
50	Charles R. Geisst, *Beggar Thy Neighbor: A History of Usury and Debt* (Philadelphia: University of Pennsylvania Press, 2013) pp. 13-16.
51	Hoffman, *Usury in Christendom*, pp. 50, 65-6.
52	Geisst, *Beggar Thy Neighbor*, p.61.
53	S.C. Mooney, *Usury: Destroyer of Nations* (Warsaw, OH: Theopolis, 1988) pp. 42-3.
54	Geisst, *Beggar Thy Neighbor*, pp. 29-30.
55	Geisst, *Beggar Thy Neighbor*, pp. 42-5.
56	Geisst, *Beggar Thy Neighbor*, p. 62.
57	Le Goff, *Money and the Middle Ages*, pp. 39, 49.
58	Mooney, *Usury*, p. 46.
59	Graeber, *Debt*, p. 288.
60	Geisst, *Beggar Thy Neighbor*, pp. 44-6.
61	Joseph P. Farrell, *Financial Vipers of Venice* (Port Townsend, WA: Feral House, 2010) pp. 165ff.
62	Le Goff, *Money and the Middle Ages*, p. 113.
63	Geisst, *Beggar Thy Neighbor*, pp. 70-2, 95.
64	Le Goff, *Your Money or Your Life*, pp. 67-70.
65	Le Goff, *Your Money or Your Life*, p. 72.
66	Geisst, *Beggar Thy Neighbor*, pp. 34ff.
67	Quoted in Le Goff, *Your Money or Your Life*, pp. 28-9.
68	Le Goff, *Your Money or Your Life*, pp. 39-41.
69	Le Goff, *Your Money or Your Life*, pp. 50-1.
70	Geisst, *Beggar Thy Neighbor*, p. 37.
71	Hawkes, *The Culture of Usury*, pp. 145ff. for what follows.
72	Hawkes, *The Culture of Usury*, pp. 150-52.
73	Hawkes, *The Culture of Usury*, pp. 52-4.
74	Hawkes, *The Culture of Usury*, pp. 58-60.

| Chapter Three |

SHYLOCK CHAINED

Defining precisely what in its most fundamental incarnation capitalism *is* constitutes one of the great disputes of substantive economic thought. In fact, before we say anything about "capital", or even "capitalism", "in the 21st century" or, for that matter, in the 20th, it is incumbent upon us to take a step back so as to ground our argument in as conceptually rigorous a fashion as possible. Indeed, already by the early 20th century, it has been pointed out, a full 111 definitions of capitalism could be found circulating in the literature on the topic.[1]

Similarly subject to intense debate is the question of the historical rise of the society we refer to as capitalist. Of course, it goes without saying that without a definition of capitalism in hand it would seem a fool's errand to try to explain its origin. It is instructive that Karl Marx, surely even in popular circles the agreed-upon major investigator and critic of capitalism, rarely, if ever, uses the term "capitalism". Rather, Marx talks about *capital*. Marx also enters the concept of a *mode of production* into the lexicon of economic history. And he refers to the *capitalist mode of production* when discussing what we today blithely dub capitalism. We will get to Marx's vital distinctions here and what they tell us about the historical rise of capitalism in a moment.

Neoclassical economics, which is currently hegemonic in the global academy, manifests a studied ambiguity with regards to both *capital* and capitalism. We capture this metaphorically in Chapter One with our story of neoclassical *Victor Victoria*. Ultimately, because neoclassical economics operates as a transhistorical theory of human behavior (which should place it in the broad field of psychology rather than *economics* – a subject for another book), it is of absolutely no help to us in differentiating among historical forms of society with their discrete "economies".

After all, simply to say people act "rationally" as self-seeking benefit maximizers is, whether true or not, a mere platitude. What we have learned about precapitalist economies from the previous chapter of this book shows that it matters little how greedy and acquisitive "evil King John" of Robin Hood fame was. This is because structural constraints were placed upon his behavior by an economy where land, the basis then of social wealth, could not be alienated. And what wealth it generated, not only appeared largely in "concrete" form as accumulation of use values for consumption, but was predicated upon work rhythms of a social class of peasants over which the ruling class of lords and kings exercised no entrepreneurial function. In short, the *economic* question, rather than the psychological one (whatever the answer to the latter research uncovers), addresses how human behavior is articulated within the context of historically specific complexes of social relations and historically constituted material substructures through which human beings reproduce their economic lives.

If mainstream economics is of no use to us, it is to Marx's writings, whatever their perceived wrinkles, that we must look to *define* capital and by association, capitalism. And it is on Marx's writings that we must rely to guide us in explaining the rise of capitalism from the detritus of feudal society. Only on the basis of crisp clarity in what we mean when we use concepts such as capital and capitalism is it possible to truly grasp the predicament in which humanity currently finds itself entrapped. Unfortunately, Marx's work has been twisted in several wrongheaded directions by followers of various stripes rendering our proposed route to producing knowledge of capitalism far from straightforward.

One problem with what has become "Marxism", as alluded to in Chapter One, is that its current illuminati continue to hold fast to the view of Marxism as a theory of history or historical directionality portending a socialist historical outcome. This turns Marx's work into a kind of astrology seeking out the correct historical alignments where the workings of capitalism will miraculously bring a socialist future into being. In the meantime, Marxists see their job as simply belaboring the ills of capitalism as they lurch after every new social protest as a harbinger of mass readiness to overthrow it.

But as we argue in Chapter One, Marx's life contribution to knowledge of our world is indubitably not a theory of historical directionality! In fact, beyond the pithy statement of "historical materialism" introduced in the early pages of the previous chapter, Marx set out very little in the way of systematic analysis of history per se. His work in thinking about the broad sweep of human history foregrounded what would become Marx's real life-long endeavor – the study of capitalism – and as he approached that endeavor, it immunized him against infection by the classical bourgeois political economy of his day which saw capitalism as a "natural" order.

Neither, to be sure, was elaborating upon the ills of capitalism in any way a chief concern of Marx. As recognized above, the growing laundry list of capitalist ills were grasped by Marx's radical contemporaries. And as the Nobel Prize for economic "science" handed out by bourgeois institutions confirms, the analysis of capitalist ills like inequality or poverty is a perfectly acceptable pursuit in neoclassical economics circles and in no way deemed systemically threatening.[2]

Again, to reinforce what was stated in Chapter One of this book, Marx's economic studies as consummated in his monumental *Capital* sought to explain how such a perverse organizing of human economic affairs like capitalism could exist as an historical society in the first place. That is to say, Marx's central question was: how can a society that converts interpersonal material relations into impersonal relations among things, and reproduces economic life for the abstract purpose of value augmentation or profit making, simultaneously meet general norms of economic life as a byproduct? This is the question seeking the "logic" or "method" of capitalist madness in our earlier words. All other questions of the march of capitalism in human history, its process of becoming, and the conditions of its historical transitoriness, hinge on that.

And answering it *is* systemically threatening because, firstly, it reveals what bourgeois economic thought from its inception in classical political economy has fought to conceal: *that capitalism is not a natural order but a historically transient society*. And secondly, it shows that capitalism is *not* just an asymmetrically wealth distributive, exploitative, alienating, crisis ridden society. Rather, it is an "upside-down", "alien" order (as Marx put it), which reproduces human material existence as a byproduct of its "extra-human" goal of augmenting abstract, quantitative value – or profit making. In this sense, for Marx, it is the limit form of what a human society should *not* be. And social change to a progressive future comes not from reading historical stars but from knowledge of capitalism furnished by Marxian political economy which outlines what has to be *undone* by human beings in our economic lives as wielded by capital to then turn material existence "right-side-up"![3]

But, and this "but" is crucial for the argument of this book: even as capitalism has wielded human societies for its abstract, "extra-human" purpose and perpetuated its ills along the way, it has nevertheless managed to meet general norms of economic life, or touch the necessary economic "bases", as we put it, to ensure material survival of human societies in its clutches. Until now! This is what makes our story here so important to grasp. And it is this which constitutes the chilling ramifications of the neoliberal decades and the resurrected predatory usury finance has unleashed on a global scale.

Making Oliver Twist

Before we explore how capitalism touches the necessary "bases" to reproduce economic life of a human society as a byproduct of its profit making let us briefly pick up historical threads from the previous chapter.

The first of our threads is that of the technological change which accompanied agricultural development across the feudal centuries. L. S. Stavrianos remarks how during a few centuries of the later Middle Ages, more was accomplished in terms of strengthening "non-human power" than during a millennium of Greco-Roman civilization. The catalogue of inventions includes water mills, the wheelbarrow, spinning wheel, canal lock and water powered bellows for smelting, leading to higher quality iron.

Simultaneously, Western Europe rapidly fostered technological innovation in shipbuilding and navigation instruments as well as in naval armament. The expansion of the Ottoman Empire and breakdown of order in the Mongol Empire "fenced" feudal Western Europe in. It impelled a search for maritime routes and the material accouterment of plying these and defending them. This early interest and its effects manifested itself in the advantage Western Europe came to enjoy in controlling the oceans of the world. It remained unchallenged in that endeavor until the defeat of the Russian navy by Japan in 1905.

European quests across the world's oceans set into motion a centripetal force siphoning wealth of the globe into the newly forming nation-state containers which would become the centers of capital accumulation. The impact of gold and silver pillaged from the Americas was immense. It amounted to a then unrivalled economic stimulus. During the 16th century alone it tripled the silver stock of Europe and augmented the gold stock by 20 percent.[4]

Britain and Europe rode the wave of the new transcontinental trading system created by the quests across the world's oceans. Trade shifted from luxury goods such as spices and silk to the new "bulk" consumer products that sprang from the exploitative plantation economies the colonial powers fashioned. Think tobacco, sugar, cotton, coffee and so forth. The new European-constructed plantation societies were economic monocultures which, conveniently for the colonial masters, had to import both food and material necessities from the master economies. Plantation economies also imported labor. This gave rise to the historical horror of the trans-Atlantic slave trade. It is true that the European colonialists were not the progenitors of the "trade".[5] But they plied it with a vengeance. Estimates are that between 12 and 20 million slaves were brutally transported from Africa between 1500 and 1867. The devastation it wreaked upon Africa is undisputable. For the development of Britain, France and Western Europe the slave trade was part and parcel of the broader "commercial revolution" bonanza. Estimates have it that capital accumulated from British colonial exploits in India and the "triangular trade" of slaves and sugar with the West Indies plantations equaled the total amount of capital invested in British industry in 1800.[6]

Trade in large European economies such as those of France and Britain increased dramatically in volume into the 18th century. Together, for example, British imports and exports leaped between 500 and 600 percent between 1698 and 1775.[7] Through the 18th century the destinations for British exports also shifted from continental Europe to British colonies. By 1772-73, 46 percent of British exports went to the East and West Indies.[8] The initial British export product was, of course, wool. In 1700 half of all British wool production was exported; at that time, 74 percent of all exports produced in country were wool products.[9]

The second thread to be picked up from the previous chapter is the transformation of socio-economic relations in agriculture. In Britain, the mid 17th century revolution saw Charles I's head on the chopping block and the ending of feudal land tenure. But it was the increased monetizing of socioeconomic relations and the impact of merchant trading activities which accelerated change. The first post-revolutionary blow to the existence of subsistence agriculture of the peasantry was the land rationalization accompanying rising exports of corn to the European market. Unhampered enclosing of land and commons by landlords contributed to a spate of 17th century agricultural improvements that heightened crop yields.

And these improvements diversified crop and fruit production in ways which changed the diet of average Britons.[10]

The wool industry, geared as it was to export, exacerbated the enclosing of lands and increase in farm size. In the period 1714 to 1820 over 6 million acres of land were enclosed in Britain. The peasantry that lost its land was reduced to languishing as relatively insecure tenants or day laborers or wandering off to cities.[11]

The Poor Law and Settlement Act adverted to in the previous chapter, and the later Speenhamland system of 1795, which replaced the early Poor Law, were all band-aid, essentially feudal, policy remedies for the above dislocations. Observers of the day went so far as to proclaim that these policy remedies forestalled a popular revolution! They fostered a new paternalism of parish priests and rural village notables. And they spawned networks of workhouses and poorhouses across the British countryside. All the policies sought in one way or another to ensure that the mass disenfranchised populace received some meager support to ensure their basic survival.[12] Wading into policy debates over this maelstrom of social carnage, writers like Jeremy Bentham hatched plans for effectively "criminalizing" poverty. Bentham's "Panopticon" was a prison which could be managed on the cheap. In the Panopticon the poor could be set to work under constant supervision lest their idle hands become the devil's playground.[13]

Debtors' prisons also continued to flourish during the 17th and 18th centuries. Instructively, while strict usury laws remained on books, enforcement turned in favor of creditors rather than debtors. Bankrupt merchants, though avoiding the literal Merchant of Venice outcome, could have their property seized as well as being imprisoned. Imprisonment continued effectively to mean death, with rape, brutalization, living and dining with hogs along the way. More often than not, the extremely wealthy and politically connected managed to avoid prison for debt. Rather, prisons were populated with debtors imprisoned for small debts. Consumer loans taken out for survival are one example of this. Wives and children of the debtor would often join them in prison. It would not be until 1844 that prison could be avoided in Britain for debts less than £20![14]

Merchant capital within the wool industry, in particular, benefitted from the social dislocation. In what is dubbed the "putting out" industry, merchants invested in small "cottage" or "proto-industrial" activities. Putting out circumvented guild restrictions as touched upon in the previous chapter. It promoted a greater division of labor by detaching work processes from craft- and apprenticeship-regulated wool production. Merchants took what was essentially a division of labor within the rural family where women and children did the spinning and men weaving, and oriented it toward production for markets. The putting out system forms ranged from piece work with merchants supplying raw material and then selling the finished good, at one end – here, family workers were in possession of their own implements within their residence – and at the other end was merchant investment in small production units gathering small groups of workers under one roof. Such production units "specialized" in one or another facet of the wool production process. Merchants then connected these in a "network" in a fashion which finally saw the finished product sold in far-flung markets.[15]

What is important for us to grasp in this context, is the distinction Marx made between "formal" and "real" subsumption of the labor process by capital. In his manuscript fragment, "Results of the Direct Production Process", Marx maintains how formal subsumption by merchant capital in various guises operated in precapitalist societies without necessarily inducing more substantive change in work relations toward capitalism. For Marx there are three determinant criteria: First is the compulsion to work. Second is the question of how "time" relating to the extent to which the income workers receive from wage work, as opposed to farming (or rural "services"), factors into reproducing their livelihoods, or is simply supplemental to it. Third is the scale of the operation where work is carried out.[16]

Fully coming to grips with Marx's propositions here necessitates our treatment of how capital touches the economic "bases" to materially reproduce human life in capitalist society. For now we can note in regards to Marx's first criterion that work in the rural "cottage" putting out industry continued to be embedded in paternalistic social relations of domination and subordination. This is particularly the case given the constraints on mobility of the peasantry even as enclosures negated precapitalist entitlements to farmland and commons. Children of the poor and "idle" could be forced into virtual slavery as "apprentices" of sundry trades. Able-bodied "idle" could be imprisoned in the aforementioned workhouses.

On criterion two, to the extent parts of the commons were not enclosed, and opportunities for family labor existed in the rural economy, the reproduction of worker livelihoods was only partially based upon their wage. Of course, this suited antediluvian merchant capital just fine. The employment it offered was precarious, contingent and casual. Wages it paid were often in kind, not cash. And they were subsidized not only by the fact that families supported themselves through access to the remaining commons and servile jobs on manors but by the laws and acts mentioned above which offered a meager "safety net". This ensured a base level of survival. Yet its effect was a further depression of wages below subsistence levels.

On criterion three, no large scale production system emerged within the ambit of the putting out model in wool production. In short, merchant capital was *not* very capitalist.[17]

It is the foregoing which, in part, makes the vogue argument among a sizeable current of Left illuminati and their academic followers so spurious. Their notion of "agrarian capitalism" is as oxymoronic as "market socialism"![18] It is true that the proto-capitalist, proto-industrial activities of wool production germinated in rural areas outside the ambit of urban guilds. But neither the production system itself nor merchant activities drawing upon it manifested dynamic tendencies toward the expanded reproduction of capital that render capitalist development and commodifying or real subsumption of the labor process a fait accompli. Merchant capital nevertheless hastened dissolution of precapitalist rural social relations. As its operations expanded, both possibilities for employment and probability of unemployment became tied to the ups and downs of its trade.[19]

The agricultural rationalization that peddlers of the notion of "agrarian capitalism" refer to was the ultimate undoing of the putting out industry. As land and its labor force became ever more specialized, landlords were increasingly prone to prohibit cottage industries and vestiges of the putting out system on their land.[20] However, that process, as we will discuss further below, began playing out in an intense fashion only from the late 18th century. Not in the 17th. From available records of enclosure through "Acts of parliament", it is from 1793 to 1815, to be exact, that enclosing land became frenzied. And, remember, the erstwhile peasants did *not* easily become sensitized to capitalist work rhythms![21] As well, during the early 16th and 17th century period of enclosures, a congeries of diverse leasing arrangements and farm sizes replaced feudal tenure. No "coordinated relationship between [these]... and capitalist farming" is evident.[22]

On the other hand, a *capitalist* agriculture, where productive farmers utilize land largely cleared of inhabitants except for a waged workforce geared to produce for the market, required an engine to pull it into the ambit of capitalist value augmentation and profit making. It could not be the engine itself![23]

In a similar vein, the argument that the intercontinental trading system engendered by Western European explorations from the 15th and 16th centuries constituted a "capitalist world system" is also spurious.[24] In terms of reading the historical evidence alone, it is firstly the case that price movements internationally, even as late as the early 19th century, were extremely haphazard. Trading areas were integrated very loosely at best, defying the sort of synchronicity characteristic of capitalist rationality.

Secondly, prior to the industrial revolution, the bulk of traded commodities were agricultural goods. Agriculture is subject to large seasonal and climatic vagaries. Such vagaries are exacerbated particularly when it is plied by peasant populations as it was across much of Europe during the period a purported "capitalist world system" is claimed to initially exist. This problem is certainly hypertrophied outside of Europe in extremely undeveloped colonial lands. And we have not even touched upon the instabilities of this era of tumult and change driven by shifting political conditions. Merchant activities were thus highly precarious. As summarized by C.A. Bayly: "Huge bottlenecks could emerge and then collapse, so that no one could be quite sure of profits, or even survival". Further, Bayly continues, major trades, even of the early 19th century, were hardly subject to capitalist forces of supply and demand. Instead, they mostly involved remittances of colonial military personnel or goods pillaged by colonial governments.[25]

Nor did anything approximating a capitalist rational mode of finance exist in the 16th or 17th century to manage trade. International financial activities such as those conducted by the Templars and Medici oligarchs, visited in the previous chapter, were not replaced for centuries. The clumsy attempt to raise funds for intercontinental trade through stock ownership, the South Sea Company of the early 1700s, collapsed unceremoniously but a half decade after its founding. Not until the late 18th century would a few enduring private banking operations emerge in Western Europe: Baring in Britain; the House of Rothschild in France. Both commenced as merchant capital and conducted affairs related to colonial investment and, of course, war.[26]

In fact, throughout the 18th and into the 19th century, states faced similar financing constraints as during the late Middle Ages. Costs of incessant wars continued to escalate. Yet, as early agricultural rationalization ran its course, with the deteriorating conditions of remaining peasantries in Western Europe, sufficient finance could not be drawn from agriculture. Nor could governments afford to alienate the great landlords they leaned on for political support. With large urban agglomerations dependent upon the fortunes of trade and government employment, raising income through taxation here was also a non-starter. In lieu of wealth effects of capitalist industrialization, governments of the era turned to their colonies. However, this fostered yet more war with rising costs of far flung fortifications and armaments further draining government coffers. Popular riots over food costs and taxes bedeviled governments with all beginning to come to a head with the French and American revolutions.[27]

In sum, there was nothing very systemic, in the sense of interrelated, mutually supporting parts of a whole, in the purported "world system" of the 15th, 16th, or even 17th century. Recent research suggests that early colonialism, for all its expropriation and pillage, did not directly manifest itself in that great disjuncture or "divergence" between "winning" advanced Western and "losing" colonial economies as argued by "capitalist world system" theorists.[28] For human existence, even in Western Europe, precariousness remained the order of the day as per A. O. Hirschman's dictum with which we began the previous chapter.

Touching the Capitalist Bases

It is more than disheartening to see popular Left gurus reinforce views that capitalism really cannot be "defined", only to claim this "thing" takes life a la world system theory in 15th and 16th century international commerce of "capitalist empires". They then follow this with the banality of how trappings of this "thing" historically exist prior to the dawn of the industrial area with which capital is identified.[29]

As emphasized across pages of this book, if we follow Marx's thinking carefully, we need not be made fools. The existence and persistence of any form of historical society is predicated upon its ability to meet general norms of economic life within the context of its social class relations. And as a byproduct of its social goal that, in turn, articulates with its class relations.

As we gathered the threads of Chapter Two's discussion in this chapter we showed how the money economy of "loan capital" and merchant trade continued its acidic melting of the feudal economic system and its structures of class power. But before we can claim that a new capitalist society has taken the place of its precapitalist precursor it is incumbent upon us to explain how that new capitalist society touches the necessary economic norms or "bases" to ensure the viability of a human society.

Marx was always clear on the fact that elements of the age of capital could be found in varying forms throughout much of precapitalist history. His famous conceptualizing of this is the notion that money, wages, commodities, finance, profits, and so forth, existed in the *interstices* of ancient worlds. But their existence was always *external* to the means by which ancient and precapitalist societies reproduced their economic lives.

What Marx's work explains is that at a particular historical conjuncture capital *internalizes* those constituents of material reproduction which theretofore had always been external to the viability of pre-existing historical societies. Capital draws all these disparate forms from across the ages into a unique symbiosis: a symbiosis through which capital wields the material reproduction of an entire society for its abstract, "extra-human" purpose of augmenting value or profit making. This is the point when *capital*, with its market principle, becomes the deep structural operating force or "software" of the economy. A *capitalist* society or *capitalism* is a society in which human economic life is shaped, predominately, by the force of capital.

If we turn our attention to Britain – not of course, because we are in any way suggesting that all historical paths to capitalism are similar, or must follow that precise pattern, but simply because Britain provides the first case of capitalist transition – the historical record tells us the following: The seismic changes in the structure of production relations in agriculture date from the late 18th century, not the mid 1600s. The earliest complete figures on national employment in Britain date from 1831. In that census, those occupying land for agriculture numbered 236,343. Of these 36 percent were *not* employing agricultural laborers. Many families, in other words, were interested not in marketing production for profits but were satisfying family needs and other "neighborhood" obligations. But by 1851, agricultural laborers, shepherds and farm servants constituted 73 percent of all those in Britain working the land.[30]

Ownership concentration in land away from subsistence agriculture also intensifies rapidly by mid 19th century Britain. In 1850, 75-80 percent of farmland was in the hands of a landlord class. It was landlords who invested most of the capital in land.

In turn, their capitalist tenant farmers "managed" the farms, contributed working capital, and hired laborers. The relationship amongst parties at this point was largely based upon impersonal legal contract.[31] This period is referred to as the beginning of modern or "high farming" which efficiently interlocked grain production as well as livestock in single farming operations. Both prosperity and overall productivity thus rise from the 1850 into the 1870s.[32]

The story of the industrial revolution begins with cotton. Cotton textile production in first Lancashire, and then Manchester, developed outside of the ambit of feudal guild regulations from the beginning. The nascent cotton industry benefitted from protective colonial policies against Indian goods. And, on the raw material import side, it profited handsomely from the slave trade. Cotton textiles also rapidly grew into an important British export. Export of cotton goods from Britain increased 10 times between 1750 and 1769. From 1770 it proceeded to capture the European market.[33]

But it would be the capture and expansion of the massive *domestic* market for cotton clothing and cloth which ultimately propelled industrial innovation towards industrial revolution. However, because powerful, well connected wool interests had government legislate against importing cotton cloth or goods from 1700, the problem the cotton industry faced was how to produce cheaply from imported *raw* cotton to satisfy the burgeoning domestic demand. This "problem" actually became the strength of the industry due to the technological development it drove. Prizes were even offered for leading inventions at that time. Initial inventions in spinning soon produced more thread than weavers could handle. That led to invention of the power loom. The loom turned from horsepower to steam by 1789. And with tweaking over the next decades, by the 1820s steam power looms supplanted hand-weaving across the industry.

Steam power, in deploying heat energy to power machines, liberated humanity from its dependence upon power of animals, wind and water. It subsequently compelled a raft of innovations in metallurgy and mining. Both coal output and quality iron output increased dramatically in the early 19th century. The need to efficiently move large quantities of goods and materials around Britain led to a spate of canal, road and railway construction. Between 1838 and 1850 Britain added over 6000 miles of railroad, for example![34]

In 1840 Britain accounted for 45 percent of total global industrial production. And between 1815 and 1861 Britain's industrial production grew at a then spectacular average rate of 3.5 percent per year. By 1881, 44 percent of the labor force in Britain was employed in industry or occupations related to it. Agriculture in that year employed only 13 percent of the working population. Much of the remaining working population found employment in varying facets of the transportation industry.[35]

When we use concepts such as the commodification of labor power and the real subsumption of the labor and production process by capital it is with respect to the wholesale transformation of socioeconomic relations that the foregoing entails. The commodification of labor power involves the effective separation of the direct producers from the means of production and livelihood. These means of production are then concentrated in agriculture in the hands of landlords and capitalist farmers and in industry in the hands of the industrial capitalist class. The working class, whether in agriculture or in industry, gains access to the product of their necessary labor *only* indirectly through the *wages* they receive. They must then purchase the full spectrum of goods required to sustain their livelihood, and reproduction as a class, in the impersonal cash nexus of the capitalist market. The capitalist market itself is populated by small independent businesses across a division of labor in producer goods, consumer goods and agricultural. The rise of the mechanized cotton industry in Britain thus heralds the first historical embodiment of paradigmatic *industrial capital*.

To recapitulate, two general norms or "bases" all viable human economies must touch for any historical society to exist and materially reproduce human life are: 1) the direct producers must at minimum receive the product of their necessary labor, and

2) society's resources must be allocated in a way that demand in society for basic goods is met without chronic waste.

Put in terms of earlier discussion, these norms or bases constitute the hardware of human material existence. Our task here is to explain how the specific operating system or software of capital manages these. Let us preliminarily look at the challenges capital faces in managing these under conditions of Marx's real subsumption of the labor and production process by industrial capital.

Marx's crucial first criterion, the compulsion for work, carries momentous ramifications for satisfying both foregoing norms. However, his argument – that paradigmatically work in capitalist economies must be "freed" from precapitalist extra-economic coercion and compelled solely by *economic* means – has been hijacked in specious debate.[36] It is true that in the precapitalist milieu of colonial possessions upon which advancing West European economies preyed, labor continued to be enmeshed in relations of domination and subordination. Activities of merchant capital even conjured up historical forms of "unfree" labor in slave plantations of the Americas. But, the historical specificity of capitalism resides in its "freeing" of labor power from precapitalist encumbrances and generalizing of economic compulsion for work.

To grasp what is at stake here it is worth thinking about the so-called factors of production – land, labor and capital. All factors of production operate in *concrete specific* ways to produce use values. Tropical soils grow mangoes. Carpenters work wood. Precision lathes fashion metal tools. But in capitalist economies the essential object is not production of use values for consumption. It is production of goods as value objects for the abstract social goal of value augmentation or profit making. Capitalist value augmentation, in other words, requires a factor of production that has both a concrete specific and *abstract general* aspect. That factor of production is human labor power. Only it can be shifted from one concrete specific form of production to another: Or, alternatively, rendered *indifferent* to production of specific use values in favor of producing *any* good as a vehicle for value augmentation.

Labor power cannot be rendered indifferent to production of specific use values unless it is "freed" from access to its means of livelihood and extra-economic social relations confining it to task and/or *place*. Capital, in other words, requires the conversion of the direct producers into a proletarian class. This is its *sine qua non*. This class then makes its labor power available for purchase on the capitalist market. With labor power available on the market as a commodity for capital to purchase as but another input into the production process, capital is able to produce *any* good according to shifting patterns of social demand and opportunities for profit making.

Capital could not operate according to its market principle to touch the necessary economic "bases" with the restrictions on mobility of workers like the Poor Laws or Speenhamland. These were thus eliminated in the early 19th century in tandem with the final enclosures of the commons. The problem (for nascent capital) is compounded under proto-capitalist conditions where work retained facets of artisanship or even when workers own and operate their own tools and implements. In both situations workers command their own work rhythms as in cottage industries. For example, the historical record of the 18th century European transitional period is replete with accounts bemoaning the work ethic of artisans and pre-industrial laborers. On deciding they had worked enough to provide for their own needs they simply took a vacation.[37] Without operationalizing economic principles like "redistribution" (for example, Poor Laws), or "reciprocity" (access to commons), as discussed in Chapter Two, the society, as such, would not be viable. With only the impersonal market principle in force it would face a perpetual inelasticity of supply, miring it in debilitating shortages.

To date with pinpoint accuracy exactly when capital's real subsumption of the labor and production process of society kicks in is not possible. We do know its steady unfolding commences in the late 18th century. It then spreads economy wide into the

19th. From the mid-19th century onward the dynamic of the real subsumption by capital sets in motion the above-referred-to great "divergence" between Europe and the rest of the world.[38]

Nevertheless, the activities of merchant capital deserve to be studied as the originating form of capital in the 18th century. Their activity, often supported by antediluvian "loan capital", in buying cheap to sell dear or using "money to make money", holds important lessons for later study of capital in its historically paradigmatic form. After all, industrial capitalists are also "merchants" interested in marketing their commodities where the highest price can be commanded. But we cannot emphasize this more. It is not possible for either merchant capital or antediluvian "loan capital" to constitute any kind of socioeconomic system on their own. That is to say, neither contains a "method to their madness" of meeting general norms of economic life, though, as treated above, the parasitic activities of each, if untrammeled, certainly corrupt that process in precapitalist society.

Why it is necessary to belabor the foregoing is that, it is true, no "pure" slavery or feudal socioeconomic system ever exists in history. The same goes, as we will see, for capitalism. To paraphrase Marx from the *Grundrisse*, there always exists one core principle of material reproduction in each form of society. Its relations "assign rank and influence to the others" and determine their "specific gravity".[39] In other words, just as markets existed in slave or feudal societies external to the principles by which these economies reproduced their economic lives, so, potentially, principles of "redistribution" and "reciprocity" appear in capitalist economies. Indeed, as we will see with "redistribution" during the "golden age", a non-capitalist principle may perform a crucial supporting role for the predominating market principle of capital. However, if the market principle of capital ceased to predominate at a point in the historical march of capital, then we could no longer talk about a *capitalist* society. Or, if circumstances arise such that economic and political practices prevent *any* principle from predominating in the touching of necessary economic bases to reproduce our economic lives, human society will face its demise.

Let us get back to the explanation of how capital, through its impersonal market principle, guarantees the meeting of general norms of economic life. A hugely important point made by Marx is the fact of capitalism as a class society where labor of direct producers must necessarily support non-laboring classes. In our feudal example, the extra-economic relations the direct producers participate in see the ruling lord command the surplus produce over and above that necessary to ensure reproduction of the peasantry as a class.

In capitalist economies the direct producers are "freed" from extra-economic compulsion. They are also "freed" from precapitalist forms of access to their means of livelihood. This is what brings them to the market to sell their power to work, or labor power. There they meet the capitalist in whose hands the means of production and livelihood are concentrated.

Our textile producing capitalist, for example, has invested $100 in machinery or means of production. The capitalist also invests $50 in raw materials. Then the capitalist turns to the market to purchase commodified labor power. The worker is offered $50 in wages. Now let us suppose that in 4 hours of working for our capitalist the laborer can produce commodities equivalent in value to the $50 in wages. And, the 4 hours of work for which the worker receives $50 is the time and money measure of the workers necessary labor. Think of the time issue in terms of our Robinson Crusoe example from the previous chapter.

However, unlike Robinson's island, no pirates arrive to force our proletariat to perform surplus labor. If we left things as above, with depreciation of means of production and exhausting of raw materials, factoring in the $150 of value these transfer to the product and the $50 worth of value added by the laborer as equivalent to his/her necessary labor, we would end up with the $200 with which we began. That is, when goods were sold, *value* equal to inputs would be materialized. But what Marx refers to as *surplus value* or profit would not.

Marx's argument for surplus value goes like this: For surplus value to be created, and the *augmenting* of value characteristic of the capitalist economy to be realized, workers must toil for *more* time than is simply required to produce the equivalent of their necessary labor. This occurs in capitalist society under its conditions where the capitalist, owner of the means of production, *sets the time of the working day*. So, in fact, with an 8 hour working day, where in 4 hours the worker produces $50 of value equivalent to his/her necessary labor, in 4 further hours of surplus labor, the worker produces $50 of surplus value or profit for the capitalist. Now, $250 dollars, pregnant with the surplus value of $50 from the original $200 investment, emerges like magic from the capitalist production process.

Yet, with this said, it is still necessary to clarify how precisely capital simultaneously meets the norms of economic life to guarantee the material reproducibility of capitalist society. We have noted that the wage must be able to purchase the equivalent of the workers' necessary labor. But we have not shown how capital "knows" the money wage it pays is sufficient. We have also not explained how capital, composed as it is of private businesses across a complex division of labor, is able to ensure that when the direct producers do go to market they will find the goods there they both need and want. After all, the "Stalinist dictator" in capital, as we put it in Chapter One, exerts its economic force on labor power in the production process by rendering it *indifferent* to production of particular goods. Rather, for their wage, workers are economically compelled to sell their life energy or labor power to capital to be applied to producing *any* good according to opportunities that arise for profit making. But, in the market as *consumers*, workers are as genuinely free as other "traders" to buy that particular array of livelihood sustaining goods suitable to them as individuals.

The answer here resides in what Marx refers to as *socially necessary labor*. Understanding this is the key to grasping the method of capitalist madness. Remember, in capitalist economies, extra-economic coercion is extirpated. Economic agents interact in the market through the cash nexus. There they respond to abstract quantitative signals of price movements. Our capitalist, the economic "agent" in whose hands the means of production are concentrated, and in whose "rational" self-seeking interest the social goal of value augmentation is pursued, is particularly attuned to these signals. Prices help the capitalist gauge the extent to which goods are in demand. Capitalists, in other words, must produce the goods that people, including the proletarian class, need and want. Prices also tell our capitalist whether their technology and production process is competitive. That is, if they produce goods in demand but with outmoded technology the market will shirk their product. Finally, because commodification of labor power is the *sine qua non* of capitalism, it is imperative for capital to maintain labor power as a commodity. If wages, the price of labor power in the market, are too high, workers will eventually buy out of proletarianization to become capitalists. If wages are too low to ensure workers the product of their necessary labor, the working class will ultimately shrink and perish. Either case spells the demise of capitalism as an historical society.

The pricing operations of capitalist markets we asserted in Chapter One are attuned to direct costs of standardized material inputs and commodified labor power. Capitalist prices in this fashion are always "backward facing".[40] As the capitalist turns to current production, the costs of technology and materials and the labor power previously applied to those have already been met. The only *new* cost to the capitalist in the current endeavor is the commodified labor power that will be set in motion. However, we have to keep in mind that businesses are all in private hands and, according to the market principle of capital, no *ex ante* decision making is assumed. Yet, notwithstanding private decision making in the hands of profit hungry capitalists, the social division of labor through which the resources of society are allocated must be organized in a fashion that guarantees the viability of capitalism as a human society. Such an "optimal" allocation of resources is signaled *ex post* in the formation of "objective" capitalist rational or "normal" prices on the market.

The possibility of impersonal market forces of supply and demand forming normal prices or reaching "equilibrium"

(Marx refers to "incessant equilibrations" of prices and uses the term "average activity"[41]) is based upon the fact that, whether we are talking about producer goods, material inputs or consumer goods, only socially necessary labor has been spent on their production. This is to say that, paradigmatically, goods are neither overproduced nor underproduced according to the prevailing pattern of social demand. Quantitative price signals emerging from market activities feed this information back to each private capitalist producer.

Put differently, socially necessary labor is the only *real* cost incurred by society in capitalist production of commodities as value objects. It is the central "social resource" that society must ensure is appropriately allocated. It is simply the case that such an allocation occurs "anarchically" by trial and error of independent units of capital competing in the market. But, when commodities do embody socially necessary labor, value will be augmented and the viability of capitalist society guaranteed as a byproduct. That the condition for human labor power in capitalist economies to be value augmenting is the same as that ensuring all commodities are produced with socially necessary labor constitutes the *differentia specifica* of capitalism as an historical society.[42]

While the "method" of capitalist accumulation entails prices of all commodities including commodified labor power gravitating toward "normal" or equilibrium levels, the "madness" of capital lurks forebodingly, ever so near. Again, as we note, means of production in capitalist economies are privately held in the hands of profit hungry private capitalists. Their inclination is always to let loose with their "animal spirits" and compete amongst each other for a bigger slice of the pie. This is where the madness of capital sets in.

The problem begins with expensive *fixed capital*, technologies such as the steam engine and power loom combo of factory system cotton production, or the giant ovens and furnaces in steel production. These are the major means of production. As the situation alluded to above where the capitalist that fails to innovate faces diminished profits and business failure, so the early innovator is lured by the promise of extra profit. But in each industry, when the technological bar has been set, all capitalists must adopt best practice or face ruin. Because fixed capital is in place and the technological bar set does not mean capitalist competition ceases. It does not. Capitalist businesses will continue with varying strategies, such as process rationalization, to covet market share and expand their operations.

Examination of the capitalist business cycle in its paradigmatic form during the era of industrial capital shows its division into two broad phases. There is the *widening* or *prosperity phase*. And the *deepening* or *depression* phase.[43] The prosperity phase plays out around the aforementioned competitive dynamic based upon a given technological foundation in fixed capital. Fixed capital entails a lengthy period of depreciation. Despite relative price stability the economy continues to grow. As it grows it begins to absorb available labor power or what Marx dubs the *industrial reserve army*. It is this absorption of the industrial reserve army which produces the phenomenon of *overaccumulation* or superabundance of capital relative to the working population. That is to say, by its own endogenous dynamic capital is wracked by a potentially fatal contradiction.

Capital, of course, is oblivious to the constraint the size of the working population places upon it. That is, capital treats it like any other input into the production process. But, labor power is not just *any* commodity as it is not a capitalistically produced commodity. Therefore it is impossible to adjust the *supply* of labor power to the demand for it as is the case with other commodities. Capital only realizes this when the industrial reserve army is completely absorbed and the continuing demand for labor power puts a strong upward pressure on wages which then sends profits on a downward slide. When profits fall, businesses respond with their own private, profit hungry, interests in mind and seek to grab market share from adversaries. While one or another firm may gain advantage from this strategy the tendency toward overaccumulation of capital in the economy as a whole is exacerbated. With profits now falling across the board, businesses begin to close and capital moves to other pursuits such as real estate or speculative activities. In response to the foregoing as well as the growing perception of risk in lending, interest rates rise. However this only offers further inducement for capital to decamp from production-centered activity where profits have been plummeting and shift toward speculative endeavors.

In the following section we will explore the role of banking and finance as subsumed under capitalist economic rhythms. For now it can be summarily pointed out that with businesses closing en masse, unemployment spiraling with its dampening effect on purchasing power, unsold inventories piling up despite price slashing, overall economic woes accelerate. At this point even the banking system is placed under duress. Finally, the economy spins into crisis and depression.

It is during the *deepening* or *depression phase* of the business cycle, when capital has been devalued across the economy as a whole, that the stronger remaining businesses grab at the chance to scrap existing fixed capital and invest in deploying newer labor saving technologies. These new technologies, capitalist history shows, generally come available in clusters. To understand this we have only to put ourselves in the shoes of the rational capitalist. In the midst of ongoing competition and profitability predicated upon existing technology (which is not depreciated), each capitalist will come to the same rational conclusion to continue expansion without incurring heavy new costs. Yet, with all businesses finding themselves in the same boat in the *depression phase* of the business cycle, stronger capitals lead the way on the basis of new technologies enjoying surplus profits to boot, with other reviving businesses following suit and so commences the recovery phase and another business cycle.[44]

Marx's writing on the business cycle, primarily in *Capital*, has been shown to have formulated most of the constituents found in later theories of business cycles up to the present day.[45] Japanese economist Thomas Sekine adds a point of major relevance for our discussion. This is how Marx's *Capital* combines in embryo the two parts of genuine economic theory of capital: its micro-equilibrium part and the macro-dynamic part. In the former the "method" or order capital imposes upon human economic life is showcased. In the latter, the fundamental disequilibrium, or "madness" the maintenance of human labor power as a commodity saddles capitalism with in perpetuity is demonstrated. The *law of relative surplus population*, through which the industrial reserve army is successively absorbed and replenished in the course of business cycle oscillations, is the "macro-mechanism" called upon to save capital.[46]

However, the capitalist operating system requires exerting of both mechanisms. It may be the case that history shows capitalism more often than not exists in a state of disequilibrium. Yet it must tend at significant periods toward equilibrium and formation of normal prices to ensure social resources, primarily human labor power, are allocated in a way that guarantees the viability of capitalism as an historical society.

In the revolutionary language of historical materialism, where Marx popularizes for the study of history *in toto* his knowledge of the foregoing dynamic gleaned through in depth study of capital, we get this: The technological accouterment of fixed capital is the forces of production. The commodification of labor power at the heart of the capital/labor relation is the relations of production. It is the capitalist relations of production within the ambit of which the maintenance of labor power as a commodity is ensured, that is threatened in the throes of the *depression phase*. To reconstitute the capital/labor relation, and save capitalism, capital is forced to incur the increased cost of investment in new technological outlays and *revolutionize* the forces of production so as to renew capital accumulation.

But, to presage what is yet to come: a use value complex of capitalistically operable technologies available for capital is never a *fait accompli*. Technology is endogenous or "outside" capital and its market principle. Rather it is embedded in society. This is but another indication of the transitoriness of capitalism as an historical society.[47] To solve the contradiction of its internal market dynamic that impels it into disequilibrium, capital must search outside its own operation for resolution – though with no certainty that such resolution will be reached.

Capital as God, Money as Avatar

To get to the question of how the money economy of finance and lending is incorporated into the capitalist social goal of value augmentation we need to backtrack a bit. Our story begins with the slam dunk that ends the oxymoronic narrative of "agrarian capitalism".

Capitalist landed property originates when land is emptied of direct producers from the precapitalist land regime. Land is then usurped by profit seeking landlords and capitalist farmers. Marx was crisply clear: Landed private property in capitalist society is irrelevant to the production of commodities as *value*! On the other hand, land and its prime activity for human sustenance, agriculture, play an important role in production of commodities as *use values*.

Land as means of production is a necessary component of the division of labor in capitalist economies. In producing commodities for sale on the capitalist market, capitalist farming must strive to be as responsive to changing patterns of social demand in terms of maintaining normal prices for its products as industry. Agriculture must approximate industry enabling the seamless flow of commodified labor power in and out of its branches according to supply and demand fluctuations. This holds in particular for supply of basic agricultural goods. If such was not the case capitalism would be unable to meet the general norms of economic life to ensure its material reproducibility as a human society.[48]

Nevertheless, landed property remains an *alien* principle for *capital*. This is the case because its origins reside in murky inheritances of the past. True, limited alienation of property did occur in the feudal era. A merchant, for example, might purchase land to gain access to noble title. But this form of ownership and acquiring property is *not* commensurate to the way titles to *property* circulate in the capitalist market. Commodities are bought and sold on the capitalist market based upon the fact that a capitalistically rational "original" price has been paid to their owner for them. It is not just a question of lineage in ownership "title" here, however. The pricing of land itself in the above context is "measureless" or arbitrary in comparison to the "measured" exchange of commodities as value objects on the capitalist market.

To remedy this capital establishes a *modus vivendi* with the landowning class. This entails the creation of a *legal fiction*. Land, of course, is bequeathed to humanity by nature. Yet at the dawn of the capitalist era, this bequeathal is found monopolized in the hands of a particular social class. Capital, therefore, must take the step of recognizing the current owners of land as "legally" entitled to it as is the case with other commodity owners. And it integrates land into the circulation of commodities in an "objective" capitalistically rational fashion as an "asset". That is, as a commodity the ownership of which constitutes entitlement to an income stream.[49] This income stream to landowners takes the form of *rent*.

Rent in capitalist economies is drawn from surplus value. The production of surplus value as the key to capitalist value augmentation is dependent upon the development of industrial capital and the real subsuming by capital of the labor and production process of society. Rent is paid out of this to those who hold the monopoly on land. Land operated albeit not owned by capitalist farmers then partakes in the capitalist social division of labor through which the material reproducibility of capitalism is forged.

Our point on the capitalist ceding a portion of surplus value as rent to owner of the "asset" land brings us face-to-face with that which bedeviled precapitalist social thinking and which Marx viewed as the most "fetishistic" concept in modern economic thought – *interest*.

Strictly speaking, our use of the terms surplus value, value augmentation and profit making interchangeably is not completely accurate. Profit is that portion of surplus value returned to industrial capital for reinvestment in its production-centered activities. Rent is the portion of surplus value ceded to owners of the asset land. However, in ceding a portion of surplus value as rent to landed property, capital establishes the principle of property ownership as entitlement to an income stream.

With that principle so established to an entity "external" to it, capital is able to apply it "internally" to itself. That is, capitalism presents *capital* as a "property" that yields the stream of income dubbed interest. Interest is therefore the most fetishistic concept in the economic theorizing of capital for Marx. This is because through its assuming the form of money making money, it expunges the role of capitalist wielding the labor and production process of society as a vehicle for value augmentation which is the source of its funds and historical marker of the capitalist era.

This, however, returns us to the question of time. In addressing this in relation to what we discuss in Chapter Two, Moishe Postone points out that, to the extent time was conceptualized in "human" terms in the precapitalist era, it was always apprehended "concretely". Time, that is, was linked to concrete "events".[50]

Thinking of time in "abstract" terms, beyond that of God's prerogative or "design", commences in a way that is socially palatable *only* when tied to a new form of social domination. This is the case, as traced by Postone, with "merchants' time". It is no accident that early utilization of inventions in mechanical clocks appeared in urban centers. The ascendance of abstract time over "natural" or concrete time, and newly reflected in urban ringing of work bells, for example, is impelled by the need to discipline labor.

When means of production are concentrated in bourgeois class hands both the production of goods equivalent in value to the workers' necessary labor and production of surplus value through performance of surplus labor hinge on capitalist control over *the time of the working day*. Hence, work bells would quickly come to signal even meal and break times! Postone sums up: "abstract time...became increasingly prevalent [in human affairs] as the commodity form slowly became the dominant structuring form of social life".[51]

The social goal of capitalism itself, value augmentation or profit making, is a question of "abstract time" writ large. What Postone dubs the "treadmill effect" refers to the way increases in the productivity of labor increase the amount of value produced per unit of time.[52] In the course of business cycles, as we have seen, capital strives to augment value under competitive conditions with its current technological complex of fixed capital. However, in the throes of the depression phase of the business cycle, stronger capitals take advantage of the general devaluation of capital to invest in new technologies to renew accumulation. All businesses, to remain viable, are forced to follow suit in adopting best practice technologies. Capitalist relations of production are thereby maintained as the process of value augmentation is reset at a "higher" level of labor productivity. And so works the "treadmill".

Capital is not only bent upon expansion of value but the "efficiency" of value augmentation. Nothing captures this better than the commonly heard phrase, "time is money". Time is money takes the notion of money making money further. It epitomizes that "quantitative, abstract, objectified view of the world", to paraphrase David Hawkes from the previous chapter, which rendered usury so infectious in a world of concrete hierarchical interpersonal material relations. Yet, as "abstract time" in commodified production relations pervaded societies in Europe, so during the 17th and 18th centuries did moral and theological strictures against money lending abate. In fact, the "beggar-thy-neighbor" bent of usury emerged as the central state policy in Europe in the *mercantilist* period. At that point the debate over usury shifted to high and low interest rates.[53]

We need to get one thing out of the way. The foregoing has little to with Protestantism vs. Catholicism. Weber, in his famous book on the "Protestant ethic" occluded discussion of Protestantism's foundational Puritan writings which castigated usury in ways that would make a Pope proud. And Puritans exported their vehement anti-usury edicts to the New World colonies.[54] No, the increasing social palatability of the money economy and lending activities was tethered to the rise of a *new*

God! This is *capital*. One has only to read Adam Smith's *The Wealth of Nations* to see that "the invisible hand was the secular surrogate of divine guidance in human affairs".[55] Of course, Smith likely did not fully appreciate how his claim of markets distilling a "common good" from disparate actions of self-aggrandizing individuals constituted a grand displacement from God to the market. Or, was the market God for Smith? In any case, by the early 19th century political leaders gravitated to the view that the logic and symmetry of market operations must be "cornerstones of God's plan for mankind".[56]

The spread of such beliefs further fuelled intellectual debate on repeal of restrictions on usury. Economist David Ricardo joined the fray as successive bills were introduced and argued passionately for in the British Parliament. Ultimately, in 1854, all existing usury laws in Britain were repealed. Processes of repeal soon spread across the capitalist world.[57]

But, by the time usury laws were repealed in Britain, the modalities of money lending throughout much of the British economy and even society at large bore little resemblance to the usury inveighed against in medieval times. That is to say, in a society of staid, concrete interpersonal economic relations based upon inalienable land with fixed output, Shylock was easily unchained in what would seem the most innocuous "loan" transactions. There was no way to "measure" repayment, as we emphasize, because measure itself in precapitalist life was embedded in precapitalist hierarchical interpersonal relations. By the early 19th century in Britain the abstract "extra-human" force detected in money lending, which was perceived in the Middle Ages to be Satanic, was embraced as God-like in market rationality. And even before usury laws were repealed money lending had been taken over by modern banking with banking itself bound to the chrematistic of industrial capital.

Much is often made about the creation of the Bank of England in 1694. However those assuming that this bank operated in a fashion ultimately conducive to capital accumulation and industrial revolution "would be wrong", assert Charles Calomiris and Stephen Haber. Rather, the role of the Bank of England and bank chartering in Britain generally concerned the financing of war.[58] In this the Bank of England served a similar function to that of finance across Western Europe. We touched on this cycle in Chapter Two: profligate monarchies, spending vastly exceeding revenues that were rooted in land and agriculture, wars fought over spoils of colonial territory, borrowers driven into the clutches of usurers.[59] Or in the case of the Bank of England, the awarding to favored sycophants of a monopoly to engage in financial schemes for financing the needs of the state in war. The "charter" of the Bank of England was renewed nine times between 1694 and 1844. On each renewal it extended a low interest or no interest loan to the government (in return for its right to beggar others).[60] Britain ultimately emerged victorious over France. However Western Europe was ravaged.

As economist Michael Hudson asseverates, citing Marx, it would be "the destiny of industrial capital…to modernize finance, turning usurious lending into productive industrial banking".[61] But to grasp how this destiny is met, it is necessary to rethink money making money and time as money from the perspective of industrial capital.

Money makes money in capitalist economies through a circuitous route. Capital successively assumes and sheds its liquid form as *money* capital, *productive* capital as means of production and labor power, and capital as the goods or *commodities* which emerge from the labor and production process pregnant with surplus value *if* they can be sold. However, capital in capitalist economies is none of the above, considered separately. It exists in part as money, and in part as commodities, though capital is found primarily in its form as productive capital. For this essential reason we refer to capitalist economies as production-centered societies given the fact that production of standardized material goods is their distinguishing economic activity.

"Efficiency" of capital derives from two main facets of its wealth augmentative ability. The first, as treated above, is the securing or "internalizing" by capital of its own fount of regeneration and augmentation as it subsumes the labor and production processes of society. The second is the conscripting by industrial capital of money lending activities and merchant buying and selling under conditions where it calls the shots.

Returning to the common saying time is money, for capital to "breed", money as capital must be invested in the labor and production process. The production process must be followed through. And the goods produced must be sold on the market at "normal" prices. Only then is money profit from surplus value reinvested as capital in the perpetually running "treadmill" of value augmentation. Of course, the byproduct of value augmentation is the economic viability of capitalist society. It is this fact which couples economic growth with industrialization, industrialization with development, and development with growing prosperity and rising living standards in capitalist societies from the mid 19th century onward. In this fashion, a link is created between the efficiency of value augmentation and its social wealth effects. Lest we forget, from the cementing of industrial capital's operations in 1850 through to the end of the century *real wages* rise steadily in both Britain and France.[62]

Modern capitalist banking arises as an essential component of this efficiency. To recapitulate, capitalist production is fundamentally anarchic in that production and investment is concentrated in the hands of private businesses scattered across a wide division of labor. As part and parcel of anarchic decision making here it is important to recognize that time horizons of investments across firms, industries and sectors as well as cash flow patterns of each business are certain to be variant. While commercial banks which operate under the umbrella of the quasi-public central bank in capitalist economies function like industrial capital in the sense of being private businesses with their own profit horizons, they nevertheless stand "outside" the units of industrial capital. It is precisely the relative independence of commercial banks from anarchically operating private units of industrial capital then which allows banks to perform an important "social" regulatory role for capital.

Given variant investment horizons and cash flow patterns of firms it is the case that at given points in the circuitous route of money making money in the hands of the industrial capitalist money will need to be withdrawn. From the perspective of the efficiency of value augmentation, whereby money as capital is invested in producing goods which are then sold with monies as profits returned to reinvest, the funds withdrawn from the circuit constitute idle money or idle M as adverted to in Chapter One. Further, in the course of business cycles, all capitalist enterprises will need to hold as idle M depreciation funds for eventual new investment in fixed capital as well as contingency funds to address pressures of competition.

Banking, as such, cannot be conceptualized as emerging through a simple transition from usurious money lending. Rather, modern banking emerges from the real subsumption of the labor and production process of society by industrial capital. Capitalism thus resets finance on a new material basis. The historical evidence is that precisely at the juncture where the real subsuming of the labor and production process by capital ramps up, major rule change permitting commercial banks to be "chartered" occurs in Britain. From 1825 such banks begin to proliferate. By 1836, 61 appeared. In 1870 there were 111 operating 1,127 branches. Simultaneously the "goldsmith" banks and other like institutions, which teetered on the edge of usurious practices, vanish from the market.[63]

Unlike usurers of old, capitalist banks *do not lend their own money*. Commercial banking performs the function of *financial intermediation*. Funds held idle according to the varying investment time horizons of private businesses, along with depreciation and contingency funds, were now deposited in commercial banks. This idle M, added to by scattered personal savings, was placed with banks as either "demand" or "time" deposits. These deposits became the basis of bank lending. Banks profited on the difference between interest paid to depositors and *lender's* interest which the banks' borrowers paid to it (banks also earned income from limited securities investment).

From the perspective of industrial capital as a whole, banks *socialize* idle M in that they made money held idle by one capitalist available to others for production-centered investment. Financial intermediation, in other words, entails commercial banks taking in idle M generated at multiple points across the economy as a whole and channeling the funds to where they are required. In this way the banking system hastens the converting of idle M into money as capital. It contributed to value augmentation by increasing the magnitude of productive capital in operation. And in the advancing of commercial credit commercial banks enabled capital to more rapidly purchase the commodities it applies to the production process.

The role played by commercial banks in advancing commercial credit to capitalist businesses is referred to as *relationship banking*. Because principal plus interest is owed to the commercial bank which originates the loan, it is important for commercial banks to avail themselves of details of the creditworthiness of a borrower. This applies as well to commercial credit offered to businesses for discounting of bills of exchange which hastens the turnover of capital and hence its efficiency of value augmentation. Relationship banking is no longer indifferent to *what* loaned monies will be used for, as was usurious "loan capital". Nor is it indifferent to *how* the loan plus interest will be paid. In the role it played socializing idle M for industrial capital relationship banking is tasked with ensuring funds were offered as credit for determinate purposes which generate income flows of interest.

The network of commercial banks under the umbrella of the central bank in capitalist economies constitutes the *money market*. Interest *rates* in the capitalist money market were determined impersonally according to the market forces of supply and demand for funds. Market forces, in turn, are subject to the capitalist chrematistic of value augmentation and the exigencies of material reproduction of capitalist society as the byproduct of that. Unlike usury, lending at interest is managed according to "objective" capitalist "rational" criteria and carried out with socially redeeming value. Its socially redeeming value is the nexus established in capitalist production-centered societies between the efficiency of value augmentation and the social wealth effects of this which financial intermediation enhances. For capitalist commodity production to viably persist, some form of relationship banking is required.

Importantly, funds traded in the money market are *not* capital. They originate as idle M *withdrawn* from the historically specific capitalist circuit of value augmentation. Once placed in the hands of banks as financial intermediaries the funds assume the form of a *commodity*. They do not share the diverse materiality of other commodities. This is what cements banking as a "capitalist-social" institution.[64] The funds may be lent to *any* capitalist irrespective of the particular form of use value production to which the funds will be applied. However, prior to being returned to the capitalist circuit, the funds become a commodity in the sense that, when deposited in the banking system, they constitute an *asset* entitling their "owner" (the bank) to an income stream for their determinate use.

Such "reconceptualizing" by capital of itself as simply a commodity or asset, the ownership of which commands income as interest, reaches its apogee with *commercial capital*. As money lending is eclipsed by relationship banking with the ascendance of industrial capital (though it may maintain existence at the margins of society), so merchant activities of buying cheap and selling dear are supplanted by a newly emergent branch of capitalists – commercial capital. Commercial capital derives from industrial capital. It takes over from industrial capital at the point Marx refers to as the *salto mortale* (deadly leap) of the commodity,[65] that is, at the point in the capitalist circuit where commodities must be sold for the treadmill of value augmentation to continue with the profits from that reinvested as capital. Commercial capital takes over the specialized task of selling commodities from industrial capital. This is the case whether it operates in wholesale or retail. In buying commodities in bulk from numerous producers and selling to varied consumers commercial capital "socializes" commodities for capital which produces them in separate businesses.[66]

More importantly for the current discussion, commercial capital is a major user of idle M deposited in the banking system. Drawing upon the commercial credit advanced to it, commercial capital pays industrial capital in advance for the goods it intends to sell. This raises the efficiency of value augmentation as it enables industrial capital to reinvest money as capital in the production process *before* goods are potentially sold to final consumers. Commercial capital thus operates to shorten the *time* by which money makes money in the capitalist production-centered circuit of value augmentation.

Commercial capital does *not* produce surplus value. Rather its profits are a portion of surplus value ceded to it by industrial capital. But this is not how things appear. The funds commercial capital deploys are drawn from the money market. When commercial profits flow back to it from its sale of commodities a portion of this is paid as interest. What remains is viewed as "entrepreneurial profit" from buying and selling. Of course, even if commercial capital did not borrow funds for its business it would still divide its profits into return on capital invested and entrepreneurial profit. The former is seen as accruing "automatically" to "capital as property" entitled to an income stream. The latter is perceived to accrue to entrepreneurial "risk taking" or "work" performed by the capitalist.

It is this last point which constitutes one of the central mystifications of bourgeois ideology. No qualitative difference exists between capitalists who "work" taking "risks" and the commercial workers hired to carry out endeavors alongside them in operating commercial businesses. Hence, capitalist and commercial worker appear as simple "occupational strata" with no fundamental class antagonism marking their relation. Capitalists are presented as commercial workers receiving entrepreneurial profit as their "wage". Extrapolating such thinking to industrial capitalist and worker is but a small step in the rarefied world of bourgeois economics.[67]

Similarly, on the question of dividing profits into interest or returns on capital invested and entrepreneurial "reward", even industrial capital engaged in production-centered activity applies such to its own operations. That is, the idea crystallizes of capital qua property as an automatically interest generating force. Even industrial capital "begins to view its own capital as 'funds' lent to it by itself" and *its* profits springing from the activity of wily entrepreneurs![68]

All traces of the *differentia specifica* of capitalism as an historical society are here extirpated. Submerged is capitalist wielding of the labor and production process of society to produce surplus value for its abstract social goal of mercantile wealth augmentation. Rather, surplus value is reduced to "property incomes" which are composed of *rent* and *interest* and entrepreneurial profit which capitalists receive for their "work" and "risk". Capital, as the new God, with Eucharistic power, transubstantiates into an *asset* to which income as interest enigmatically accrues.[69] Piketty, instructively, largely holds to such a view in his self-styled "definition" of "capital".[70]

We will return to treat the phenomenon of capitalist transubstantiation in regards to the emergence of joint-stock companies and the stock market in the following chapter. Here it is necessary to bring this long yet critical chapter to a close with a brief overview of how capitalist financial intermediation plays out in business cycle crises oscillations.

In standing "outside" the circuit of industrial capital and socializing its idle M, commercial banks play a "social" regulatory role for industrial capital as we note. But capital in its paradigmatic production-centered activity is beset with a potentially fatal contradiction in its drive to expand on the basis of a given level of technology. However, though crises of industrial capital are rooted in its cyclical overaccumulation in relation to the size of the industrial reserve army, the crises break out in the realm of finance. The "regulatory" role for industrial capital played by banks is shown to be impotent in the face of capitalist contradictions.

Held implicit in the above discussion of relationship banking and industrial capital is the assumption of the commodity money based *gold standard*. We will treat the implications of the gold standard and its demise in the next chapters. For now, quite simply, the gold standard implies gold as the monetary reserve. The gold stock of the country is secured in the vault of the central bank. The gold reserve of the central bank is the basis for credit creation by commercial banks operating under its umbrella and for "legal tender" or money/banknotes which it issues. The latter circulate within the economy at large. Under the gold standard in the era of industrial capital there is essentially *no* need for state monetary policy. *Active money*, or active M, circulates according to demand for it in commodity transactions. Idle M deposited in commercial banks is "socialized" among capitalist businesses to enhance their efficiency of value augmentation.

The famous 19th century controversy between "schools" of banking and finance, Thomas Sekine explains, disregarded two vital points:

The first is that the "socializing" of idle M in the banking system and subsequent allocation of credit follow the process of material reproduction of industrial capital. During the widening or prosperity phase of the business cycle, multiple credit obligations seamlessly clear appearing to obviate the reserve requirement of gold. In fact, evidence from the 1852-1857 period of economic expansion in Britain is that banknote circulation itself declined as reliance upon self-liquidating bills of exchange increases dramatically.[71] The relation between the rate of profit and rate of interest in the prosperity phase reflects the "optimal" allocation of resources for ongoing accumulation.

The second is that as competition heats up with absorption of the industrial reserve army, rates of profit and rates of interest initially rise in tandem. However, banks have their eye *not* on the capital/labor relation at the heart of accumulation. Instead banks are fixated on the "thing-to-thing" relations of the capitalist market. Lured by profits, credit is expanded with abandon as the reproduction process expands beyond what is socially warranted. The time of the capitalist circuit is shortened. Money is rapidly reinvested in what is fast becoming excess capacity. It is also reinvested in clearing of inventories by commercial capital. Hence the increased volume of circulating bills of exchange. But, as real wages and prices rise across the board from this overheating, rates of both surplus value and ultimately of profit begin to plummet.

The crisis explodes as interest rates rise simultaneously with a falling rate of profit. Production-centered businesses begin to close as capital moves into speculative endeavors. In response to the foregoing as well as a growing perception of risk in lending, interest rates continue to rise. With businesses now closing en masse, more and more workers becoming unemployed and without ability to purchase goods, unsold commodities continue to pile up notwithstanding price slashes. At this juncture the capitalist inter-firm discounting of bills seizes up as do lines of credit both for short term payments and turnover of commercial capital. Even the banking system veers toward collapse facing nonperforming loans and runs on deposits. Gold as monetary reserve now *does* matter as the economy thus spins into depression.[72]

This stylized depiction of industrial capitalist crises which break out in the realm of finance is largely corroborated by cyclical economic crises experienced by British banks in 1825, 1836-39, 1847, 1857, and 1866. That these cyclically recurring decennial crises entailed a so-called boom-bust dynamic was not lost by any means on observers. As one so aptly put it:

> [T]he commercial world has been disturbed by a succession of...terrible convulsions... Each...have resembled each other in occurring immediately after a period of apparent prosperity...So uniform is this sequence, that whenever we find ourselves under circumstances that enable the acquisition of rapid fortunes, otherwise than by the road of plodding industry, we may almost be justified in arguing that the time for panic is at hand.[73]

It was this dynamic which stimulated debate over enhancing the capacity of central banks as lenders of last resort.

The Bank of England would only fully assume this capacity with all this was understood to involve over the course of the 19th century. That followed examination by government policy makers of multiple crises from which they drew insights over potential policy remedies.[74]

Of course, for Marx, who had immunized himself against the enchantment of bourgeois political economy of his day, state "policy" always meant human beings "conforming" to capitalist dynamics. That is, the capitalist market was upheld as a God-like natural force in the face of which human beings could only seek to shelter themselves from its wrath. However there was never any possibility that the decennial cyclical oscillations of industrial capital could be "stopped". Their manifestations in the financial realm were linked to the barrier the forces of production embodied in the technology complex of fixed capital posed to further accumulation. The central bank can certainly play its capitalist-social role in seeking to ameliorate the most deleterious impacts of crises. But nothing short of the revolutionizing of the forces of production by industrial capital would spark further capital accumulation and value augmentation with material reproduction of capitalist society as its byproduct.

Endnotes

1 Jürgen Osterhammel, *The Transformation of the World: A Global History of the Nineteenth Century* (Princeton, NJ: Princeton University Press, 2014) pp. 668-69.
2 *Reuters*, "Deaton wins economics Nobel Prize for work on consumption, poverty", http://www.reuters.com/article/2015/10/12/us-nobel-prize-economics-idUSKCN0S614W20151012.
3 See, for example, Westra, *Exit from Globalization*.
4 Stavrianos, *A Global History*, pp. 321-4, 330.
5 Elikia M'bokolo, "The impact of the slave trade on Africa", *Le Monde diplomatique*, April 1998, https://mondediplo.com/1998/04/02africa.
6 Stavrianos, *A Global History*, pp. 388-9, 409-9.
7 Stavrianos, *A Global History*, p. 409.
8 Hill, *Reformation to Industrial Revolution*, p. 234.

9 Albritton, *A Japanese Approach to Stages of Capitalist Development*, p. 71.
10 Hill, *Reformation to Industrial Revolution*, pp. 149ff.
11 Stavrianos, *A Global History*, p. 410.
12 Polanyi, *The Great Transformation*, pp. 92ff.
13 Polanyi, *The Great Transformation*, pp. 106-7.
14 Geist, *Beggar Thy Neighbor*, pp. 104-5, 125, 147
15 Albritton, *A Japanese Approach to Stages of Capitalist Development*, pp. 72-3.
16 Karl Marx, "Results of the Direct Production Process", *Economic Works of Karl Marx 1861-1864*, http://www.marxists.org/archive/marx/works/1864/economic/
17 Albritton, *A Japanese Approach to Stages of Capitalist Development*, pp. 73ff.
18 See for example, Ellen Meiksins Wood, "The Agrarian Origins of Capitalism", *Monthly Review*, 50, 3 (1998) http://monthlyreview.org/1998/07/01/the-agrarian-origins-of-capitalism/.
19 Polanyi, *The Great Transformation*, p. 92.
20 Hill, *Reformation to Industrial Revolution*, p. 271.
21 E.L. Jones, *Agriculture and the Industrial Revolution* (Oxford: Basil Blackwell, 1974) pp. 93, 101-2.
22 Mark Overton, *Agricultural Revolution in England: The transformation of the agrarian economy 1500-1850* (Cambridge: Cambridge University Press, 1996) p. 205.
23 Albritton, *A Japanese Approach to Stages of Capitalist Development*, pp. 83-4.
24 On this the central players are, Immanuel Wallerstein, *The Modern World-System I: Capitalist Agriculture and the Origins of the European World-Economy in the Sixteenth Century* (Berkeley: University of California Press, 2011); and, Andre Gunder Frank, *The World System: Five hundred Years or Five Thousand* (Basingstoke: Routledge, 1993).
25 C. A. Bayly, *The Birth of the Modern World 1780-1914* (Malden, MA: Blackwell, 2004) p. 135.
26 Geist, *Beggar Thy Neighbor*, pp. 131-2.
27 Bayly, *The Birth of the Modern World*, pp. 92-4.
28 Osterhammel, *The Transformation of the World*, pp. 650-51.
29 See, for example, Graeber, *Debt*, p. 345.
30 Overton, *Agricultural Revolution in England*, p. 178.
31 Overton, *Agricultural Revolution in England*, p. 204.
32 Jones, *Agriculture and the Industrial Revolution*, pp. 191ff.
33 Hill, *Reformation to Industrial Revolution*, pp. 252ff.

34 Stavrianos, *A Global History*, pp. 410-13.
35 Bayly, *The Birth of the Modern World*, p. 173.
36 See, for example, Graeber, *Debt*, pp. 350ff. Though, to be sure, a cottage industry of writing on "unfree" labor under capitalism has arisen of late.
37 Duplessis, *Transitions to Capitalism in Early Modern Europe*, pp. 262-4.
38 Osterhammel, *The Transformation of the World*, pp. 650-1.
39 Karl Marx, *Grundrisse*, http://www.marxists.org/archive/marx/works/1857/grundrisse/ch01.htm.
40 Robert Albritton, "Buy Now, Pay Later: Resisting the Powers of the Commodity Form", unpublished typescript.
41 Karl Marx, Chapters 10 and 50, *Capital*, Volume 3, http://www.marxists.org/archive/marx/works/1894-c3/index.htm.
42 For those interested in pursuing underlying theoretical constituents to this argument, which involves understanding the relationship between value and price as explored in Marx's *Capital* see, for example, John R. Bell, *Capitalism and the Dialectic: The Uno-Sekine Approach to Marxian Political Economy* (London: Pluto, 2009) pp. 66ff. On the infamous "transformation problem" in Marxian economics, see Thomas T. Sekine, *An Outline of the Dialectic of Capital*, Volume 2 (Basingstoke: Macmillan Press, 1997) pp. 3ff. The key point for our discussion is that whatever the fluctuation of prices in the market, those prices for the gamut of basic goods which guarantee access of the direct producers to the product of their necessary labor must settle at a level where workers are able to purchase those goods with their wage, or capitalist society would not be viable.
43 Notwithstanding the economic approach to business cycles and economic crises, business cycles are viewed in broad terms of prosperity and depression phases. See, for example, Gottfried Haberler, *Prosperity and Depression: A Theoretical Analysis of Cyclical Movements* (London: George Allen & Unwin, 1958) pp. 257ff.
44 For the contextualizing of the foregoing in terms of specialized debate in Marxian economics see Richard Westra, *Political Economy and Globalization* (London: Routledge, 2009) pp. 28-35.
45 Trevor Evans, "Marxian and post-Keynesian theories of finance and the business cycle", *Capital & Class*, 28, 2 (2004).
46 Sekine, "General Equilibrium and the Dialectic of Capital", pp. 192-4.
47 Sekine, "General Equilibrium and the Dialectic of Capital", pp. 194-5.
48 Sekine, *An Outline of the Dialectic of Capital*, Volume 2, pp. 70-4.
49 Sekine, *An Outline of the Dialectic of Capital*, Volume 2, pp. 130-3.
50 See Moishe Postone, *Time, Labor, and Social Domination: A*

	reinterpretation of Marx's critical theory (Cambridge: Cambridge University Press, 1996) pp. 200ff.
51	Postone, *Time, Labor, and Social Domination*, p. 213.
52	Postone, *Time, Labor, and Social Domination*, p. 289.
53	Geisst, *Beggar Thy Neighbor*, pp. 118-21.
54	Hoffman, *Usury in Christendom*, pp. 220ff.
55	Geisst, *Beggar Thy Neighbor*, p. 124.
56	Bayly, *The Birth of the Modern World*, p. 136.
57	Geisst, *Beggar Thy Neighbor*, pp. 145-7.
58	Charles Calomiris and Stephen Haber, *Fragile by Design: The Political Origins of Banking Crises & Scarce Credit* (Princeton: Princeton University Press, 2014) pp. 84-5.
59	Bayly, *The Birth of the Modern World*, p. 100-1.
60	Calomiris and Haber, *Fragile by Design*, p. 91.
61	Michael Hudson, *Killing the Host: How Financial Parasites and Debt Destroy the Global Economy* (Dresden: ISLET, 2015) PP. 108-9.
62	Stavrianos, *A Global History*, p. 418.
63	Calomiris and Haber, *Fragile by Design*, p. 123.
64	Sekine, *An Outline of the Dialectic of Capital*, Volume 2, p. 152.
65	Karl Marx, Chapter 3, *Capital*, Volume 1, https://www.marxists.org/archive/marx/works/1867-c1/index.htm.
66	Sekine, *An Outline of the Dialectic of Capital*, Volume 2, p. 178.
67	Sekine, *An Outline of the Dialectic of Capital*, Volume 2, p. 183.
68	Kōzō Uno, *Principles of Political Economy* (Brighton: Harvester, 1980) p. 116.
69	Sekine, *An Outline of the Dialectic of Capital*, Volume 2, p. 197.
70	Thomas Piketty, *Capital in the Twenty-First Century* (Cambridge, MA: Belknap Press, 2014) pp. 47-9.
71	Charles P. Kindleberger and Robert Z. Aliber, *Manias, Panics and Crashes: A History of Financial Crises*, Fifth Edition (Basingstoke: Palgrave, 2005) p. 65.
72	Sekine, *An Outline of the Dialectic of Capital*, Volume 2, pp. 154-6, 159-62.
73	Quoted in Richard S. Grossman, *Unsettled Account: The Evolution of Banking in the Industrialized World Since 1800* (Princeton, NJ: Princeton University Press, 2010) p. 65.
74	Grossman, *Unsettled Account*, pp. 100-2.

| Chapter Four |

TROUBLES IN CAPITALIST PARADISE

To adequately treat the development of capitalism into the 20th century we need to reflect back on a point we make in Chapter One. That is, "the sleight of hand of Biblical proportions" played by classical and neoclassical economics. Beginning with Adam Smith, we note, both traditions conflate two very different meanings and kinds of "exchange" – value in use, or use value *and* value "in exchange", or simply *value* – as a mercantile quantity *indifferent* to use value. This sleight of hand became the foundation for the self-indentifying of their discipline as "economics". Economics, as such, purports to study that which is transhistorical: human material or economic life. Its proponents are unperturbed by the fact that prior to the capitalist era it was nonsensical to refer to such a thing as an "economy". And no one did. No one did because human economic life was enmeshed with a welter of social practices – religion, politics, culture, and so forth – and was indistinguishable from these.

It is an inconvenient truth for the mainstream economics profession that the very condition of possibility for the systematic study of "the economy" is that it appears "transparently" in the capitalist era. While the possibility of economic theory requires the historical existence of capitalism, however, the problems for economic theory only begin here. When we use the term "transparent" to describe the way economic life appears to "levitate" out from other social practices in the capitalist era this does not mean that theorizing capital as the "operating system" of capitalism is possible without disciplined thought and appropriate scientific procedure in the service of truth. This brings us back to value and use value.

Use value, again, is the transhistorical foundation of all human material existence. Without the metabolic interchange between human beings and nature which furnishes the goods or use values of human sustenance, human life and society would be impossible. Value, on the other hand, is the historically specific and transitory principle of capital. It is abstract and quantitative and embodied in mercantile wealth. Capitalism is historically delimited because its existence is tied to a constellation of goods and technologies appropriate to produce these which lend themselves to suppression of concrete, qualitative considerations in material life in favor of abstract, quantitative ones. This fact underpins what Marx dubs the "contradiction" between value and use value.

Value, and the augmenting of value as the social goal of capitalism, must necessarily co-opt use value life. But the co-opting of use value life must be such that it does not compromise value augmentation or profit making. This is what we capture in the notion of capital reproducing human economic life as a *byproduct* of value augmentation. Now there are two big questions which flow from this. One has to do with economic theory. The second relates to what is the subject focus of this chapter. Let us dispense first with the question of economic theory. Then we can move to the more practical matters of capitalist development through to the late 20th century which set the stage for our argument on the unleashing of usury with the putrefying of capitalism into the 21st century.

While economic life appears "transparently" for theory to explore in the capitalist era it does so in the "upside-down" way capital organizes it. This is precisely why we need economic theory. If we begin with hunches shaped by the reigning ideology of the day, as did Adam Smith, we are likely to be misled, as he was, into believing that economic life per se and capitalism is the same thing. From there it is but a small step to construct the fantasy world of "economics" according to our ideological penchant. The fantasy world certainly contains bits and pieces of capitalism. It would have to. After all, the only real world cues about economic life it has to work with necessarily spring from capitalism whence economic life first appears "transparently" (whether this is admitted or not). But it carefully exorcizes all the telltale signs that might expose capitalism for what it really is. Like *Victor Victoria*.

Marx, on the other hand, problematized the historically peculiar and unique phenomenon of economic life in the capitalist era appearing "transparently". This is what led him to elaborate upon value augmentation as the social goal of capital. And to further develop in the economic theory of *Capital* the economic categories that explain how capital manages use value life to accomplish this. When we pick up a neoclassical economics textbook as many readers here might have done we quickly see that "economics" is presented as an "abstract theory" or "model" which seeks to explain economic life in terms of quantitative variables. But the warrant in terms of approaches to knowledge we have for this is never explained. And we know as discussed in Chapter Two that in precapitalist society an abstract, quantitative rendering of the world was so disconcerting as to be considered Satanic.

Marx however located the roots of abstraction in economic theory in the way value *abstracts* from the qualitative heterogeneity of use values to bring them into the quantitative, homogenizing "thing-to-thing" relations of the impersonal capitalist market. His constructing of an abstract theory in *Capital* was not based on ideological whims with mathematical tools of high physics then grafted on to these. Rather it was based on the real world capitalist tendency of market cash nexus activities and capitalist value augmentation to abstract from concrete, qualitative, interpersonal use value relations of past societies. This explained why, in the capitalist era, economic life appears "transparently" for the first time in human history. And it also provides the foundation for economic theory. It does so because economic theory captures the abstract, impersonal, one-dimensional commodity-based economic society that capital builds. Economic theory exposes this society for what it really is and really does (the *truth* about capital). And it underpins our comparative analysis of economic life in past historical societies. It also constitutes the basis for creative thinking about how economic life might be organized on a non capitalist basis.

Now let us return to implications of value and use value for grasping the political economy of the 20th century. In exposing the "truth" about capital, Marx well understood the possibility of capital building its one-dimensional, impersonal society, with its abstract social goal, hinged upon value "neutralizing" use value obstacles. As we put it above, the historical existence of capitalism is predicated upon a constellation of goods and technologies appropriate to produce these which lend themselves to suppression of concrete, qualitative considerations in material life in favor of abstract, quantitative ones. That is, in the simplest terms, not all use values are amenable to being co-opted by capital as vehicles for value augmentation. Agriculture, dependent as it is on the vagaries and rhythms of nature is highly resistant to capital. Attempting to co-opt nature and the biosphere for value augmentation, for example, has been one of the fatal conceits of capitalism and its ideologues. Space technologies, for a further example, with their products of space stations, manned rockets and so on are use values that could never be vehicles for value augmentation "traded" in markets. They bring to bear the combined activities of vast collectivities of governments, academic institutions and large TNCs. Their social costs in terms of allocating labor and resources are unrecoverable in any market calculating quantitative sense.

Cotton production and its related industrial accouterment, on the other hand, was in many ways the ideal use value complex for capitalist development. Its technologies from steam engines through spinning machines to factory infrastructure were engineered in society by eccentric inventors and even entrepreneurs themselves. Businesses were small and entrepreneurial. Capital investment requirements were low with entrepreneurs financing and expanding their own businesses with their savings and reinvested profits. Modern capitalist farming followed the entrepreneurial investment model of industry and mechanized with its earnings. Transactions took place in impersonal, self-regulating markets according to information conveyed through price signals. Banks provided relationship services of financial intermediation. Banks also played an active "capitalist-social" role in allocating idle M for determinate purposes across production-centered and commercial capitalist businesses. The state, for its part, did little. It printed legal tender. There was some rudimentary investment in public education. And the state maintained a minimal defense apparatus. In the mid 19th century, for example, government spending in Britain amounted to about 5 percent of GNP. At the close of the century it had risen to about 7.5 percent of GNP.[1]

Indeed, if we take the neoliberal mantra of today, "that optimal outcomes will be achieved if demand and supply of goods and services are allowed to adjust to each other through the price mechanism, without interference by government or other forces"[2]... well, post industrial revolution Britain is about as close in history to such a condition ever being approximated. Even the maintenance of human labor power as a commodity, labor power being a potentially combustive element of human use value life for capital to neutralize, occurred through supply and demand fluctuations in the context of the capitalist business cycle as dealt with in the previous chapter. All social classes, including both workers and the bourgeoisie, in mid-19th-century Britain, exhibited a sense of fatalism over prosperity and depression oscillations whatever their impacts on employment or business success.[3]

Following Britain, Belgium was the second capitalist economy to experience industrial revolution, the first on the European continent. Industrial revolution spread further in the decade of the 1850s, into France, then into Germany and Austria where it ultimately drove efforts toward political unification, and even into Northern Italy to some extent. Recent studies have also served to dispel views that the nascent organization of capitalist industry in the textile sector in early "follower" capitalist developers was substantially different in terms of its entrepreneurial character from Britain.[4] Nevertheless, in cotton production, the initial capitalist industry of industrial revolution, British production, was never rivaled through the 19th century by American, French, German or Austria-Hungarian contenders. Britain also dominated world trade in manufactured exports.

That Britain maintained a role as "workshop of the world" and center of international trade, despite having only 2 percent of the world's population, relates in part to the waves of emigration from it to the white settler colonies. Of course, that industrial revolution occurred first in Britain explains its initial rise to the apex of global development. But the transplanting of colonialists with common language and culture and imbued with ideologies of laissez faire government and capitalist market economy to the US, Australia, Canada, played a major part in what Kees van der Pijl refers to as the formation of a "Lockean heartland" at the core of an increasingly integrated global political economy.[5]

It is at this point in world economic history that we can begin to speak of a capitalist "world system" or capitalist "empire" in a meaningful systemic sense. As Costas Lapavitsas puts it, "the world market as a set of institutions, mechanisms, practices and customs is a creation of industrial, commercial and financial capitals which have become dominant in their respective national economies".[6]

In the mid 19th century the key international "institution" and "mechanism" of world market intercourse was the global monetary system of the gold standard. The process of integrating national markets in Europe and spread of industrialization would not have been possible without standardization of international monetary practice. The monetary stability such standardization provided is what enabled the British pound sterling to play its international role. From 1821 British law brought into being the system whereby the Bank of England and other commercial banks were required to exchange banknotes into gold. No restrictions were placed on gold exports or imports. And the price of gold was fixed in pounds. Gold, as we have already pointed out in the previous chapter, was the reserve for all money.[7]

The monetary standard hatched by industrial, commercial and financial interests in Britain evolved into an international monetary system with far-reaching import. That system, the gold standard, ultimately constituted a projection of the domestic monetary system of one country – Britain. This was a historically unique phenomenon where the international monetary system entailed a seamless integration of international, national and local monetary relations. Its ultimate roots were the dominance of global production and trade by Britain. This produced an international economic constellation which was based largely on *economic* dominance and compulsion rather than on political or military power.[8]

Any economy by the late 19th century seeking the mantle of "modern" adopted the gold standard. Its adoption mandated a congruence of domestic economic policies amongst participating states. In this way the gold standard has been apprehended as encumbering global participants with an implicit "moral order". That is, the gold standard "universalized the values of classic liberalism: the autonomous individual pursuing his own interests, a reliable and predictable business environment, and a minimally active state". And it promoted a global trading system predicated upon "free" laissez faire policies.[9] In other words, a globalization of the principles of a Lockean commodity-based economic heartland was attempted.

The Use Value Identity

In our earlier discussion of business cycles in the period of the capitalist "stage" of liberalism, the touching of "bases" by capital to ensure the material reproduction of capitalist society occurred in as "pure" or market self-regulating way as ever existed in capitalist history. This meant that transformations and replacement of fixed capital we discussed, which revolutionized the forces of production to preserve capitalist relations of production by resetting the forces at a "higher" technological level, were always those that capitalist market operations could accommodate. This is not to say they were minor. In his *Capital* Volume 1, in Chapter 15 on "Machinery and Modern Industry", Marx elaborates upon how inventions such as the steam engine not only were subject to important modifications but led to multiple new applications which spread across industries. Further, demand for dedicated machine parts and tools was concomitant with new applications. These processes were further amplified by new mechanisms of transmission which connected machinery throughout factory operations – and so forth.[10] Such concatenating of technological changes absorbed the inventions which appeared in clusters during the roughly decennial periods of business cycles. The innovations would then be incorporated initially by the stronger capitals in the depression phases of the cycle.

But what Marx was definitely *not* talking about here was the momentous and deep-seated change which swept the capitalist world beginning in the decade or so following his passing in 1883. Not only the development and technological refinement of cotton production, but growth in factory size, plus the momentous increase in trade this enabled, called forth extensive investments in transportation and communication infrastructure including a spate of railway construction, shipbuilding, port facilities and so on from the mid 19th century as alluded to. However, exigencies of survivability placed upon capital to meet the demands of a frenetically expanding global economy by the final decades of the 19th century forced its business units to turn to a series of new technologies and materials which had come available in Europe in the 1860s and 70s. While cotton was the key use value of the industrial revolution with iron as its infrastructural "frame", the central use value of what would become the frame and driver of capital accumulation in the "second" industrial revolution was *steel*.[11]

However, though it is ideologically attractive for mainstream economics to treat seismic transformations in technological systems as a seamless outcome of market forces – and similarly politically expedient for a cross-section of Marxist illuminati to claim such change as a reflection of capitalist "logic" – nothing could be further from the truth. This is where the theoretical insight Marx's economic thinking offers into the contradiction that use value always poses for value augmentation is brought to the fore in the clearest empirical terms. That is to say, the concrete, qualitative factors of the new use value complex erected significant barriers for value augmentation which capital had to surmount for accumulation to continue. And, paradoxically, in surmounting the obstacles the new constellation of use value production posed for capital, the economy necessarily became *less* capitalist! Nor did the new frame arrive without significant social and economic tumult.

The sign of troubles in the liberal, laissez faire capitalist paradise was the long economic downturn and successive financial crises that wracked major economies from the mid 1870s. What has been described as the "great crash" is notable for the contagion which spread amongst states recently interconnected by the international financial and trading order shaped by the projection of Britain's domestic monetary system. Crisis erupted first in Germany and Austria in 1873. It soon hit Italy, Holland, Belgium, the US, and even Britain itself, France and Russia. "[T]the whole world has become a city", declared one observer of reverberating market panics. The collapse of the venerable Barings bank in 1890 spread further contagion to areas as far-flung as Argentina, Australia and South Africa, and to the US until 1893.[12]

The *prima facie* case is that the crisis broke out in finance. It entailed a wave of price deflation brought on by growing pains of an international monetary system based on the gold standard. The growing pains were in no small part related to the web of international debt fostered by intensified demand for capital in the interconnected financial and trading order.[13] There was also the question of the limited supply of gold as monetary reserve which arose when the financial systems fell under duress. Transfer of gold from banks of one state to coffers of another had a destabilizing impact here. The solution, hence, appeared to be the "gold rush" discovery of new supplies from the 1880s in the US, Australia and South Africa. And, as global prices for key traded goods again steadily rose, more and more states internationally acceded to the gold standard, further intensifying global economic integration.[14]

But the rejuvenation of capitalism from its first major systemic crisis, which ultimately would see accumulation renewed from the mid 1890s to World War I (WWI), was *never* a *fait accompli*.

Mass production of steel and the heavy chemicals required for this not only fostered a broader interconnection among industries but brought about the application of science to industry. Unlike cotton, steel production was not directed toward final consumers. But steel was essential to the new frame of the early 20th century global economy and the advanced economies within it. Besides the place of steel in expansion and sophistication of transportation infrastructures, it was the mainstay for the capital equipment that produced the foregoing as well as new electrical machinery, the internal combustion engine, and the array of dedicated machine parts and tools which supported all industries. The demands of steel production on this scale in turn harnessed new technologies of power generation such as the steam turbine which enabled generalized electrical power in industries. And the production of steel itself entailed a qualitative increase in the capital intensity of production. The technology story of the "second" industrial revolution is best told in the work of David S. Landes.[15]

It is not just a matter here of technology being endogenous to workings of the capitalist market. When we take account of the following factors – the competitive economic scale of operations, necessitating multiple blast furnaces operating in concert along with the generating of power for these; the vertical and horizontal integration of industrial processes (including backward linkages to obtain material inputs, and forward linkages to sales of finished products in transportation or even armaments) bringing to bear what were once separate industries within a single concern; the exorbitant costs of the massive fixed capital outlay; and, finally, the extended time of often several years from the completing of facilities to their operationalizing – all these demonstrate that to manage the production of a heavy use value like steel, capital necessarily had to adopt a new, qualitatively different *form*.

The new steel companies adopted the nascent corporate limited liability joint-stock legal form (a point to be returned to regarding morphing conditions of business finance). The legal foundations of joint-stock companies were promulgated in the mid 19th century in Britain, in some US states from the 1830s, but joint-stock companies were initially prevalent only in transportation and utilities.[16] Following the great crash of the 1870s, they would spread across the steel industry in Europe and the US. The diffusion of the joint-stock form to other commanding heights industries followed.

The application of science to industry along with the organizational demands of large scale monopoly corporate operations compelled a transformation of management away from entrepreneurial owner-operated business toward a professionalized managerial class. It was the specialized knowledge of businesses in the hands of this class which yielded many of the efficiency gains of the new corporate form of enterprise.[17] In fact, management of work itself became "scientific" with deployment of "Taylorism" which sought to regiment work activities on the factory floor.[18]

The emergence of the professionalized managerial cohort synchronized with the new business ownership model. Shareholding disperses ownership in a fashion which facilitates a level of control by large shareholders far greater than their actual capital investment. This does not mean separation of control from ownership. Rather, whether large shareholders manage the business themselves or delegate the role to a professional management stratum, what we are talking about here is the "concentrating of controlling power" amongst shareholder "owners". Professionalized management is the tool of this.[19]

Giant steel companies also manifested tendencies toward monopolization of industry. The nearly two decades crisis had offered opportunities for the largest and most powerful businesses to take over smaller, weaker companies en masse. Monopolization, or strictly speaking, oligopolization of industry, stemmed further from the trend towards vertical and horizontal integration of industrial processes and the businesses which had plied these. In the US, for example, the 100 largest corporations grew in size by a factor of 4 between 1896 and 1905. A full 40 percent of total US capital stock would be agglomerated in their hands during the period. Already by 1901 US Steel Corporation controlled 63 percent of steel production. Under such conditions of monopolistic and oligopolistic dominance, commanding heights firms increasingly eschewed market pricing. Their power enabled them to set prices in ways that secured surplus profits at the expense of the remaining competitive sector.[20]

Monopoly pricing strategies by large firms commenced a process by which capital came to "govern" the market. Under monopoly governing of the market the sheer magnitude of outlay on fixed capital meant that its potential devaluation, or even destruction, during cyclical market oscillations became anathema. Giant oligopolies managed business cycles with their price fixing in ways enabling them to expand production and incorporate incremental technological modification during the prosperity phase of the business cycle. Such a strategy increasingly saddled large firms with overcapacity. The capitalist tendency toward overaccumulation therefore came to manifest itself in overproduction and gluts of commodities paralleled by diminution in business profits. Much of the brunt of this dynamic is borne by the small business sector through the siphoning away of their profits under conditions of monopoly price distortions.[21]

Both the perception of oligopolies governing the market along with the realization in major economies of the era that giant companies were "too big to fail" helped crystallize the view that the state could no longer act as "night watchman". Rather, it was recognized in the changed use value milieu that the state had a *policy* role to play in managing ups and downs of accumulation along with social conflicts which potentially arise from that.

One of the central policies of the state in the era of monopoly accumulation was tariff protectionism. Protectionist policy helped giant oligopolies maintain their monopoly price and profit regimes secure from foreign competition in their home markets. US tariffs on imported manufactures averaged 44 percent, for example.[22] Protectionism, of course, has its pitfalls when other states deploy it in turn. As well, monopoly pricing is constrained by levels of real wages as it is one of the "bases" which capital must touch under any circumstance to materially reproduce a human society where workers can purchase the equivalent of their necessary labor with their money wage. Monopoly profits could also not be allowed to drive profits in the competitive small business sector below rates of interest.[23]

The second state policy, which in fact is the signature policy of the era, is *imperialism*. Correctly apprehended in its basic *modus operandi* by Marxists of the era, Rudolf Hilferding and V.I. Lenin, the policy arose in the requirement that capital find an outlet for the capital overaccumulation in the domestic market that occurred due to the monopoly pricing and profit regime. What in effect amounted to large pools of idle M could only be profitably invested in colonial and imperialist territories captured by imperialist states. These territories would then be sealed off as preserves for exploitation by the "national" capital of imperialists. Excess commodities could also be "dumped" there at fire-sale prices. Profits from the imperialist endeavors would then be reinvested to promote those industries in imperialist territories which supported major export industries in the "national" economy, such as steel, or to secure supplies of raw materials.

The evidence for imperialist capital outflow, largely as portfolio investment, is robust. From 1870 to 1913 international portfolio investment averaged around 50 percent of global GDP. Capital outflow from Britain in the 1900-1914 period amounted to a whopping £920 million. From 1910 to 1913 alone Britain's net foreign investment equaled over 53 percent of its domestic savings.[24] In 1913-1914 a full 42 percent of British foreign investment went to Latin America, Asia and Africa. This entangled much of what today is the non-developed world in the imperialist system of control and exploitation.[25] Only 15 percent of global industrial output resided beyond Europe and North America. Much of this represented primary processing of cash crops and mineral production. While some recipients of imperialist portfolio investment benefitted, essentially the orchestration of imperialist policy was by "national governments which encouraged the commercial interests of their own citizens to preempt rival mining, telegraph, railway or commodity companies".[26] When this "preempting" had finally divided the non-developed remainder of the globe into imperialist-dominated "economic territories", imperialists turned toward potential coveting of territories from each other. So began the military build-up which preceded WWI.

The third policy of the period of state support of oligopolistic capital accumulation was a broad thrust of state political and ideological management and creation of vast bureaucracies for that purpose. Part of this was directed at political management of stirring labor activism. The increased scale of industrial operations in steel production fostered growing collectivities of workers. By 1907, 75 percent of workers in German iron and steel factories labored in plants with upward of 1000 workers.[27] The largest oligopoly firm in Germany, Krupp, had over 70,000 workers at the time of WWI.[28] The extension of the democratic franchise toward universal male suffrage as a sop to workers proved a double edged sword. In Germany this produced a socialist working class party that proceeded to eke out electoral gains. Government responded by co-opting components of the socialist program which entailed public investment in rudimentary social insurance programs.

Government also invested heavily in higher education in order to organize science in the service of capital accumulation. But supporting oligopoly capital through spreading technical education was not the only reason for state investment in mass education. Rivalries amongst imperialist states meant inculcation of mass publics with a vehement *nationalism*. We would not be overstating the matter to see nationalism as the key ideology of the era. Primary education replete with nationalist symbolic trappings such as flags in the classrooms of children and daily singing of national anthems became *de rigueur*. Education would also become the platform for disseminating ideologies of "methodological individualism" during the imperialist period to counteract the encroaching collectivization of material life by monopolies and the state. It is certainly no accident that neoclassical economics with its cult of so-called rational individual choice becomes hegemonic at this juncture. The compartmentalizing of education where "economics" is cordoned off from politics and sociology is part and parcel of that.[29]

Fourthly, imperialist states directly invested in providing so-called public goods such as power generation. They also invested in transportation and infrastructure. When we look at figures on state spending as a proportion of GDP, a qualitative rise from the mid 19th century is glaringly evident. In 1913 state economic activity as a percent of GDP in Britain rises to 13.3, in Germany it is 17.7, and in Japan 14.2. Even in the US, state investment constituted 8 percent of GDP in 1913.[30]

It is, however, in the realm of finance where the transformation of the very form of capital, in the most substantive sense, occurs. The capital investment requirements for the fixed capital outlay of giant monopolistic firms, along with the complex measures involved in bringing facilities on line, demanded a mobilization of funds the extent of which the resources of entrepreneurs or even their family partnerships could never supply. The idle M held in the banking system, which "socialized" funds for industrial and commercial capital investment, also proved inadequate for the qualitatively greater magnitudes of capital necessary to finance monopoly industries. The viability of capital accumulation in heavy steel and chemical industry thus hinged on a further and new mode of mobilizing idle M from the hands which were then holding it within society at large: a rentier cohort of erstwhile small capitalists "bought out" by oligopoly firms who then became "rentiers"; the new class of managers and white collar managerial functionaries with considerable personal savings, and the landlord classes.

The transformation of the capitalist credit system with the emergence of stock or equity markets carried important ramifications for capital accumulation with effects continuing to this day as we will explore in the following chapter. For now, a first ramification is that the new credit system of equity markets now enabled the largest stockholders to deploy even more immense quantities of socially available funds along with their own paid-in capital to concentrate "controlling power" of joint-stock monopoly-oligopoly firms at the expense of other shareholding "owners". A second ramification is the disjuncture between the capitalist production-centered circuit of value augmentation and the goings-on of stock markets. That is to say, the paid-in capital of giant oligopolies continues its operation as capital in the production-centered circuit of profit making, notwithstanding activities of individual shareholders. Individual shareholders can withdraw from the business by selling their shares. But this transfer in ownership does not disrupt the capitalist production-centered circuit. This is the case because stocks are "fictitious" capital in the sense of simply being commodity or "property" entitlements to share in the profits of business in the form of periodic *dividend* payments.[31]

More importantly, equity valuations are different from rates of interest. The latter vary according to supply and demand for funds in money markets. Equities, on the other hand, are *not* "produced" or supplied in response to "demand" for them. Rather, they bought and sold in the *capital* market. The "reconceptualization" of capital by itself, adverted to in Chapter Three, assumes a qualitatively more complex form with the growth of equity or capital markets. Through the capital market, the transubstantiation of capital into a commodity or asset the use value of which is to earn an income stream, occurs through the fictitious converting of real production-centered capital into money capital as the equity of the firm. That equity is then divided into marketable shares. However, again, real production-centered capital continues its circuit independently of this. Shareholders do not necessarily own the equivalent in equity of what they advanced in their initial share purchase. That depends, on the one hand, on the relationship between the rate of interest and the rate of profit.[32] On the other hand, it hinges on perceptions of future profit of joint-stock companies and potential speculative activities of investors in that regard. As emphasized by Lapavitsas, grasping the disjuncture between the motion of real capital and fictitious (equity) capital as such, and how this interfaces with the money market and banking system, is integral to understanding the gargantuan accrual to finance today of "profits without production".[33]

A third ramification of the transformed credit system is the relation the requirement of massive investment in fixed capital engenders between giant oligopolies and banks. The early 20th century imperialist era not only sees the rise of bigger government but also bigger banks. The sheer size of capital investment commitments compounded by the time scope of setting these in motion dictated that banks themselves grow and cultivate enduring affiliations with large companies. Banks' interest in the long term stability of their oligopolistic affiliates led them to discourage competition and spur mergers. The latter was facilitated by the joint-stock form of business in the way it allowed for cross-holding of equity among businesses and banks. Rudolf Hilferding dubs this arrangement *finance capital*.

Germany is often upheld as the paradigmatic exemplar of finance capital given its predicament of "late" or "catch-up" industrialization. However, Landes argues that banks in Britain would ultimately turn from their global exploits to domestic business investment in kind as demand arose.[34] And banks in Britain got big. By 1920 the so-called "Big Five" banks in Britain accounted for 80 percent of all lending and deposits.[35] In fact, it is at close of the 19th century that central banks as *the* biggest banks among the bigger banks began to emerge as lenders of last resort to expand credit in times of crises.[36]

The "organizing" of capitalism and governing of the market dampened the sorts of business cycle oscillations idiosyncratic to mid 19th century capital. But all the machinations of oligopoly firms, their supportive infrastructure of large scale credit granting financial affiliates, the readiness to spring into credit creating action of central banks and the newly widening role of bigger government could not forestall the bigger social and economic tumult which struck the global economy first in 1907. In the US President Theodore Roosevelt was forced to turn to the banking house of Morgan to shore up the financial system as panic set in. The US central bank, Federal Reserve System (FED), was established forthwith in 1913.[37]

Then came the Great Depression of 1929. The world economy did not effectively emerge from it until 1945.

The Use Value Ultimatum

The story of the Great Depression is replete with proximate causes. The fallout from WWI certainly figures prominently as one. Economist Michael Hudson, in his landmark book, *Super Imperialism*, offers the clearest explanation.[38] According to him, US financing of its European Allies in the WWI period left a festering sore at the heart of the global financial system. Twin veins of this "sore" were the transposition of international finance from a regime dominated by private flows to one of intergovernmental finance: and the rise of the US as a global creditor state. The former saw Allied states debt expanded in a way which wildly exceeded the productive resources of the continent. Such would not have occurred under the suzerainty of private lenders who would have exercised greater prudence in lending given their private exposure to potential default (given lending conditions of the time, of course). European debt was problematic under conditions of ramped up US trade protectionism. This meant there was no chance that European debtors might be able to at least partially export their way out of debt travails.

Nevertheless, a peculiar "triangular flow of payments" was instigated, argues Hudson, which brought private lending back in to support Europe in its irredeemably indebted time of need. Billions of dollars were lent to Germany (as asset after asset in Germany was placed on the auction block) which it then used to pay war reparations to Allies, who then used the money to service their debt to the US government. Bracketing here the question of the complete lack of long term sustainability of such an arrangement in itself, from 1928 private flows turned away from Europe to booming US stock markets. US investors were soon followed by European and other investors attracted by the Wall Street bonanza which in turn led to a contraction of credit elsewhere in the world, impelling other economies into recession. The dearth of global liquidity and spreading recession around the world soon exacerbated the travails of the US economy.

The empirical evidence here is compelling. The Dow Jones Industrial Average (DJIA) leaped from 191 in the beginning of 1928 to 381 by September 1929. This doubling of equity prices dwarfed potential returns from US investments overseas where capital had previously flowed. Simultaneously, the net outflow from the US of $900 million in 1927-28 became but an annual trickle of $86 million from 1929 to 1931.[39]

What were the "travails" of the US economy? The *prima facie* case is that it had much to do with exuberance over Wall Street stock market opportunity. Mass public information about the security of stock investments lagged behind the widespread acquisition of "common stock" holdings. Individuals owning common shares numbered a half million in 1900. By 1930 that number had multiplied to 10 million.[40] There was also the issue of rising consumer debt. From the early 20th century a raft of consumer goods became available in the advanced economies. Personal incomes had doubled in these economies between 1870 and 1913. Demand for the new consumer goods including telephones, personal sewing machines and eventually automobiles also doubled during this period.[41] As consumer goods proliferated so did credit to obtain them. In the 1920s consumer debt would double. There was $6.4 billion in US consumer debt before the 1929 crash. Yet, the new credit revolution in fact only involved 10 percent of the population![42]

There is also the question of policy mismanagement. Was the 1929 crash caused by insider squabbling within the FED system, lacking a "maestro" to pull the trigger with "high powered" money at the right time?[43] What about the policy fixation on so-called market solutions? This discourse was certainly quixotic given that capitalist economies were now processed by oligopoly firms, bigger banks, bigger government and the "organizing" of the economy was managed in ways which dampened the sorts of business cycle oscillations that occurred from mid to late 19th century. Nevertheless, market ideology screamed for what is politely dubbed "austerity". The statement of President Herbert Hoover's treasury secretary, Andrew Mellon, on the Depression was simple: "Liquidate labor, liquidate stocks, liquidate the farmers, liquidate real estate".[44] "Liquidationism" is but acquiescence to the inevitable. Austerity clears the rot. And, as in the 19th century, entrepreneurs will weave their market magic, kick starting another business cycle upswing a-la-Adam Smith. Such policy beliefs held sway as the cataclysmic Great Depression began to unfold.[45]

Lurking, however, beneath the foregoing is what we may conceptualize as a use value ultimatum delivered to capital. Steel production, the leading early 20th century sector, had grown dramatically to meet demand for railways, port facilities, communications infrastructure, industrial and civic construction, and ultimately WWI weaponry and transport accouterment. Yet by the 1920s it stalled as the engine of capitalist growth. Most global rail track had been laid by that time. Global trading and communications infrastructure was already emplaced.[46]

In the US, the sunrise industry of the mid 20th century world economy, automobile production, was experiencing its earliest stirrings. In 1913, 1.7 million automobiles, 75 percent of these in the US, roamed roads of the globe. By 1916, Ford alone produced 730,000 automobiles. In 1929, the US would produce 5.4 million vehicles of various sorts. The automobile industry was then the demand source for 20 percent of US tin, nickel and steel and a full 50 percent of "strip steel". It absorbed over 30 percent of US aluminum, 75 percent of plate glass and rubber.[47] It thus seemed self-evident that expanding automobile production, given its sheer material accouterment, extensive backward and forward linkages, potentially constituted the new growth industry which could spin capital into a sustained boom. And rejuvenate steel production to boot. This was easy to envision...traumatic to accomplish.

Looking at this from the demand side of the real economy, we know that the market for automobiles grew very rapidly in the US given the geospatial expanses of the country. Yet the expense of the automobile rendered it an upper middle class, and elite, market item. Even Henry Ford's famous "five dollar day" did not allow auto workers to purchase cars. The latter was simply a device to thwart worker turnover considering that in 1913 Ford required around 14,000 laborers to run a plant.[48] Upper middle class demand was certainly fuelled by rising farm incomes in the WWI period. As global agricultural supply resurrected, however, the US was saddled with chronic overproduction in that sector. Declining income from agriculture impacted automobile demand. It also impacted construction. Thus, a housing boom and bubble amounting to 8 percent of GDP was collapsing by 1927.[49] By 1933, a full 43 percent of US farm households responsible for 52 percent of all mortgage debt were in default.[50]

From the supply side of the real US economy the picture is more complicated. French economists Gérard Duménil and Dominique Lévy make the best sense of the varied evidences.[51] The auto industry, the major industrial sector in 1929, was divided between large, relatively strong firms and numerous smaller companies. The industry was further marked by extreme technological heterogeneity. Larger firms innovated rapidly. The smaller and medium sized companies did not. Technological heterogeneity was driven by the fast pace of technological change within the industry paralleled by rising costs of labor. In effect, the foregoing rendered a "large segment of the economy obsolete". It is no surprise that approximately 50 percent of *all* automobile establishments were shuttered by the Great Depression. Evidence further shows the problem of technological obsolescence to be endemic across major businesses in the US economy by 1929.

Let us sprinkle some issues of finance into the mix. Going back to agriculture and housing it is instructive that as the boom unfolded so banks proliferated across the US. Many banks were small and depended upon a narrow customer base. Of 31,000 banks in 1921, only 15,000 would remain in existence by 1933. When we look at industry a peculiar relationship is discovered, according to Duménil and Lévy, between its technological heterogeneity and its financing. Equity and bond financing played an inordinately large role in financing fixed investment in the lead up to the Great Depression. This in part suggests an unjustified exuberance on the part of investors over the potential of industries such as automobiles. Between September 1929 and June 1931 industrial share prices plummeted 59.7 percent.[52] Banks were also caught up in lending to small and medium sized firms the viability of which was in question. The larger businesses which ultimately survived the Great Depression had cut borrowing and maintained cash reserves when profit rates initially began to fall.

Such factors concatenated with the financial travails of the aforementioned global imbalances and ultimately the "fetters" the global gold standard placed upon government action and led to waves of global capital flight. And, of course, it was adherence to rules on expansion of credit set by the gold standard which, along with ideology, mandated austerity as the policy response.[53]

In short, as we have seen, capitalist breakdown and crises erupt in the realm of finance. This is the case given the vital capitalist-social role banking and finance play in the capitalist production-centered circuit of value augmentation. In particular, banking and finance militate against the anarchy of capitalist production. Of course, notwithstanding a more pronounced capitalist-social role played by "bigger banks" with affiliated oligopoly firms to govern the market, the anarchy of capital based in private units competitively bent upon value augmentation is impossible to override. The anarchy of capital is amplified when we factor in private oligopoly units of capital competing on the world market from their base camps in nation states. In the age of steel production and imperialist state policies the final chapter in monopoly firm overproduction of capital is the drive to war to enhance market share. Though that resolved little. By the early 1930s steel production with its massive economies of scale was operating at approximately 50 percent capacity in the US, for example.[54]

Looking back at troubles in capitalist paradise from the vantage point of the Depression and the emergence of the post World War II (WWII) "golden age" two patterns emerge: First, seismic transmutations of capital, which entail not just technological upgrading of fixed capital but shifts to producing a qualitatively divergent constellation of use values with their wholly new technological outlays, is a hugely disruptive if not potentially fatal process for capital. Intervening periods between major phases or stages of capitalist development are therefore punctuated by decades of economic crises, social dislocation and/or war.

Second, the only historical period of capitalism in which accumulation unfolded largely according to the market principles of capital was the liberal, *laissez faire* era of textiles and light consumer goods from the mid 19th century to the 1870s. As capital faced the management of use value obstacles inhering in heavier or "bulkier" forms of use value production such as steel and heavy industrial chemicals, it assumed a *less* characteristically capitalist form. As we shall see, for capital to shift to mass production of consumer durables as the basis of sustained accumulation, it must adopt a wide array of extra-economic, extra-capitalist practices for support. So what is referred to as the post WWII "golden age" of capitalism is paradoxically the least characteristically capitalist phase of capitalist history.

The emergence of a new stage of capital accumulation, as we have emphasized at several points, is never a *fait accompli*. To begin with, some capitalistically manageable use value complex which can pull accumulation into a sustained boom must exist on the horizon. Capital found this in the automobile industry. The new use value structure of accumulation came alive initially in the US. By the late 1960s and early 1970s it would directly employ 800,000 workers in the US. When linkages it fostered with other industries from highway construction to service stations and insurance are factored in, it employed 1 out of 6 Americans. In the 1950s it contributed to a full 20 percent of US GNP. In 1955 over 60 percent of total global output of automobiles was produced by three giant US transnational corporations (TNCs). These TNCs – General Motors (GM), Ford and Chrysler – dominated 94 percent of the US market.[55]

The TNC *form* capital paradigmatically assumes in the post WWII period is qualitatively different from the monopoly capitalist form of early 20th century steel production. The TNC form was found not only in automobiles. It emerged in other commanding heights industries including petroleum and chemicals, agricultural machinery, electronics and electrical appliances, transportation equipment and so forth.

Production of complex consumer durables such as the automobile required coordinating the supply and distribution of thousands of standardized parts and components. TNCs integrated these along with research and design, advertizing, marketing and so forth in multidivisional, multi-plant behemoths which function like centrally planned communist states. TNC transactions are largely "internalized" among their corporate divisions. This means that transactions rely on the device of "transfer pricing" rather than markets. As a result of TNC activities global trade itself becomes dominated by *intra-industry* and *intra firm* flows in ways which further eschew market pricing.

The TNC form of capital that spawned in the morphing of the strongest firms surviving the Great Depression shed the mode of direct bank financing dubbed "finance capital" by Hilferding. Rather, if capital manifested a novel trend in its TNC form during the "golden age" it is toward self-financing with its massive retained earnings and selective turns to capital markets. The General Motors Acceptance Corporation (GMAC) is an example of TNC capital developing its own financing arm. Evidence shows that 65 percent of funds acquired by US nonfinancial corporations in the 1946-1970 period was generated internally. During the same period data demonstrates that equity represented only 3.5 percent of all funds generated by US nonfinancial corporations.[56]

Superintendence of both TNC operational financing and strategic planning of its integrated activities fell into the hands of management. TNCs incorporated specialized departments for cultivating managerial expertise. Management worked in pyramidal structures with top management based at company headquarters in turn delegating responsibility for operating decisions to divisional management. The command over financing endowed management with untrammeled capacity for advancing the firm's profit oriented, market capturing interests.[57] Top management also invested in the TNCs they ran. A 1957 study showed that TNC top management in the 100 largest US companies owned an average of 9.9 percent of their businesses' stock and drew significant income from that.[58]

Commanding heights industrial sectors in the "golden age" were structured in an oligopolistic fashion. They avoided price competition and lesser firms tended to tacitly follow the dominant oligopoly in setting prices in each sector. This system led to increased concentration of manufacturing assets. From 1947 to 1968 the percent of total US manufacturing assets in the hands of the top 200 oligopolies leaped from 47.2 to 60.9 percent.[59]

While the monopolistic steel industry with its product market rooted in other businesses primarily in railroads, shipping and armaments encouraged imperialist policies, oligopolistic consumer durable industries advance policies of *consumerism*. For TNCs themselves this meant accepting a high wage labor force and embracing unionization where big labor organizations pressed wage demands commensurate with productivity increases. The industrial model of TNC consumer durable production entailed high throughput of semiautomatic assembly line production which lowered unit costs. In this way it was possible to include the expensive consumer durables the production of which was central to value augmentation in the consumption basket of direct producers in advanced economies.[60]

Including automobiles and consumer durables in the consumption basket of labor power makes sense in terms of our discussion of the way capital meets the general norms of economic life to materially reproduce a human society. In conceptualizing this Marx always recognized that what precisely constituted the consumption basket of workers is historically relative. It would have to be, as the possibility of capital touching the required "bases" also means that the total labor power of society is organized in a division of labor that meets the demand for goods in society that people need and want. Between 1950 and 1971 the percent of the workforce in major OECD economies in manufacturing sectors rises from an average of about 34 percent to nearly 40 percent with the US coming in at 36 percent in 1966, Belgium at 47 percent in 1957, and Germany with 49.3 percent of its workforce in manufacturing in 1970.[61] If we factor in the percent of manufacturing assets in the hands of giant TNCs producing consumer durables in advanced economies, and take account of the enormous economy of scale requirements, we can see that a monstrous misallocation of social resources would follow under such labor market conditions if real wages were not able to purchase consumer durables.

The centerpiece of this modus vivendi between capital and labor is the post WWII "golden age" *class accord*. Just prior to the Great Depression the giant oligopolies had employed goon squads, numbering in thousands of thugs, to thwart worker action. But, commencing in the US and ultimately spreading across advanced democracies, the "golden age" saw class struggle purged from the labor agenda. Labor and their union reps traded political quiescence for a rising wage and benefit package. Real income for US families skyrocketed during the "golden age". From 1946 through 1974 real *disposable* income *never* fell!

US family income also grew equally for each quintile between 1947 and 1979. And the share held by the top 1 percent fell to just over 20 percent of total US income. Indeed, mainstream presses loudly proclaimed how workers lost their class identity. Ideologies of mass consumption and the hyper-individuality of the "consumer" became prevalent. Credit for purchase of consumer durables abounded. Pejorative notions of "consumption loans" from the days of usurious money lending were banished. In their stead the term "consumerism" was entered into the lexicon of finance.[62] This was reinforced by an omnipresent corporate mass media and corporate advertizing firms. The political legitimacy of advanced state governments themselves were bound to ensuring the consumption fete never ends.[63]

Policy support of capital by "bigger" government began in the phase of imperialism. During the "golden age", however, government performed herculean policy feats to ensure ongoing capital accumulation. "Bigger" government became Big Government.[64] During WWII, the state ramped up its investment act, financing 61 percent of US total investment in 1943.[65] Following the war, Big Government rolled out an elaborate welfare state: policies for social welfare, unemployment insurance, health insurance in varying doses, pension entitlements, workplace disability compensations and so forth. What is important to grasp here is that the major oligopolies which emerged as TNCs from the Depression had themselves experimented with precisely such policies and found them productivity enhancing and labor force stabilizing. TNCs thus wholeheartedly backed Big Governments' efforts and expenditures. As Jeffry Frieden bluntly states: "Modern societies may simply have required social democratic welfare states to survive".[66]

Arguably the signature policy of the "golden age" was Big Government support for ever-expanding mass consumption of consumer durables. Such support is provided largely by macroeconomic fiscal policy though monetary policy is also brought in to play. The key fiscal policy was countercyclical demand management to maintain the economy in a state of quasi boom. Building on ideas of economist John Maynard Keynes the key question for advanced economies was boosting effective demand. This can be accomplished by Big Government through increased spending as signs of recession appeared. Such spending carried a "multiplier effect" in its impact upon the private sector where jobs would be kept which otherwise would have been lost. Employment from direct government spending and that in the private sector spurred by it ensures that workers will have active M in their pockets to consume with. Deficits incurred by the government are sure to be short lived as revenues from economic activities it supports return to its coffers.

But there is another side to the workings of Big Government here. When we think back to the Chapter Three discussion of the micro-equilibrium and macro-dynamic tendencies of capital it is clear that "golden age" Big Government is necessarily implicated in both: touching the "bases", as we put it, to ensure the material reproducibility of capital as an historical society; as well as maintaining human labor power as a commodity under conditions of capitalist disequilibrium and revolutionizing of the forces of production.

The early 20th century world of monopoly capital already saw attenuated business cycle oscillations. Tendencies toward overaccumulation of capital were deflected by imperialist policies of capital export and the dumping of its heavy use values in captive imperialist territories at cut rate prices. In the "golden age" economy dominated by the TNC form of capital a very different process of governing macro-dynamic oscillations of capital was invoked. With TNCs producing expensive consumer durables like automobiles, the cycles instead oscillated around expansions to full capacity utilization followed by contractions of output with maintenance of overcapacity where price levels of key consumer durables fluctuate minimally.[67] Even during the Great Depression, for example, consumer durable prices fell only 8 percent. Agricultural commodity prices, on the other hand, fell 52 percent between 1928 and 1933. Steel and construction material fell 18 percent in that period.[68]

Generous "golden age" social wages, along with acceding of capital and Big Government to unionized collective bargaining over wage/benefit packages, partially decommodified labor power. Yet, when we set this within the context of macroeconomic countercyclical fiscal policymaking of the state we can see how, paradoxically, partial decommodification of labor power served to maintain labor power as a commodity. That is, production decisions in the golden age were still anarchic in that they were made by individual oligopolies with their own private profit-making strategies and horizons at heart.

Already in the imperialist era monopoly power enabled firms to innovate selectively at various junctures in the business cycle. In combining economies of international *scope* with those of scale, TNC capital of the golden age was further empowered to maintain less productive technologies alongside more productive ones according to the competitive conditions it faced. Nevertheless, competition still impelled cycles of overaccumulation of capital and falling profits, the cumulative effects of which ultimately led to the demise of the golden age by the mid 1970s as we will see.

The "golden age", in other words, did not replace market operations by planning as did Soviet-style states. Rather, Big Government engaged in what may be understood as economic "programming". Such programming is, however, essential to ensuring an "optimal" allocation of resources. Macroeconomic policymaking kicked in *ex post* as business cycle indicators displayed signs of looming recession. The maintenance of labor power as a commodity was therefore mediated, on the one hand, by falling profits and resultant unemployment/curtailing of production (with resultant overcapacity) at that point, above which wages cannot rise in the prosperity phase of the cycle. On the other hand *ex post* macroeconomic countercyclical policymaking ensured wages did not fall below that point required under exigencies of corporate capital accumulation. Therefore no "pure" depression phase of the business cycle materialized that would see exorbitantly expensive capital outlays destroyed.

Remember, already in the imperialist period there was consensus in government and business that big capital was too big to fail. In the "golden age", it was much too big to fail!

With Big Government, the "golden age" heralded the ascendency of Big Bank. As Nomi Prins opines, the reputation of banking, sullied during the Great Depression, was restored by WWII bank support for the state. Nothing, of course, demonstrates "support" better than money. By end June 1946, public debt in the US had increased five-fold to $270 billion. Government debt itself amounted to 60 percent of all debt. And commercial banks wound up holding around a third of US debt securities equivalent to 71 percent of their total assets. In other words, the Big Government-Big Bank nexus forged in war became the foundation of rejuvenated banking during the "golden age".[69]

While we will visit the issue of the new post WWII international monetary system momentarily, it is vital to apprehending the "golden age" Big Government-Big Bank nexus to be clear on the point that gold no longer constituted monetary reserve. Rather, differing from both the mid 19th century period of liberal, *laissez faire* capitalism and the early 20th century imperialist era, national money systems transmuted from commodity money to *fiat money*. In fiat money systems the aforementioned government debt securities serve as the reserves of the new monetary system. It is thus the holdings of government bonds between the central bank and the commercial banks connected to it which determine the level of the monetary base and the extent of credit creation in the economy. For example, in the US, if the FED buys securities from commercial banks with its reserves, the monetary base increases. But money in the economy at large only increases if commercial banks then engage in lending. Most importantly, unlike the gold standard system of *laissez faire* capitalism, *no automatic mechanism* exists to trend money supply and credit issuance toward its "optimal" or "equilibrium" level. Attempts in that direction can *only* be achieved through policy.[70]

In the US policymaking produced a raft of regulations which transformed the financial sector. The Glass-Steagall Act created a firewall between commercial (relationship) banking which accepted deposits and investment banking that specialized in securities transactions. Regulation Q set bounds on interest rates in the deposit accounts. The Federal Deposit Insurance Corporation (FDIC) guaranteed savings of the mass public to a given limit. Even institutional mechanisms to subsidize credit for homebuyers and farmers were rolled out.[71]

To be crisply clear here on the pervasiveness of financial regulation across the advanced capitalist world, the fact of the matter is that in 1960 interest rates in all 22 OECD economies were set by state policy or state-sanctioned banking organizations. Policy regulation yielded a remarkably stable financial system. From the end of WWII until 1974 there was no major bank failure in the advanced capitalist economies. Nor did the banking population change much. Such was the case in the US along with Canada, Japan, UK, among others.

Notwithstanding the policy regulative constraints on the financial sector, commercial banking exhibited both robust growth and profitability. The over 4 percent average growth in GDP per capita of major economies between 1946 and 1972 tells part of the story here. Though interest rates were capped by Regulation Q, market rates on bank assets rose. Large banks with expanding deposit bases therefore prospered. As well, the internationalizing of production and commerce by TNCs from the 1950s internationalized banking in its wake. Big Banks themselves became TNBs and profited handsomely in that milieu.[72] If regulation handed commercial banks a protected domain of operation, so too investment banks had a monopoly in securities trading. Trading in securities was also profitable despite the fact that total financial assets of broker-dealers never increased more than 2 percent of US GDP between 1946 and 1980.[73]

Finally, advanced economies' Keynesian "economic nationalist" projects were cocooned by the Bretton Woods international monetary system (BWIMS).[74] Rebuilding each war-torn economy along with the fostering of prosperity in the US economy demanded a significant degree of macroeconomic policy flexibility. It also required varied interest rate regimes to deal with divergent national circumstances for gathering idle M and encouraging investment. Internationally, attempting to revive world trade necessitated currency stability. BWIMS' fixed exchange rate regime liberated TNCs' trade and investment activities from the specter of foreign exchange risk. TNBs similarly had no need to cultivate the gargantuan currency trading operations required by banks today. BWIMS mandated capital controls to ensure that long term productive capital investment rather than short term speculative financial flows took advantage of the divergent policy regimes.

In one fell swoop the BWIMS offered a contract among nations for resurrecting the capitalist world economy. BWIMS instated the US dollar as the new hub international currency replacing gold. While it was clear to BWIMS architects that this would confer potential benefit on the US, to keep the US honest, the dollar exchange rate was fixed to gold and subject to free convertibility at $35 to the ounce. With the dollar then deemed "as good as gold" the exchange rates of all the world's other major currencies were fixed to it.

BWIMS liberated "golden age" advanced economies to manage their fiat currencies according to their chosen "economic nationalist" ends. Fiat money became the intimate partner of macroeconomic policymaking. Under the gold standard, inflationary fiscal policies to bolster effective demand would have been met by capital flight followed by assaults on wages and other austerity measures so as to lower costs and keep currency exchange rates stable for trade. Fiat money under state management, on the other hand, can be applied to maintenance of full employment along with high profits without forcing currency devaluation.

BWIMS even solved the problem of global liquidity. In the US as elsewhere war rationing confined consumption within strict bounds even among those with money and savings. Thus, in the aftermath of war it was certain that resultant pent up demand would bring large profits to businesses investing to meet that. The problem was that with businesses around the globe devastated by the Depression and war, and those in the US having to reconvert from military to civilian production, the idle M that firms in the normal course of the business cycle would have saved for new capital investment in plant and equipment was in short supply. Idle M held by banks had also been diverted away from private lending toward investment in government bonds in support of the war effort. However, with the dollar as a managed currency domestically, and the US dollar as world money, the US, through the BWIMS, was able to satisfy the international hunger for liquidity and jumpstart the global economy.

Lastly, BWIMS birthed two novel supranational institutions. The role of the International Monetary Fund (IMF) was to secure policy compliance from member states to deal with balance of payment (BOP) difficulties. The World Bank (WB) was hatched as an intergovernmental organization flush with billions of dollars to lend to individual states for development. Such *political* organization of the global economy constituted one of the more significant and telling changes in the history of capitalism.

Paradise Lost

Despite the herculean policy exertions of Big Government and Big Bank, the "golden age" economy fell prey to what remained of its capitalist substance. Rising profits which fuelled investment in the leading consumer durable manufacturing sector of "golden age" advanced economies built up a massive and expensive technologically efficient fixed capital structure. As we note, both market-eschewing price setting activities of TNCs along with Big Government countercyclical macroeconomic policymaking averted major cyclical devaluations of capital. Instead, the capital outlay simply compounded as oscillations revolved around expansions to full capacity utilization followed by contractions of output with maintenance of overcapacity.

The problem is that in the relatively closed "economic nationalist" economies of the "golden age" the absorption of the high throughput of consumer durable industries depended firstly on expanding markets. Signs of market saturation had appeared already in the US by the 1970s. By 1980, for example, there would be over 10 million more registered cars in the US than licensed drivers (and this figure says nothing about automobiles that are not sold in a given year)![75] Then there was the crucial question of rising wages for manufacturing workers. Ultimately, rising real wages and rates of capacity utilization reached their "upper bound". Such overaccumulation of capital in relation to the effective demand embodied in the real wage placed a downward pressure on profits. It also led to growing pools of surplus funds from industry, or idle M, as rates of productive investment slowed.[76] We should point out here that the "golden age" already contained a propensity for generating greater amounts of idle M than in previous stages of capitalism. But much of it was mopped up by the Keynesian welfare state social wage policies (along with warfare state policy in the US). And in the US, it was further put to use by early forays of major TNCs in foreign direct investment (FDI).

The corollary to pooling idle M as the "golden age" progressed was the expansion of private debt among TNCs. Franco Modigliani and Merton Miller in their "MM theory" gave the debt explosion and the greater leverage it granted to TNC investment strategies respectable academic grounding. MM theory, which generated a series of Nobel Prizes as "quant" economists at the University of Chicago and across MBA programs refined it, maintained that properly deployed debt will enhance TNC profit making.[77]

Economist Hyman Minsky approached the question of TNC debt from another angle. He argued that mounting debt was endemic to capitalist economies with increased accumulation of durable capital assets such as the "golden age" case where the economy is dominated by TNCs.[78] Sekine importantly points out, in relation to Minsky, that while Minsky does not problematize capitalism in this regard, it is not capitalism *per se* which must confront the problem of durable capital assets. Rather it is the phase or type of capitalism that crystallized in the post WWII era.

The increasing "roundaboutness" of capital accumulation in the production of consumer durables brought to bear expensive investments in fixed capital by layers of interconnected businesses producing inputs into final consumption consumer durable use values. The temporal exigencies of such layered interconnections among businesses generated demands for complex modalities of financing. TNCs, during the "golden age", therefore had to become arbitragers or "money managers" as well as producers. That, in turn, is what saddled the system with a permanent "instability".[79] Big Government and Big bank, for Minsky, are able to contain such financial "fragility" for a time. But the sheer volumes of funds pumped into economies for that purpose foment inflation.[80]

BWIMS did not just ensure global liquidity for post war reconstruction and development. Its funds provided a conduit for US exports of its technologies along with the business structures and practices which animated them. So successful was the rebuilding of Western Europe and Japan that exports from *their* TNCs soon challenged the US in its own home market. Even US TNC capital invested in Europe through FDI exhibited productivity gains which in the end challenged US domestic production. The US role in the Cold War, including its ringing the world with military bases and military interventions in Korea and Vietnam, misallocated resources in its domestic economy in ways avoided by its global competitors. It also added to the inflationary pressures of state macroeconomic programming and welfare policies.[81]

The weakening of the US economy and US dollar saw demand rapidly grow for conversion of US dollars into gold at the BWIMS rate of $35 per ounce. As US gold stocks depleted then President Richard Nixon slammed the gold window shut, unilaterally breaking the BWIMS "social contract" among nations. Predictably, the US money supply increased: 40 percent between 1970 and 1973 to be exact. Between 1972 and 1973 the UK money supply increased by 70 percent. Price inflation exploded around the world. The quadrupling of oil prices by Organization of Petroleum Exporting Countries (OPEC) added to global inflationary woes. But OPEC was not the main villain of the piece. It was the unilateral closing of the gold window. Under BWIMS states would have had to curtail price rises to maintain fixed exchange rates. In any case, recession soon spread across the industrial world in the worst downturn since the Great Depression. In 1975 industrial output shrank 10 percent as the US stock market value halved from its 1972 level.[82]

In desperate attempts to turn back the clock on paradise

lost two strategy thrusts characterized advanced economies. One was massive expansion of state economic activity. Big Government was becoming *very* Big Government. Millions of jobs were created in advanced economy public sectors. Big Government on average increased its spending from 33 to 42 percent of advanced economy GDP between 1971 and 1983. By the latter year Big Government accounted for an average of one fifth of all jobs, in some cases one third of jobs, in major economies. Much was financed by borrowing.[83] However, while borrowing was an attractive strategy with inflation galloping ahead of interest rates, the desired impact of Big Government spending never materialized. Further inflation was fostered. And the Keynesian "multiplier" was negated by the TNC international relocating of production as touched on below. Chronic US government deficits thus originate at this juncture.

Big central bank was also called upon in significant fashion to serve its function as lender of last resort. The first major stress faults in the advanced economy banking systems developed around exchange rate volatility and the currency trading the demise of BWIMS gave rise to. The 1974 failure of Franklin National Bank of New York, the largest bank failure in US history up to that point, followed its $45.8 million in foreign exchange losses.[84] The FDIC covered its deposits to the then stipulated $40,000. The FED looked after its remaining liabilities. With the writing on the wall regarding bank failures the Bank for International Settlements (BIS) was awakened in 1975 to consider guidelines for "national responsibility" for bank liabilities.[85]

Notwithstanding the coming into fashion of "monetarist" theories, the US money supply exploded. In 1974 it was near $1.2 trillion. By 1984 it veered close to $3 trillion. If all this Big Government and central bank money infusion huffing and puffing was intended to rejuvenate investment in the real production-centered consumer durable economy – well…nothing of the sort occurred. The late 1970s saw labor forces slashed and unemployment become structural; TNCs began disinternalizing production-centered facilities as state economies, the US in the lead, hollowed out industries. The story of the late 1970s in the

US, and mirrored in other major economies, is that of *stagflation*. This is the toxic combination of recession and inflation.[86]

The money infusion cited above in fact fed the second strategy thrust of advanced economy capital. This was the impelling of surplus funds on a frenetic trek across the globe. International capital flows jumped from $258 billion to $921 billion between 1974 and 1984.[87] In 1965, 13 US banks had 211 overseas branches with assets of $9.1 billion. By 1975, 126 US banks had 762 overseas branches holding assets worth $145.3 billion.[88] During the 1976-1980 period alone, US TNCs and TNBs tripled their foreign investments to $530 billion.[89] But, this expansion of cross-border flows of funds, note Kindleberger and Aliber, carried the "Minsky story" with them to the global economy. And, if the IMF was the intended international lender of last resort, it never rose to the occasion.[90]

To sum up, the prime global beneficiaries of the declining productivity growth and falling rates of investment in advanced economies which impelled TNC and TNB funds across the globe were a clutch of so-called newly industrializing economies adjacent Japan on the Pacific Rim. South Korea in particular and Taiwan to a certain extent would achieve measures of full scale industrialization that initiated them into the international club of advanced economies. Webber and Rigby put it well: "As capital sought to unbind itself from constraints of labour and demand in industrial capitalist countries so it has brought additional economies into the bounds of those constraints".[91]

As we shall see, the prime beneficiary of the 1970s economic crisis and demise of the BWIMS among advanced economies of the "golden age" era was the US. Not, of course, in the sense of business as usual. But in the way it rode the wave of the US dollar as hub currency, now no longer tethered to anything but US treasury IOUs (T-bill IOU), into an excrescent surrogate economy of and by Wall Street.

Endnotes

1. Martin van Creveld, *The Rise and Decline of the State* (Cambridge, MA: Cambridge University Press, 1999) pp. 214-9, 235.
2. See Colin Crouch, *The Strange Non-Death of Neoliberalism* (Cambridge, Polity Press, 2011) p. 17.
3. Giulio M. Gallarotti, "The Advent of the Prosperous Society: The Rise of the Guardian State and Structural Change in the World Economy", *Review of International Political Economy*, 7, 1 (2000) p. 5.
4. Bayly, *The Birth of the Modern World*, pp. 175-6.
5. Kees van der Pijl, "International Relations and Capitalist Discipline", in Albritton, Itoh, Westra, Zuege (eds.) *Phases of Capitalist Development*, pp. 5-8.
6. Lapavitsas, *Profiting Without Production*, p. 19.
7. Osterhammel, *The Transformation of the World*, pp. 730-3.
8. Albritton, *A Japanese Approach to Stages of Capitalist Development*, pp. 143-4.
9. Osterhammel, *The Transformation of the World*, pp. 735-6.
10. Marx, Chapter 15, *Capital*, Volume 1, https://www.marxists.org/archive/marx/works/1867-c1/ch15.htm.
11. David S. Landes, *The Unbound Prometheus: Technological Change and Industrial Development in Western Europe from 1750 to the Present*. Second Edition (Cambridge: Cambridge University Press, 2003) p. 249-51.
12. Kindleberger and Aliber, *Manias, Panics and Crashes*, pp. 117-9.
13. Osterhammel, *The Transformation of the World*, pp. 741-2.
14. Jeffry A. Frieden, *Global Capitalism: Its Fall and Rise in the Twentieth Century* (New York: W. W. Norton, 2007) pp. 16-8.
15. Landes, *The Unbound Prometheus*, pp. 251ff.
16. Jonathan Barron Baskin and Paul Miranti, Jr., *A History of Corporate Finance* (Cambridge: Cambridge University Press, 1999) pp. 139ff.
17. Baskin and Miranti, Jr., *A History of Corporate Finance*, pp. 171-4.
18. Albritton, *A Japanese Approach to Stages of Capitalist Development*, pp. 188-9.
19. Kōzō Uno, *The Types of Economic Policies under Capitalism* (unpublished translation by Thomas T. Sekine).
20. Albritton, *A Japanese Approach to Stages of Capitalist Development*, pp. 184-5.
21. Uno, *The Types of Economic Policies under Capitalism*.
22. Frieden, *Global capitalism*, p. 65.
23. Bell, *Capitalism and the Dialectic*, p. 201.
24. Calomiris and Haber, *Fragile by Design*, p.128.

25 Osterhammel, *The Transformation of the World*, p. 740.
26 Bayly, *The Birth of the Modern World*, pp. 177-9, 231.
27 Frieden, *Global Capitalism*, p. 63.
28 Albritton, *A Japanese Approach to Stages of Capitalist Development*, p. 184.
29 Albritton, *A Japanese Approach to Stages of Capitalist Development*, pp. 198-203, 214-21.
30 Angus Maddison, *The World Economy: A Millennial Perspective* (Paris: OECD, 2006) p. 135 Table 3.9.
31 Bell, *Capitalism and the Dialectic*, pp. 194-5.
32 Sekine, *An Outline of the Dialectic of Capital*, Volume 2, pp. 198-201.
33 Lapavitsas, *Profiting Without Production*, p. 58.
34 Landes, *The Unbound Prometheus*, pp. 349-51.
35 Calomiris and Haber, *Fragile by Design*, p. 127.
36 Kindleberger and Aliber, *Manias, Panics and Crashes*, pp. 196ff.
37 Baskin and Miranti, Jr., *A History of Corporate Finance*, p. 176.
38 See Michael Hudson, *Super Imperialism: The Origin and Fundamentals of U.S. World Dominance* (London: Pluto Press, 2003).
39 Frieden, *Global Capitalism*, p. 174.
40 Baskin and Miranti, Jr., *A History of Corporate Finance*, p. 182, 196.
41 Frieden, *Global Capitalism*, p. 62.
42 Geisst, *Beggar Thy Neighbor*, pp. 186-8.
43 Kindleberger and Aliber, *Manias, Panics and Crashes*, pp. 204-5.
44 Quoted in Mark Blyth, *Austerity: The History of a Dangerous Idea* (Oxford: Oxford University Press, 2013) p. 119.
45 Blyth, *Austerity*, pp. 120-1.
46 Landes, *The Unbound Prometheus*, pp. 460ff.
47 Frieden, *Global Capitalism*, pp. 59-62.
48 Albritton, *A Japanese Approach to Stages of Capitalist Development*, pp. 228-9.
49 See Maria N Ivanova, "Not just another crisis: How and why the Great Recession was different", in Richard Westra, Dennis Badeen and Robert Albritton (eds.) *The Future of Capitalism After the Financial Crisis: The Varieties of Capitalism Debate in the Age of Austerity* (London: Routledge, 2015) p. 172.
50 Gérard Duménil and Dominique Lévy, "The Great Depression: A Paradoxical Event", http://www.jourdan.ens.fr/levy/dle1995e.pdf.
51 Duménil and Lévy, "The Great Depression".
52 Landes, *The Unbound Prometheus*, p. 372.
53 Frieden, *Global Capitalism*, pp. 182-3, 186.
54 Westra, *The Evil Axis of Finance*, p. 30.
55 Albritton, *A Japanese Approach to Stages of Capitalist Development*,

	pp, 229-30.
56	Baskin and Miranti, Jr., *A History of Corporate Finance*, p. 242.
57	Baskin and Miranti, Jr., *A History of Corporate Finance*, p. 236-7.
58	Westra, *The Evil Axis of Finance*, p. 34.
59	Albritton, *A Japanese Approach to Stages of Capitalist Development*, pp. 232-3.
60	Westra, *Political Economy and Globalization*, pp. 56-7, 80.
61	Charles Feinstein, "Structural Change in the Developed Countries During the Twentieth Century", *Oxford Review of Economic Policy*, 15, 4 (1999).
62	Geisst, *Beggar Thy Neighbor*, p. 216.
63	Westra, *The Evil Axis of Finance*, pp. 35, 38-40.
64	This term draws upon Hyman Minsky, *Stabilizing an Unstable Economy* (New Haven, CT: Yale University Press, 1986).
65	Duménil and Lévy, "The Great Depression".
66	Frieden, *Global Capitalism*, p. 242 and passim.
67	Thomas Sekine, "Fiat Money and how to combat debt deflation", in Kiichiro Yagi, Nobuharu Yokokawa, Shinjiro Hagiwara and Gary Dymski (eds.) *Crises of Global Economies and the Future of Capitalism* (London: Routledge, 2013) pp. 208-9.
68	Frieden, *Global Capitalism*, p. 175.
69	Nomi Prins, *All the Presidents' Bankers: The Hidden Alliances that Drive American Power* (New York: Nation Books, 2014) pp.181-2.
70	Sekine, "Fiat Money and how to combat debt deflation", p. 218.
71	Calomiris and Haber, *Fragile by Design*, pp. 189-94.
72	Grossman, *Unsettled Account*, pp. 255-9.
73	Westra, *The Evil Axis of Finance*, p. 99.
74	Westra, *Political Economy and Globalization*, p. 89.
75	Tom Osenton, *The Death of Demand: Finding Growth in a Saturated Global Economy* (Upper Saddle River, NJ: Financial Times Prentice Hall, 2004) p. 30.
76	Weber and Rigby, "Growth and Change in the World Economy Since 1950" pp. 259-60.
77	Geisst, *Beggar Thy Neighbor*, pp. 212-3.
78	Minsky, *Stabilizing an Unstable Economy*, pp. 210ff.
79	Sekine, "Fiat Money and how to combat debt deflation", pp. 211-2.
80	Minsky, *Stabilizing an Unstable Economy*, pp 215-8.
81	Westra, *The Evil Axis of Finance*, pp. 73-4.
82	Frieden, *Global Capitalism*, pp. 364-6.
83	Frieden, *Global Capitalism*, p. 367.
84	Grossman, *Unsettled Account*, p. 267.
85	Kindleberger and Aliber, *Manias, Panics and Crashes*, pp. 232-3.

86 Grossman, *Unsettled Account*, pp. 260-1.
87 Westra, *The Evil Axis of Finance*, pp. 74-6.
88 Grossman, *Unsettled Account*, p. 268.
89 Frieden, *Global Capitalism*, p. 371.
90 Kindleberger and Aliber, *Manias, Panics and Crashes*, pp. 249, 255.
91 Weber and Rigby, "Growth and Change in the World Economy Since 1950", p. 261.

| Chapter Five |

MERCHANTS OF VENICE ON WALL STREET

Our narrative began with the reconstituting of Western European civilization following its brush with near annihilation during the Dark Ages. The feudal system that arose transformed social relations in agriculture, "freeing" the direct producers from the chains of chattel slavery. But it tethered them to the land they farmed with a form of extra-economic compulsion via "the divine right of kings" and military force concentrated in the hands of ruling lords and princes. The social goal of feudal society was the maintaining of staid social relations of domination and subordination and the distribution of use values according to the relative needs of these relations. The key economic principle which held feudal society together, we may recall, was *redistribution*. Redistribution moved surplus goods directly from the hands of peasant producers into those of landowning classes and ultimately princes and later kings at the center of the social order.

Whether we are talking about the direct producers satisfying their needs with the means of production they possess or the ruling landed classes to which surplus produce was redistributed it was always concrete, subjective, use value considerations that were paramount. Even when things passed from hand to hand or were "exchanged" with the use of money in feudal society it was still use value in consumption which was the end game of the transaction. And transactions were always gauged in subjective, interpersonal terms according to hierarchical relations of parties.

Usury was particularly bedeviling for its "measurelessness". The concrete, interpersonal socio-material relations reproducing economic life in feudal society evolved their own form of "measure" which was extra-economic. The worth of things and how they moved from person to person or even between social classes through redistributive mechanisms were all calculated in concrete terms and by how such contributed to maintaining traditional life. Usury, in short, had no socially redeeming value in precapitalist society. It and the money economy of merchant arbitrage corrupted all social classes and fostered widespread indebtedness and expropriation. And it fomented War. The unraveling of feudal social relations of material reproduction once more drove Western civilization to the precipice.

Following over a century of social dislocation and social tumult, capital, with its market principle of abstract mercantile exchange, took over the management of human economic life. Capital established a new social goal for capitalist society, the augmenting of abstract mercantile wealth or profit making. What was seen in medieval times as the Devil's infection to be expunged before it spread was now embraced as the new God. Capital generated its own system of "money-lending" via commercial banking. And it evolved its own operations of mercantile buying and selling via commercial capital. Both activities are endowed with socially redeeming value. In commodifying the means of production and human labor power, the wellspring of social wealth, capital augmented wealth by the production of surplus value. Money making more money and arbitrage of buying and selling in capitalist society contribute to the efficiency of this production-centered circuit of value augmentation.

Be this as it may, the fact that usurious "loan capital" and merchant capital existed as the earliest historical forms of capital continues to maintain a peculiar ideological force in capitalist society. This ideological force is what we explained, in Chapter Three, as driving the "reconceptualizing" by capital of itself. Such "reconceptualizing" flowed initially from the fact of idle M being withdrawn from the production-centered circuit of value augmentation and deposited in the banking system. There, money no longer operates as real capital. Rather, it is represented as taking the form of a commodity or asset, similar to land, the ownership of which constitutes entitlement to an income stream. The income stream is calculated by reference to the rate of interest at which money as a commodity is "traded" on the money market.

With the generalization of the giant joint-stock oligopoly form of enterprise, and ultimately the TNC, the "reconceptualization" of capital by itself assumes a qualitatively more complex form. The viability of capital accumulation in heavier and more roundabout forms of use value production hinges on mobilizing idle M from varying hands which hold it within society at large. The growth of equity or capital markets engenders a new modality of credit in capitalist economies. Through the capital market, the transubstantiation of capital into a commodity or asset, the use value of which is to earn an income stream, occurs with the "fictitious" converting of real capital into "money capital" as the equity of the firm.

In the TNC form of joint-stock enterprise the private nature of capital tends to be effaced. The "cunning" of capital here is its self-portrayal as a social enterprise rather than one of private accumulation for its bourgeois social class owners. Most importantly, with the "trading" in the money market of idle M socialized in the banking system, and "trading" of idle M siphoned from society in the equity or capital market, capital so "reconceptualized" cements itself as a *perpetuum mobile*.[1] To leave it as money, idle, anywhere in society, is tantamount to the perishing of its use value. And as minions of capital as the new God, the function of human beings is to be restless in the infinitizing of abstract mercantile wealth.

This brings us to the juncture at which Chapter Four left off. Capital, in "reconceptualizing" itself as an asset, the ownership of which miraculously constitutes entitlement to an income stream, holds to the dream of shedding its materiality.

But capitalism as an historical form of society *only* exists to the extent that *capital* subsumes the labor and production processes of society. Neither money making money as antediluvian "loan capital", nor money making money as merchant arbitrage, could meet the test of reproducing a human society. Both preyed upon and deranged precapitalist societies at best. They devastated precapitalist society at worst.

The possibility of capital subsuming the labor and production process of society arises with social demand for a particular constellation of goods and availability of technologies to produce these which lend themselves to suppressing qualitative considerations in economic life in favor of quantitative ones. And, as capital subsumes the labor and production process of society to wield it as an engine of surplus value production and value augmentation, capital must nevertheless provide society's general requirements of economic life as its byproduct. This, as we explained, besets capital with the balancing act Marx captured with his notion of the "contradiction" between value and use value.

The light use values and technologies of cotton production proved to be easily subsumable by capital. Hence, the laissez faire era of industrial capital offered the purest historical instance of the market principle of capital simultaneously augmenting value as it reproduced material life of the mid-19th century capitalist society as its byproduct. The heavy, more "roundabout" forms of use value production commencing in the early 20th century attenuate the market principle of capital. The "golden age" of capitalist consumerism strongly dampened the operation of the market principle of capital and increasingly activated the economic principle of redistribution through its welfare state social democratic policies. To the extent this extra-economic support overpowered the operation of "pure" capitalist market pricing, Bell and Sekine argue, the "golden age" period does not qualify as a stage of capitalism *stricto sensu*.[2]

We have remarked on the paradoxes of the "golden age". We can add here that as complex and expensive a use value as the automobile is, its use value characteristics lend themselves to the quantitative calculus of capital. Gargantuan, standardized mass production output of automobiles is testament to this. The "golden age" decades of consumer durable industries also drew the largest percentage of employed population into production-centered manufacturing activity in capitalist history. Nevertheless considering the herculean exertions of the state and ideological apparatuses in support of accumulation, the vast collectivist operational and financing characteristics of the TNC, the role of Big Bank and fiat money creation, it is abundantly clear the market principle of capital could never have augmented value nor reproduced material life to the extent achieved in "golden age" capitalist society on its own. Even the international dimension of capital organized around the BWIMS "social contract" among nations entailed significant decommodification.

But, with this said, though it was a programmed economy, a planned economy in the Soviet style, the "golden age" was not. Notwithstanding the family resemblance in extra-economic support structures among key advanced "golden age" economies, and the network of supranational political management institutions revolving around BWIMS, financial and profitability crises exploded across the "golden age" landscape.

The progressive step for human society at this juncture would have been an orderly transition to strengthened social democracy. Duménil and Lévy maintain that the supranational institutions crafted around the BWIMS, the IMF and WB, might have provided the foundation for this at the international level. Limits on capital mobility for speculative pursuits and the regime of fixed exchange rates among currencies could have been ensured by democratic investing of these supranational bodies with increased independence from private interests.[3] There were also historical precedents for backstopping this global institutional social democratization by international money other than the gold standard or the US dollar.[4]

Further, the argument can be made that in deepening social democratic institutional structures, and expanding public ownership, existing national regimes of fiat money could reconfigure their economies away from dependence on automobiles and consumer durables. After all, even the sober mainstream business analyst has recognized that consumer durables no longer constitute engines of capitalist economic growth into the future. Nor do new industries such as biotechnology or ICT carry anywhere near the necessary material accouterment or size to act as a major engine of extended growth for either an individual state or the global economy (we will return to this). Business consultant Tom Osenton asserts:

> *There is currently no sector experiencing growth rates necessary to drive any economy...*there will be no economic turnaround and no getting back on a growth track... The lifeblood of capitalism is dead, the victim of hundreds of years of progress. A century ago expectations were low and sacrifice was high. Now in the first decade of a new century, expectations are high and few in developed countries have ever experienced real sacrifice.[5]

From the perspective of this book, the automobile and consumer durable complex mark the final use value chapter for capitalist production and value augmentation. That no use value complex exists on the horizon which can be capitalistically managed as the engine of a new phase or stage of capitalism, demonstrates that capitalism as a mode of reproducing human material life has been outpaced by history. This consigns humanity to the twilight zone of an intervening period prior to its bringing into being a new mode of production. So doing is not guaranteed, however. Hence, our capacity to meet the general norms of economic life is in a perilous state with global barbarism knocking at the door.

The Killing

My argument here certainly must strike the reader as

counterintuitive. After all, the automobile sector of the "golden age" persists as the largest manufacturing sector of the global economy. Even ICT, in the broader consumer durable category, is generating a smorgasbord of sci-fi-like home entertainment and personal communications devices with no end seemingly in sight.

But the world that emerged from the depths of the mid 1970s crisis was radically altered in the most perverse ways. We left off Chapter Four with the US and other major advanced economies mired in stagflation. For the US economy, the malaise of stagflation was compounded by its relative industrial decline which prompted rebellious global stirrings to replace the US dollar as hub currency. This brought about unilateral US action which effectively opened the neoliberal era. Duménil and Lévy refer to this action as the "Volcker Coup".[6] It saw US interest rates manipulated to astronomical heights from early 1980. The "coup" reference is apropos because with the US dollar as world money, dollars were at the center of global borrowing. Thus, the unilateral action ostensibly carried out to deal with the inflationary malignancies of the US economy, impacted the world.

In that world, idle M pools had escaped declining investment possibilities in advanced economies and flowed from the OPEC price spike to an eager coterie of TNBs. Taking advantage of the availability of such funds in inflationary times had been prudent for borrowers. On the one hand, this enabled non-oil producing countries to finance oil importation trade deficits. On the other hand, it empowered states to expand import substitution industrialization (ISI) strategies.

The striking of the Volcker Coup saw nominal interest rates explode to around 20 percent. As inflation choked, real interest rates jumped. Average *real* interest rates among major capitalist economies increased to about 5.6 percent between 1980 and 1987. This created an absurd economic situation. Under conditions of lingering fallout from the "golden age" demise, interest rates were over double the growth rate of the advanced economy national product. This near decade long high interest rate environment was marked by ever more funds being leeched from production-centered activities world-wide. Funds, instead, streamed toward financial markets like Wall Street and the short-term arbitrage opportunities that were being hatched there. Even the "entrepreneurial culture" of capitalist production-centered activity was being elbowed into the dustbin of history from this juncture.[7]

For most of the third world, the ISI dream came to a screeching halt. When the Volcker Coup struck, global TNBs found themselves in the position of having direct exposure to approximately $700 billion of outstanding third world debt.[8] The eight largest US TNBs had exposure to 25 percent of the debt of the four major Latin American debtors, an amount equivalent to 147 percent of their net worth. It was in the context of Volcker interest rate hike-induced debt crisis that the IMF and WB found their new neoliberal calling: creating a breathing space for creditor banks with "rescue packages" to support continuing debt service while "structural adjustment" programs could be cobbled together to guarantee debt was serviced for the long durée. Development in the third world would, from this point forward, be held hostage to the foregoing.

In the US and other advanced economies full scale industrial structures were increasingly disintegrated as TNCs disinternalized their production-centered activities, frenetically disarticulating them around the world. The effect of the Volcker Coup was dramatic for US labor as well, increasingly rendering remaining employment temporary and contingent.[9]

For purposes of our argument, the hastening by the Volcker Coup of advanced economy TNC disarticulating of their production-centered activities across the globe and the holocaust the coup visited upon the third world are two sides of the same coin. By 1998 only slightly more than 20 percent of the US labor force remained in manufacturing.[10] In just over a decade the figure would fall to 11 percent.[11] This tendency has played out across the OECD.[12]

FDI to the third world, as an indicator of the disarticulating or "offshoring" of TNC production-centered activities, soared from $6.3 billion in the 1970s to $140 billion in the 1990s and, ultimately, $394 billion by the 2000s. The share of the non-developed world in global FDI jumped from 22 percent in the 1970s to around 35 percent in the early 2000s. Though, to be sure, the share of global *stock* of foreign investment continues to be held predominately in advanced economy hands.[13] Nevertheless, FDI to the non-developed world continued to grow considerably in the 21st century. By 2012, 52 percent of FDI was directed to the third world. This was the first time the third world share of FDI surpassed that of advanced economies.[14]

Notwithstanding this FDI spurt, the virtuous coupling of industry with development, development with growth, growth and rising living standards for mass publics, as occurred in the previous century of capitalist development, was never sustained or to be repeated. Remember, as Webber and Rigby cited in Chapter Four put it, the coming on line of other full scale industrialized economies such as South Korea, only "brought additional economies into the bounds of those constraints" advanced economies had been struggling to escape from. Besides the competitive pressures of giant TNCs saddled with burgeoning overcapacity, and fighting to capture markets for the same complex of consumer durables, the total market size also reached its limitations in declining global rates of population growth and increasingly aging populations as the 20th century closed.[15]

Capital, following the Volcker Coup, desperately sought to "free" itself from all of this. Sekine's take on Minsky, touched on in the previous chapter, captures what is at stake. In advanced "golden age" economies the complex, layered financing instabilities spring from the wholly integrated, full scale industrial structures of TNC capital. Massive, long term investments of TNCs are always "risky", even in the face of the dampened business cycle environment created by oligopoly TNC operations. Big Government and Big Bank, therefore, must step up to the plate to deal with the essentially irresolvable problems TNC capital faces in each advanced economy. Exogenous crises such as the Volcker Coup only exacerbate these. One major advanced production-centered economy may be able to export its way out of the rut. However, not *all* such economies can attempt this simultaneously![16] Big Government deficit spending and Big Bank accommodations are, much to the chagrin of neoliberals, the only *capitalist* policy solution for "golden age" Big TNC capital discontents.

However intended, the Volcker Coup provided the requisite "shock" for a full spectrum disintegration and disarticulation of that "golden age" production-centered economy in the US. And, with the dollar as world money, the "shock" reverberated across the globe. What is important to grasp here is that the radical disintegration and disarticulating of production-centered economies, following the Volcker Coup, obviated the need to maintain mass commodified labor forces and massive scale fixed capital economies for consumer durables anywhere in the world. Let us examine the architecture of this.

Manufacturing as a percent of gross value added in advanced economies therefore plummeted from the 1980s (Germany is somewhat of an exception). In 2010, in the US, it fell to around 13 percent.[17] Simultaneously, manufacturing activity exploded in the non-developed world – though, not the third world as a whole. Major pieces of disintegrated and disarticulated global manufacturing were emplaced in a clutch of East Asian "miracle" economies in the orbit of Japan. The institutional development of the latter had proceeded under the unique historical conditions of the Cold War. US policy had supported the fashioning of East Asian economies into "showcase" bulwarks against communism.[18] China's subsequent growth paradoxically piggybacked on this edifice initially constructed to contain it. It is instructive that the 13 percent increase in share of China in global manufacturing output in the period 1970 to 2008 is virtually mirrored by the 12 percent decline of the US share during those years.[19]

Manufacturing activity, however, was endowed with a distinctly new, neoliberal look. That is, manufacturing was sliced and diced into "global value chains" (GVCs). GVCs "unbundle" production in ways which have reconfigured patterns of global trade away from trade in goods to "trade in tasks". To the extent material things do move through global trade networks it is largely as *intermediate goods* or *sub-products*. Non-developed economies increase in FDI driven manufacturing manifests itself in a rising share of intermediate goods in their trade in manufactures. Growing third world trade in manufacturing intermediaries is part and parcel of the expanded export orientation and dependency of their economies as a proportion of GDP.[20] The hypertrophic export orientation of much of the third world in turn follows upon their tenderizing by the Volcker Coup and the subsequent structural adjustment programs imposed upon them by the IMF and WB. The routine is familiar: currency devaluation, privatization of public enterprises, closing of government development banks, slashing of wages slashed, "deregulation" removing impedances to global flows of funds, export-driven production, and so on.[21]

Advances in ICTs enabled TNCs to manage the fragmentation of production systems of GVC networks through revolutionized communication, coordination and logistics for geospatial dispersion. Hence, a shrinking proportion of any particular good is made in a single country. TNCs morphed into "brands", largely divesting themselves of the business of making things, running factories, or maintaining pesky, and expensive, mass commodified labor forces.[22] TNCs headquartered in advanced economies have retained their "core competencies", including design, research and development (R&D), finance, marketing. The business of production under TNC auspices is increasingly outsourced to low wage countries. While the subsidiary in the low wage country remains wholly owned, ever more production is making its way into the hands of varying shades of contract suppliers. Some contract suppliers have become TNCs in their own right. But the buzzword in TNC suzerainty of international production is the "non-equity mode" (NEM) of control. And, more often than not, third world economies host TNCs and their suppliers in special economic zones (SEZs). Alternatively dubbed export promotion zones (EPZs), there TNCs and their affiliates enjoy low/no tax environments, infrastructure subsidization and "liberalized" rules on profit repatriation. In 1975, 25 countries hosted SEZs. By 2006, 130 did.[23]

On a 2010 count TNC foreign affiliates employed 68 million workers and had sales of $33 trillion, amounting to one tenth of global GDP.[24] NEM arrangements alone employed 20 million workers globally and generated $2 trillion in sales in 2010. NEM control by TNCs is responsible for 90 percent of production costs in toys and sporting goods, 80 percent of production costs in consumer electronics, 60 to 70 percent of production costs in the automotive component sector.[25] Of the 100 largest TNCs in the world their global operations accounted for 60 percent of assets, 65 percent of sales and 58 percent of the employment by these TNCs. It is estimated that in 2012, GVCs under TNC auspices accounted for 80 percent of global trade. By 2009-2010, 51 percent of total world manufacturing exports flowed through TNC global production networks. Between 1990-1991 and 2009-2010 the share of the third world in this "trade" grew from 18.5 percent to 47.3 percent.[26]

US TNCs continue to be best in class. Though, in the US and other advanced economies, it tends to be the ICT sector and sundry service and retail TNCs, such as Wal-Mart, which constitute the commanding heights industries. As already noted, TNCs core competencies have remained in house, in the TNC "home" domicile. And, in those sectors, including ICT, where material goods of some sort appear in TNC branded business, it is to these core competencies and the expanded quotient of knowledge intensity they impart to the goods to which value added accrues. Hence, yes, as figures provided by Canadian Marxist guru duo Leo Panitch and Sam Gindin attest, 70 percent of *value* of goods and services of US TNCs are accounted for by their US operations. Yes, 85 percent of their R&D expenditures, similarly, are made at "home". But, when Panitch and Gindin declare that such disqualifies US corporations as TNC entities, one wonders what planet they are living on?[27]

During the "golden age" of wholly integrated production-centered operations a case could be made that US corporations were "American", their international operations simply supplementary. But the fact that it was international competition from European Union (EU) located US TNCs in the US domestic market which contributed to the demise of the "golden age" economy (as touched on in Chapter Four), renders Panitch and Gindin's position questionable even here. Today, it is hard to imagine commanding heights US TNC "brands" existing at all without their transnational operations and labor forces.

On the operations side of the question not only has the share of TNC revenues accumulated from overseas operations steadily increased, but both the total amount of TNC profits held overseas along with the percentage of pre-tax TNC profits held abroad are disproportionately high.[28] The four top US tech TNC giants, including Apple and Microsoft, according to the Bureau of Investigative Journalism, hold $255 billion in cash, cash equivalents and marketable securities in accounts of their overseas subsidiaries. This booty is immune from US tax authority.[29] Retail operations of Wal-Mart, for another example, contributed 9.3 percent of *all* US imports from China during 2001-2006. In just 2006, Wal-Mart imports from China were worth $26 billion.

On the labor force side of the question, the numbers on US TNC employment cited by Panitch and Gindin ("two-thirds of their global employment") are misleading at best. In 2012 Apple, for example, employed 60,000 people in the US. Its global *subcontractors*, however, employed 700,000 workers in that year. Foxconn, Apple's China based assembler, had a labor force of 1.2 million in 2012 (not all dedicated to Apple), with 230,000 workers at the iPhone assembly plant in Foxconn City alone![30] In fact, a recent report by the Economic Policy Institute estimates 2.4 million US manufacturing jobs were lost to China due to its expanded role in US and other TNC capital dominated GVCs and exports from China into the US domestic market during 2001-2013.[31]

This brings us to the crux of the argument in this section. The commodification of labor power is the specific means by which capital manages the metabolic interchange between human beings and nature in capitalist economies. For such "management" to occur in a way that ensures the viability of capitalist society, capital must meet the general norms, or touch the "bases", of economic life. We described this earlier as the method of capitalist madness. The first key "base" capital must touch is ensuring the direct producers receive the product of their necessary labor. In other words, the commodification of labor power is not simply about workers of various sorts receiving a wage. It is about the wage, whatever it amounts to in money terms, being sufficient to guarantee that labor survives and is able to reproduce a workforce. That in turn is dependent upon an allocation of social resources, most importantly human labor power, to producing with minimal waste those goods which people in society, particularly workers, need and want.

When the market principle of capital is operationalized to viably reproduce economic life of a human society, prices, including the price of commodified labor power, must adjust in the course of business cycles to "normal" or "equilibrium" levels. Such was approximated in as "pure" a fashion as possible under mid-19th century laissez faire accumulation conditions. The above movement of prices then indicates that socially necessary labor has been applied to the production of all commodities. Capitalist prices, as we note, are "backward facing". That is, the formation of capitalistically rational or equilibrium prices proceeds "optimally" when it is direct costs of commodified material inputs and labor power which factor into the abstract, quantitative calculus of business profit making according to market principles. But the foregoing hinges on the existence of a production-centered economy the historical possibility of which is predicated upon a delimited range of standardized mass producible use values and technologies appropriate to their production.

Again, during the "golden age", the use value recalcitrance posed to accumulation by the complex of consumer durables, particularly the key use value – the automobile – forced capital to recruit a welter of extra-economic, extra-capitalist supports to manage the labor and production process of society as a process of value augmentation. Automobiles and heavy electric goods such as refrigerators or electronic use values like televisions were amenable to standardized mass production. These use values also initially brought to bear a significant proportion of direct costs into the capitalist production calculus. Here, effective demand was provided by the de/semiskilled proletariat in the advanced "golden age" economies, who constituted a proportionately large percentage of the total labor force (in the range of between 35 and 50 percent among OECD economies). This socio-economic configuration infused into the "golden age" economy its modicum of capitalist market rationality despite the oligopoly structure of capitalist business. Big Government with its macroeconomic countercyclical fiscal policy and Big Bank playing a major capitalist social role in TNC finance helped smooth the "optimal" allocation of social resources for ongoing accumulation and meeting norms of material reproduction as a byproduct.

The big lie of the neoliberal era, swallowed hook, line and sinker by many Marxist illuminati, is that post Volcker Coup so-called deregulation, liberalization and privatization reloaded the *capitalist* market. This, however, is nonsense. With the production-centered economy disintegrated and the manufacturing labor force eviscerated, the virtuous connection between capitalist surplus value production and meeting of general norms of economic life through maintenance of labor power as a commodity was severed. This is the reason why, as will be fleshed out in the next chapter, exorbitant "profits" are increasingly being made in the US and other advanced economies *without* capitalist production.

Let us approach the question of end of capitalist production-centered society from the perspective of capitalist investment. With the disintegration of the US economy, as we noted in Chapter One, the total stock of fixed capital was 32 percent lower by 2008 than it would have been had the trajectory of "golden age" accumulation been maintained from the 1980s. In the 2000s, as the report by Atkinson, Stewart, Andes and Ezell illustrates, "the overall amount of fixed capital investment (defined as investment in structures, equipment, and software) made by manufacturers as a share of GDP was at its lowest rate since World War II, when the Department of Commerce started tracking these numbers".[32]

In another measure of investment in the US economy it is shown that the US "investment ratio" – that of gross fixed capital formation to gross operating surplus – dropped from a peak of 69 percent in 1979 to 46 percent in 2012. In the EU, similarly, the investment ratio dropped from 51.7 percent in 1995 to 47.1 percent in 2012. The significance of these numbers, following up on our discussion in Chapter Three, is that with access to idle M socialized in the banking system there is nothing stopping businesses under optimal conditions of capital accumulation to achieve an investment ratio of *over* 100 percent through borrowing where opportunities for greater profit making beckon.[33] Even the US 1979 investment ratio of 69 percent was thus meager. To see nonfinancial businesses in the US transfer an amount 5 percent *greater* than their already skimpy capital expenditures into hands of *rentiers* between 1985 and 1997 tells us much about what "capital" in the late 20th century was really all about.[34]

Employment figures reveal another side of the dearth of capitalist production-centered economic investment. From 1990 to 2008, a full 98 percent of all employment in the US economy was in the non-tradable sector with service sector government and health care employment as the numbers one and two job generators. Government and health care employment, however, combining for about 40 percent of the employment gains in the above period, is heavily dependent on Big Government spending. Overall private sector employment in all sectors grew only 1.1 percent between May 1999 and May 2009.[35] Indeed, in the 2000s, the US lost 5.7 million manufacturing jobs. This represented a decline of 33 percent of all manufacturing employment, a greater rate of manufacturing job loss than occurred during the Great Depression.[36]

When ICTs are factored into the mix of extirpated manufacturing employment and bloating service sector employment the possibility of such a society allocating resources according to market principles is further corrupted. Remember, the condition for human labor power in capitalist economies to be value augmenting is its abstract general aspect. Capital renders commodified labor power indifferent to production of particular goods, applying it rather to production of *any* good according to shifting opportunities for profit making. The condition for human labor power to be value augmenting is simultaneously the condition that ensures all commodities are produced with socially necessary labor. The latter is the metric by which capital allocates social resources to guarantee the economic viability of capitalism. This nexus constitutes the *differentia specifica* of capitalism as an historical society.

Services, of course, are found in every form of society in history. They even have an important place in capitalist economies. Many services, ranging from management to retail, are essential to operations of capitalist businesses, contributing to the efficiency of the capitalist circuit of value augmentation. Unlike commodified labor power, however, services are traded in the capitalist market for their *concrete specific* attributes. They do not *directly* produce surplus value. More importantly for us here, not only is a "service economy" an oxymoron in the sense that no human society could survive without a labor and production process. But no human society can allocate resources in a way that guarantees its economic viability on market principles with workers bound to specific tasks as is the case with services.

Prices for services are also largely set according to *subjective* criteria. The arbitrary allocation of resources in an economy attempting to deploy the market principle which follows from the impact of a swollen service sector on pricing is exacerbated by ICT. As we note, to the extent ICTs factor into remaining production-centered activities they saddle material use value production with an increasing proportion of indirect costs and further subjective determinations in pricing entailed by the latter. Indirect costs, or "intangible assets", such as ICT patents are estimated to "account for between one third to half of the US corporate sector". The sheer extent of indirect costs across the commanding heights of the economy has been proven to vex not only TNC allocations but systems of national accounts generally.[37] No society can survive for long with such haphazard allocation of social resources.

It is instructive that Nobel Laureate Joseph Stiglitz, in his critique of Piketty, belabors what he sees as the expanded role of rent seeking in advanced economies as the root of current burgeoning inequality.[38] Stiglitz, however, tends to define rent seeking narrowly in neoclassical terms of monopoly power in skewed pricing.[39] But, from our perspective, *capitalist* rational market pricing through which a resource allocation is achieved that ensures the viability of capitalist society is compromised by *the infusing of subjective determinations of both services and ICTs into prices*, whether monopoly power is involved or not.

Remember, rent in Marxian economic analysis is, along with profit, interest, and dividends, a deduction from surplus value. Rent as we saw in Chapter Three, initially referred to income accruing to landed property for its monopoly over this resource. What we confirm in our stark example of the iPhone from Chapter One is that at least 60 percent of its price reflects precisely that of indirect costs flowing to "brand" Apple. Much accrues as rent to technology patent owners. In fact 26 percent of the iPhone 4 cost was made up of the flash memory holding the phone's apps, music and operating software; the working memory (DRAM); finally the applications processor making the phone work. These technologies come courtesy of Apple's arch competitor, Samsung. Only a pittance accrues to the actual production workforce of Apple iSlaves.[40]

A similar story of rent flows can be sketched in relation to sporting equipment or fashion apparel industries where exorbitant fees accrue to designers for "brands" and sundry "services" of "stars" representing them. Apparel for example is dependent on a third world labor force of over 25 million.[41] Yet around 70 percent of its value added accrues to services in advanced economies. And, even there, incomes disproportionately stream upwards to "professional" services and downwards to transportation or retail (think Wal-Mart employees).[42] Without the anchor of commodified labor power, and the requirement that resources are allocated to ensure the direct producers receive the product of their necessary labor (which places objective limitations on surplus value), such subjective skewing of incomes cascades down through the "service economy" as a whole. This is what renders "inequality" a substantively different phenomenon today from that produced by specifically capitalist social relations of production during the 19th and 20th centuries.

ICTs also transform the very field of work accelerating the global shift away from the commodification of labor power. What a pair of MIT researchers recently discovered is that ICT "is destroying jobs faster than it is creating them". This is the case even in the third world including its East Asian corner where significant components of disarticulated production are emplaced. Apple contractor Foxconn, for example, is planning the gradual installation of 1 million robots across its system. Reports claim that in some Foxconn departments, three quarters of the labor force has already been displaced by technology applications.[43]

While sexier monikers are regularly applied to the third world – think "emerging markets" – the stark reality is, as we have emphasized, no state from the kaleidoscopic third world in the post WWII period, outside of South Korea (and to some extent Taiwan), has achieved full scale industrialization.[44] Today, conditions more reminiscent of late feudal economies and putting out systems of manufacture reign across the third world. Ever more production-centered activity disarticulated into GVCs is even being hived off within third world economies into SEZs as noted above. SEZs are essentially apartheid economic enclaves where foreign ownership is rife. Little in the way of positive spillover effects from SEZ activities reach third world domestic economies thus impeding their transition to modernity. Of course, that is why putrefying remnants of "capital" in the 21st century are in the third world in the first place!

Populations across the third world remain embedded in agriculture which itself is degraded inter alia under compulsions of debt service. They swarm in and out of slum ridden urban agglomerations to meet demand from GVCs for contingent and precarious work.[45] Labor power is not commodified as wages fall far below the product of necessary labor. Material reproduction of this "precariat" demands supplementation by their rural familial base. China is the poster economy for such destitute existence where over 400 million peasants or 40 percent of China's total labor force languish with no hope of ever experiencing the wealth effects of capitalism.[46] Let us not forget that the estimated 211 million migrant or "floating" labor force in China (2009 count), projected to grow to 350 million by 2050, germinates in these twilight zone conditions for work.[47] And do not expect change here either. From the early 1990s through to the years preceding the global meltdown, there was *no* increase in the total number of manufacturing jobs in China.[48] When labor does shift out of agriculture in China it shifts into services.[49]

We cannot overstate what is at stake in all of this in terms of material reproduction of human livelihoods. In the US there is no "floating population". There is simply no work for it to float to. January 2016 Bureau of Labor Statistics shows 95 million Americans 16 years old and over *not* in the labor force.[50] Shadow Government Statistics captures the true US unemployment rate at around 23 percent.[51] Nor does a fallback option in subsistence agriculture exist for the US populace. Rather, in the US over 46 million residents are food stamp recipients courtesy of Big Government. The number of US food stamp recipients exceeds the total population of such countries as Kenya, Ukraine and Argentina.[52] Five percent of Americans are the purchasers of 40 percent of all consumer goods while 60 percent of American residents buy little of anything.[53] These figures, however, are really just the surface indicators of a monstrous misallocation of social resources.

To conclude this section, we show there is a paucity of opportunity for investment in production-centered activity today. The latter is but skeletal remains of its former self. This provides the context for the Wall Street centered global financial system operating as a reincarnation of ancient usury. The other part of the story to be explored is the fact that "capital" in the 21st century no longer scarce. We thus find ourselves at a peculiar historical conjuncture where oceans of it swell as idle M with no possibility of being converted into profit making capital. Antediluvian usurious "loan capital" thrived before the dawn of the capitalist era. Only with the waning of the capitalist production-centered economy is historical space opened for its devilish resurrection.

Money for Nothing

Our endeavor to trace the steps in the modern reincarnation of antediluvian usury as casino capital will be best served by briefly summarizing the tenets of capitalist finance. Capital, we explain in Chapter Three, generates its own mode of financing: commercial or relationship banking. The role of commercial banking is to take the idle M that it holds in the money market and "activate" it in socially redeeming production-centered activity. Commercial banking operates "outside" the capitalist circuit of value augmentation. And, in activating idle M without use value restrictions, it plays an important capitalist-social or regulatory role for production-centered capital as a whole. Central banks constitute the ultimate capitalist-social backstop to financial intermediation and credit provision of commercial banks.

Stock markets proliferate in the capitalist production-centered economy during the imperialist phase of heavy steel industry as discussed in Chapter Four. Their initial calling was in the service of what Hilferding dubbed finance capital. Stock or equity markets tap into sources of idle M throughout society and place it at the disposal of monopolistic business and affiliated banks.

Equity markets ultimately transform the capitalist system of credit provision. We may recall from Chapter Three how interest *rates* in the capitalist money market are determined according to the market forces of supply and demand for funds. Equity valuations, however, differ from that of interest rates. Equities are *not* "produced" or supplied in response to "demand" for them. Rather, they bought and sold in the *capital* market according to fictitious values. "Fictitious", as explained, due to the disjuncture between stock ownership change on equity markets and the motion of real production-centered capital in its circuit of value augmentation.

Though the era of finance capital a-la-Hilferding was short lived, equity markets continued their spread into the post WWII "golden age" economy. Equity or capital markets brought to bear but another institutional layer of financial intermediation in modern economies. This is *investment banking*. Investment banks, as Lapavitsas puts it, "are denizens *par excellence* of capital markets".[54] Investment banks not only superintend the business of issuance and sale of securities. Investment banks "make markets". They do so in the crucial sense of creating the liquidity for trading of securities. Though investment banks profit from securities transactions by trading on their own account, largely investment banks profit from essential services they provide for securities transactions, the most vital being liquidity creation. It is investment banks with which so-called institutional investors – the congeries of funds: pension, insurance, mutual, money market, hedge, and so forth alluded to in Chapter One – primarily transact in securities markets. Though funds of institutional investors originating in social savings also involve tapping into available idle M within society as is the case with money and capital markets.

Credit provision, whether through money markets or capital markets, while evidencing discrete historical antecedents, nevertheless involves important linkages. All credit provision entails drawing upon idle M. Rates of interest established in the money market provide a touchstone for security valuations on capital markets.[55]

With these institutional arrangements in mind we can explore the making of our Merchants of Venice on Wall Street. Again, it was the contradictions inhering in capitalist production of consumer durables which drove the "golden age" demise. But, as is the case for the radical disintegration of the production-centered economy, so with neoliberal saddling of the world economy with Himalayan financial claims, it is the policy response of the Volcker Coup which is the villain of the piece.

From a macroeconomic standpoint the trends are crisply clear. In the period 1952 to 1968, the expansion of credit proceeded on average 5 percent per year. This contrasts with GDP growth on average of 3.9 percent annually. Though this leaves a gap of 1.1 percent, it is arguable from our earlier discussion that the demand for credit was driven by exigencies of capitalist growth under conditions of complex layered financing a-la-Minsky in the "golden age" production-centered economy.

On the other hand, from 1968 to 2007, credit expanded at an average annual rate of 4.9 percent. Yet GDP grew on average 3.1 percent annually. The gap here averages 1.9 percent per year. When we look at credit in the aftermath of the Volcker Coup it explodes from end 1982 to end 1987 at an annual average rate of 10.1 percent (adjusting for inflation). The gap between expansion of credit and GDP growth averages over 5.6 percent during this period. Where did the debt accrue? No surprise here. Neoliberal even *bigger* Big Government "solutions" under Ronald Reagan ratcheted up public debt 188 percent. Then, from end 2000 to end 2007, we see a second inordinate growth of credit. It expands on average 6.4 percent annually while GDP growth averages only 2.4 percent per year. Neoliberal Big Government is joined here in the debt fest by finance and households as we shall see.[56]

Indeed, for Richard Duncan, such a quantum jump in credit creation and subsequent enlarging of debt across the US economy and society, signals a morphing in the very nature of the economic system. This is the case on the one hand, Duncan maintains, because expanding credit well out of proportion to economic growth proves that demand for credit is not driven by growth. Rather credit is spurring whatever feeble growth is being eked out of the current morass. On the other hand, the transforming of the economic system follows from the fact that it is neoliberal Big Government and its Big Bank machinations with fiat money in the wake of BWIMS demise which is behind the explosion of credit. On these grounds, Duncan argues, we can no longer talk of capitalism. Rather, capitalism has been transfigured into what he dubs "Creditism". And persistent stagnation in the wake of the 2008-2009 global meltdown, suggests to Duncan that the debt-fueled growth illusion of Creditism has reached its limit.[57]

Duncan's work offers another angle on the leeching of capitalist rationality from the current US and global economy. Yet, there is something far more insidious going on in the mounting of financial claims which greatly eclipse GDP than the fact that debt simply cannot be repaid. What we are alluding to not only further contributes to the misallocation of social resources impeding the ability of society to meet general norms of human material reproduction. It will devour humanity if not stopped dead in its tracks. Let us explore the internal architecture of the financial claims to make our case.

We have already touched upon the debt stranglehold the third world was placed in by the Volcker Coup. Given the extent of the exposure of TNBs to the debt, orchestration of the third world "rescue" which brought ostensibly public international institutions such as the IMF and WB into a bailout gambit with the US government, constituted manna from heaven for US commercial banks. In the words of Nomi Prins: "A reckless precedent had been approved...to use the power of the [US] presidency to feed the power of the private bankers as they left financial landmines around the world".[58]

However, our interest here is in what the Volcker Coup and subsequent third world debt debacle fomented beyond bailouts of commercial banks. That is, the Volcker Coup also became a catalyst for a sweeping transformation of lending. The changes promised to "free" commercial TNBs from the liquidity constraints they had faced when their assets (and more, as we have seen) were tied up in "relationship" loans to third world borrowers.

So commences the era of global *securitization*. Securitization, quite simply, allows banks to take illiquid assets off their balance sheets by packaging them off to an investment "vehicle". For the commercial banks, securitization paid off quickly with the process backstopped by the IMF and WB. Securitization of old and new debt reduced debt on TNB balance sheets across the 1980s.

As the near death experience of third world debt for TNBs subsided, and TNBs set about savoring the taste of securitization with its secondary market casino opportunities, the BIS moved in with its Basel I accords in 1988 for the then G-10 advanced economies. The key feature of Basel I was the order for major TNBs to maintain capital equal to 8 percent of their "risk-weighted assets". Part of the problem was gauging risk and the percent of capital banks needed to hold for differing asset classes in such a "risk-bucket" approach. Basel II, in 2005, would seek to remedy this lacuna by prompting banks to develop their own proprietary "risk" weighting models. Yet again, banks quickly learned how to game the rules. As Eric Gerding argues, the evolving of ever more arcane securitization instruments not only endowed TNBs with capacity to create "guarantees" virtually *ex nihilo*, but also increased their leverage, while nimbly skirting capital adequacy ratios.[59]

In relation to securitization of third world debt the newly crafted tool of choice for financial gamesmanship was the *swap* derivative. For the uninitiated, a *derivative* is a contractual obligation deriving its value from the performance of some underlying instrument or "asset". A swap entails borrowers' trading obligations, usually fixed for variable or floating ones, over interest rates or currencies. Swaps, in the new universe of securitized third world debt, were classified as *off-balance sheet* (OBS) liabilities. Through their use banks could "trade" flows on interest rates or currencies, garnering revenue in handsome fees, without putting new loans on their books. Banks claimed the swaps market was a "hedging" arena mitigating financial system risk. Yet as the popularity of swaps grew, the risks to investors that swaps purportedly mitigated were displaced onto banks. And it is not difficult to appreciate the popularity of swaps for the speculators who swooped into them. Swaps, as Charles Geisst tersely states, "completely obfuscated the relationship between debtor, creditor, and the nature of the obligation itself".[60]

This, however, is the point. Remember, it was the flight of idle M to the third world from a dearth of investment activities in advanced economies which accelerated third world debt in the first place. However, the Volcker Coup dashed third world dreams of full scale industrialization which would have provided them with wherewithal to pay off debts from profits of subsequent capitalist production-centered wealth creation. But the Volcker Coup left a wasteland in its wake. In Latin America, 1989 GDP per capita was 8 percent below what it was in 1980.[61] Indeed, output of the third world as a whole dropped to such an extent that it would not be until 1996 that it would reach the level it had attained in 1979.[62]

At that point, under the impetus of global disarticulation of production into TNC-dominated GVCs, industry had been decoupled from industrialization with growth decoupled from development as we highlight above. Debt chains, therefore, are certain never to be cut. Between 1980 and 2002, in fact, the third world remitted $4.6 trillion, an amount equal to 50 Marshall Plans (calculated in 2003 dollars), to private financial institutions in OECD states.[63] By 2007, of the total $3.36 trillion third world debt, 80.4 percent would be owed to private lenders.[64] And, of course, lest we forget, the stabilizing of flows to private lenders through securitization was supported by IMF and WB resources and austerity enforcements in the third world.[65]

To be sure, opportunities for limited financial play in international markets antedated the Volcker Coup. The "Eurodollar" market had commenced holding dollar deposits during the BWIMS era. Its origins were the Soviet Union's efforts to place dollar deposits in banks beyond the regulatory reach of the US. London, in particular, was welcoming. Holdings at the outset were comparatively miniscule, however. Their mushrooming began with recycled petrodollars following the OPEC hike of 1973. And they increased with the decay of the "golden age". But the experience of the nascent Eurodollar market was merely a "hedging 101" lesson. Deposits, loans or investments could be shifted among currencies in anticipation of exchange rate or interest rate fluctuations.[66]

Rather, it was the Volcker Coup, along with the third world debt crisis, which triggered the crafting of the arcane financial instruments of securitization. And it was precisely these innovations packaging burgeoning third world debt that speculators holding enlarged pools of idle M, comforted by concerted US government and IMF/WB "rescue" actions, and driven by giddy prospects of short term gain, were interested in diving into. But the emerging international casino economy around third world debt arbitrage was just the beginning. Neoliberals had their sights trained on deregulating and liberalizing the US banking system itself and changing its orientation to the world.[67] Commercial banks would increasingly play the part of investment banks and hedge funds. That is, "as quasi-insurance companies willing to partially underwrite any sort of known financial risk for a price".[68]

The problem here, of course, is that commercial or relationship banking in capitalist economies was never intended to engage in what amounts to financial disintermediation. Even for investment banking financial disintermediation through securitization and derivatives carries little of the socially redeeming purpose of equity markets in tapping wider sources of idle M for capital accumulation. In fact large scale financial intermediation involving extended money market play with idle M also falls *outside* the capitalist rational ambit of commercial banking. Idle M in capitalist economies was to be kept within reasonable bounds. It was to be duly activated by relationship banking in socially redeeming production-centered activities as per the efficiency requirements of the capitalist circuit of value augmentation. Relationship banking in some form, as maintained in Chapter Three, constitutes a necessary feature of capitalist production-centered economies. Hence, the neoliberal policies which set out to "free" TNBs from perceived "golden age" tethers, and "liberate" idle M funds to operate on their own account, to the extent commercial banking was undermined in the process, ended up starving what remained of the capitalist production-centered economy.

Large commercial TNBs, however, were cheerleaders for neoliberal deregulation. The borrowing opportunities in

Eurodollar markets and from non US TNBs that deregulation afforded US TNCs had severed a major customer base. No less than Alan Greenspan on his appointment as FED Chair went to bat for TNBs over the threat of US loss of financial competitiveness. As well, from the late 1970s US commercial bank deposit bases were increasingly depleted as savings fled toward high interest rate offerings by unregulated private finance companies and money market mutual funds – the private financial intermediary (PFI) forerunners of the *shadow banking system*.[69] Shares of US financial sector assets of commercial banks were also falling. That fall was paralleled by rising shares held by institutional investors. Between 1978 and 1993 financial sector assets in the hands of institutional investors jumped from 32 percent to 52 percent. A similar pattern was detectable in Britain, France and Germany.[70] Institutional investors were also drivers compelling further deregulation and financial innovation in global markets.[71]

While the neoliberal ideology of deregulation and liberalization as the "freeing" of "capital" swept across academic and policy circles, writings of the endgame were fast appearing on the wall. The Depository Institutions Deregulation and Monetary Control Act of 1980 (DIDMCA) "preempted state usury laws" by weakening Regulation Q restrictions on interest rate charges and allowing banks to set variable interest rates on mortgages according to assessed "risk". As banks competed with nascent shadow banking funds on the interest rate field, the fund industry in turn pressed the Securities and Exchange Commission (SEC) to tweak their valuations in a fashion that enabled funds to present their products to investors as offering the safety and liquidity of bank accounts.[72] Then there came the Garn-St. Germain Depository Institutions Act which permitted banks and so-called Savings & Loan (S&L) "thrifts" to raise interest rates payable on deposits.[73] That was followed by further deregulation of the sorts of assets, particularly dodgy real estate assets, in which S&Ls could invest (other people's money).[74]

Concatenating of the Volcker Coup interest rate shock and nascent neoliberal deregulation and liberalization brought a significant part of the US banking system to its knees. The episode is often referred to as the S&L crisis. But major US commercial banks also crashed during the period. In 1984, for example, Continental Illinois was bailed out by the US government under the increasingly familiar "too big to fail" refrain. In total, 1,043 S&Ls also failed between 1986 and 1995. A study by the Congressional Budget Office estimated total losses to the US economy at over half a trillion dollars.[75] The bailout plan crafted by George H. W. Bush not only saw the FDIC pay out on deposits, but Wall Street banks made good money as part of the bailout plan selling the assets of the failed thrifts.[76] And, to put the costs to the public in perspective here, Big Government "rescues in the late 1980s and early 1990s wound up *surpassing* the portion of national deposits lost in the failing institutions that had *actually shut down* in the years surrounding the 1929 crash".[77]

Unperturbed, banks pressed on along the same trajectory. Big Banks became much bigger Big Banks with a wave of banking mergers and acquisitions (M&A) commencing in the early 1990s on a scale not witnessed since the 1950s.[78] Between 1995 and 2000 a total of 11,100 bank mergers occurred.[79] Enabling legislation, precursors of which had unfolded piecemeal, and often under the political radar, arrived in the form of the Riegle-Neal Interstate Banking and Branching Efficiency Act of 1994. Megabank JPMorgan Chase was forged shortly after in a 37-bank merger. It would amass $2 trillion in assets by 2011. Bank of America was created in a merger of 50 banks in total. Its merger with NationsBank in 1998 truly made it the "Bank of America".[80] By 2012, the new so-called "Big Six" US banks, JPMorgan Chase, Morgan Stanley, Citigroup, Goldman Sachs, Bank of America and Wells Fargo held $9.5 trillion in assets. That was equivalent to approximately 65 percent of US GDP in 2012. Their trading revenues (much with borrowed money) amounted to around 93 percent of *total* trading revenues of *all* banks in the US.[81]

Current mainstream discourse on the 2008-2009 meltdown turns on questions of banking size as the key variable in both bank and systemic banking risk.[82] But what banks are doing and why they concentrate on the activities they do has received less critical attention. As commercial banks grew in size, deregulation and liberalization of finance proceeded apace. Legal reinterpretations of existing legislation relating to capital market activities also abounded prior to repeal of Glass-Steagall.[83] Already by 1993, the 20 biggest US banks had OBS exposure amounting to 39 percent of their assets and 573 percent of their core capital. As well, the 20 had proprietary trading accounts equaling 45 percent of their assets and 749 percent of their core capital.[84] But, the Gramm-Leach-Bliley or Financial Services Modernization Act of 1999 "rendered moot the slow-drip approach" to breaching the firewall separating spheres of commercial banking, investment banking and insurance. Investment banks were in turn empowered to operate as "true middlemen in the shadow banking web" as commercial banks increasingly invested in shadow banking instruments.[85]

Ostensibly, neoliberal deregulation and liberalization and the "freeing" of capital was supposed to breathe life into, if not the "golden age" economy itself, at least a close approximation of its prosperity. But the deregulating and liberalizing of activities of commercial banks only helped bring into being a surrogate "economy" of casino play with the bloating pools of idle M for which there were scant opportunities for investment in real production-centered capitalist activities as we have noted. As neoliberal policies continued to run their course, it is true that small, local and regional commercial banking persisted in the US.[86] This necessarily is the case given that elements of small business commodity production continue to exist and the capitalist-social functions of commercial banking were required to facilitate that. But the commanding heights commercial TNBs that were the cheerleaders for deregulation and liberalization of finance largely turned to speculative pursuits that have little to do with relationship banking.

Our citing of Richard Duncan above on the macro-economic trajectory of deregulated and liberalized credit expansion in the end devolved to increased debt across various sectors of the economy. Duncan presented two broad trends. Let us, however, look closer at the credit deluge. Again, as effects of the Volcker Coup spread, debtors of all stripes found their conditions transformed from Minsky's "speculative" financing at inflation induced zero interest rate bands of the 1970s into that of his "Ponzi" financing.[87] Total credit market debt leaped from around 160 percent of US GDP in 1982 to approximately 260 percent in 1997. Duncan highlighted Big Government debt. By 1997 it made up approximately 19 percent of the credit market debt total. Debt of financial businesses grew from around 20 percent of GDP to over 60 percent then. These debts represented 22 percent of total credit market debt. Household debt reached near 70 percent of GDP by 1997. Importantly it constituted 26 percent of total credit market debt at that time.[88] Of course it would almost double as a percent of total credit market debt between 2000 and 2007.[89]

What is important to take from these figures is something Altvater and Hubner, cited in Chapter One, emphasize. This is the "dynamic" of debt. That unlike the case of non-financial profit making production-centered businesses (we will turn later to the issue of diminishing TNC profits and their turn toward "financialization"[90]), financial claims on the aforementioned sectors depend on future wages and taxes. On his parsing of household data at the close of the 20th century, what Doug Henwood deftly reveals is that both household debt as a percentage of after tax income and household debt service as a percent of after tax income rise meteorically in the neoliberal 1980s (the latter dips temporarily as interest rates fall in the early 1990s only to climb steeply again). Debt and debt service increase, in turn, are tethered to expansion of consumer credit and the inflating of mortgage debt as a percent of the value of owner occupied housing. Borrowing in this fashion, precisely at the time jobs of "golden age" high wage commodified labor power are being zapped and outsourced to proto-capitalist relations of production in the third world, compensates for declining incomes. Yet consumption continues to increase, now fueled by debt.[91]

In the US, as household debt, consumer debt and mortgage debt exploded, effectively becoming un-repayable, banks commenced the process known as "asset securitization". The earliest credit card asset backed securities (ABSs) appeared in 1987. Yes, government sponsored agencies (GSEs) such as the Government National Mortgage Association (Ginnie Mae), Federal National Mortgage Association (Fannie Mae) and Federal Home Loan Mortgage Corporation (Freddie Mac), had begun asset securitization in the 1970s. But they did this as *government* agencies. No *private* financial intermediaries or PFIs had attempted it to that point. The process worked for GSEs because it was assumed the agency would back the security if its mortgage "collateral" failed and that the US Treasury would support the agency if it failed. In other words, the perceived risk did *not* rest with the "asset" securitized. Caution thus met the early private ABS forays.[92]

Nevertheless, credit card securitization compelled a greater transformation of consumer lending than the innovation of the credit card itself. In 1989, approximately 11 percent of consumer debt that had been securitized was based on revolving credit. In 2009, 43 percent of total securitized consumer debt was based on revolving credit. Securitization enabled any finance company with access to cheap money to enter the credit card business. Such PFIs also made inroads into the wholesale lending market for business. Their funding emanated from commercial paper (a form of promissory note) rather than deposits thus placing them beyond the regulatory reach of the FED. Enlargement of this shadow banking system begat with money market mutual fund PFIs created a vortex increasingly drawing in commercial banks. As with TNB activities in the swap derivative game around third world debt, domestically operating commercial TNBs felt as though they had discovered El Dorado. Wall Street investment banks certainly benefitted from underwriting and securitizing fees. Consumers benefitted from easy credit.[93]

In the end, the orgy of securitization sounded the death knell for commercial, relationship banking. The shadow banking system served as its model going forward. This "originate to distribute" (OTD) model of banking, engendered by the perfect storm of receding *real* investment opportunities for idle M, swelling global debt and securitization of household debt, is based upon financial disintermediation. Banks "originate" loans only to sell them off or "distribute" them through securitization, garnering fat fees in the process. The socially redeeming facet of relationship banking is thus leeched away, as is any responsibility in lending. Banks evince little interest in creditworthiness of borrowers or to what end loans might be put as both principal and interest is paid to end buyers of securities, *not* banks.

From 1990 to 2003 the number of Americans with credit cards jumped by 75 percent. Their credit card spending quadrupled from $338 billion to $1.5 trillion. Fees to credit card issuers climbed from 28 percent of profits in 2000 to 39 percent by 2004.[94] Such fees often entailed the usurious ratcheting up of interest rate charges for cardholders who simply made a late payment. At end 2007, 1 billion credit cards were in use in the US. By 2008 75 percent of credit card debt was securitized. In mid-2008 almost a trillion dollars in revolving credit was outstanding in the US. Of that approximately 60 percent of credit card bills were not fully settled on presentation, taking advantage of the revolving option. This of course was a boon to securitizers of credit card receivables given the exigencies of ABSs. Credit card customers were incentivized to make minimum payments lest bondholders suffer "repayment risk".[95]

Coined during the Great Depression in the US, the notion of an "American Dream" encapsulated the view that the rite of passage into middle class life came with a family home, automobile, and access to consumer durables. The post WWII "golden age" veered as close as possible in really existing capitalism, in the US and advanced OECD states in any case, to actualizing such a paradise for the broader mass public. It would be the chimera of this American Dream that appeared decades following the "golden age" demise in the guise of access to credit and a home mortgage. These in turn depended upon future income potential which, other than as articulated in hollow neoliberal political promises, had by then become elusive at best. Yet, in 1977 during the waning years of the "golden age", the Community Reinvestment Act (CRA) was passed as an inducement for banks to better service communities hitherto excluded from bank residential lending. The Riegle Community Development and Regulatory Improvement Act, which was passed in 1994 simultaneously with the Riegle-Neal Interstate Banking and Branching Efficiency Act, combined with the CRA to similarly pressure newly minted nationally operating megabanks to expand home ownership in the above direction.[96] As one analyst quipped about US government housing policy toward the urban poor, "let them eat credit".[97]

Mega TNBs were soon joined by GSEs in mongering the novel adjustable rate mortgages (ARMs) at 3 percent down payment (down from the early 1990s' 20 percent) to applicants in lieu of previously required good credit rating and employment/income history for 30 year, low risk, fixed rate mortgages. Such placating of the CRA with its urban poor constituency ultimately impacted borrowing conditions for *all* US income brackets. Middle and upper middle classes could also trade up to the symbolic "McMansion" in the suburbs under the same arrangements. In 1999 only about 10 percent of US home purchases were made with down payments of 3 percent or less. By 2003 the figure was near 15 percent. By 2007 well over 40 percent of homes were purchased with down payments of 3 percent or less.[98]

So-called subprime and *Alt-A* or "alternative to agency" mortgage loans (the latter signaling the loan quality would not have passed the sniff test to be taken on by GSEs in days past) accounted for only 8 percent of all new mortgage lending in 2001. By June 2008, as one new calculation has it, there were 28 million subprime and Alt-A loans outstanding with a total value of around $4.8 trillion. The mortgage originators in league with the GSEs operating under the new underwriting standards were, for the most part, a cabal of four of the "Big Six" banks – Bank of America, Citibank, JPMorgan Chase and Wells Fargo (mega originators Countrywide and Washington Mutual were ultimately merged into these). GSEs, of course, enjoyed *explicit* Big Government protection even though their operations were deregulated. Mega commercial TNBs enjoyed *implicit* Big Government protection under the *too big to fail* rule which had been applied to the eminently smaller Continental Illinois in 1984. All thus drew high bond and debt ratings from the likes of nefarious rating agencies, Moody's and Standard and Poor's (S&P).[99]

However, while the house of cards was built on mortgage loans which should not have been made, the very possibility of such subprime and Alt-A loans being made was due to their securitization.[100] Mega commercial TNBs had gotten out of the capitalist-social relationship business of lending on the basis of deposits and into originating and distributing loans that left principal and interest paid not to them but to end buyers of securities. It also obviated interest in the creditworthiness of borrowers or to what end loans might be put. And, not to be outdone, CEOs of major US investment banks that were the top fundraisers for re-election of George W. Bush in 2004 – Goldman Sachs, Morgan Stanley, Merrill Lynch, Lehman Brothers and Bear Stearns – secured license from the SEC to radically lower their capital requirements. That enabled them to increase their leverage from 12 percent to between 30 and 40 percent.[101]

Again, the endgame of loans and leverage was casino speculation: just making money. GSEs bought mortgages from banks and converted them into an ABS-like instrument, the mortgage backed security (MBS). As investors purchased MBSs new mortgage credit was made available to homeowners. Banks that originated mortgage loans could then purchase the MBSs with all the guarantees that an AAA-rated asset (from a GSE) on their books offered to "freeing" their capital for further speculative pursuits. This reduced the total amount of capital the financial system as a whole had to hold against mortgage lending. In turn, banks repackaged MBSs along with other debts into collateralized debt obligations (CDOs). CDOs were derivative-like instruments which allowed banks to "bundle" MBSs of varying quality in a single vehicle. Finally, both investors in MBSs and CDOs as well as originators of these instruments could buy a peculiar derivative form of insurance against "credit events" on their speculative vehicles, called a credit default swap (CDS).[102] The CDSs further "turbocharged" credit markets, if such is imaginable, by offloading credit risk, enabling financial institutions that purchased CDS to offer new loans and assume new credit risk.[103] Finally, CDOs were themselves securitized as CDOs "squared", as CDSs were "hedged" by second and third credit derivative contracts. "Rinse, lather, repeat, and long, convoluted chains of risk transfers form".[104]

All in all, across 2002-2007, it was the major US TNBs and PFIs that created around 80 percent of the nearly $14 trillion worth of MBSs, ABSs and CDOs (and other assorted "concoctions"). International banks were responsible for the other 20 percent.[105] International banks, particularly in the EU, purchased an estimated 40 percent of toxic US MBS products leading to EU banks bearing almost half of meltdown losses.[106] The GSE-TNB-investment bank liquidity mill of securitization had effectively imported the model of revolving credit card financing into the mortgage lending market. The meltdown contagion spread across every sector of the financial system including sovereign wealth funds and pension holdings. And given the exigencies of ARM contracts, years and years are necessary for the crisis to work its way through the system.[107]

One of the more disconcerting revelations of the post meltdown period is that when up against the wall, many homeowners walked away from their mortgages and properties while maintaining their credit card payments. At the height of the good times bubble, 2004-2005, consumption reached around 78 percent of US GDP. The fete was buttressed by novel loan products (home equity loans or HELs and home equity lines of credit or HELOCs) which enabled consumption as well as the meeting of credit card obligations to feed upon property equity. If securitization facilitated the mass public need "to eat credit" for ongoing consumption, the meltdown brought on "cannibal consumption" where the temporary fruits of eating credit were themselves eaten.[108]

Let us conclude this chapter with three points which gather further insights from the unfolding of the meltdown into the way capitalist substance is leeched from the US economy (and by association the global economy given Wall Street's international financial role). First, while early stirrings of the shadow banking system compelled deregulation and liberalization of commercial banking, ultimately banks turned from competing with shadow banking to participating in it. The signal enabling legislation for this was the granting by US Congress of bankruptcy exemptions for "repurchase agreements" or *repos*.[109] Indeed, it is certainly not overstating the case to suggest repos are "one of the primary reasons financial institutions created the entire shadow banking system."[110]

Quite simply, a *repo* entails a borrower selling a security below its "market" price. An agreement is made by the borrower to repurchase the security at an agreed upon higher price in the future, often at an "overnight" rate. The price difference is the "haircut". The magnitude of both leverage gained by one party and collateral held by the other is based on the size of the haircut. For OTD banking, repos constitute the principal source of funding.[111] This contrasts with relationship banking where it is demand deposits which are the basis for bank lending. While there is no way of accurately calculating the size of the shadow bank repo market, estimates had it at around $11 trillion as the meltdown struck in 2008. Calculations are complicated by the "rehypothecation" of collateral. That is, where collateral "churns" in the hands of investment bank broker-dealers it is "pledged" with, as they reuse it for other own account securitization transactions.[112]

What came to light only as the meltdown unfolded was the fact of repo collateral being the liability of a theretofore unknown financial Frankenstein product, a "special investment vehicle" (SIV). SIVs were "pools" created by TNBs of varying cash flows and risks. They were backed by commercial paper. Use of commercial paper for short term funding by large corporations had been a staple of the financial system for some time. But its shadow banking adoption commenced with credit card loan securitization as we note above. SIVs then turned to mortgage related assets. Investment in medium term ABSs and CDOs with ever elevating leverage further exacerbated the "mismatch" between the short term liabilities (of commercial paper) and the medium term assets. As indicators of troubles in the housing market spread, hedge funds run by the investment bank Bear Sterns (with investments in mortgage related instruments) faced mounting haircuts and increased suspicion over their collateral in the repo market from where they obtained their funding.[113]

Prior to the repeal of Glass-Steagall in 1999 the failure of an investment bank would have remained more or less an isolated incident. But with the intertwining of commercial TNBs and investment bank broker-dealers with shadow banking, the failure of Bear Sterns shook the financial system. The stock market was also impacted. And other hallowed investment banks, GSEs and major commercial banks were ultimately brought down. Big Government with its Big Central Bank was forced to step in as lender of last resort to save the casino securitization economy as a whole.[114] Despite the huffing and puffing of complex financial engineering, "Marx's fundamental remark about capitalist crises was confirmed: financial institutions were in urgent need to hold value in the form of money, but they could not obtain it commercially because liquidity was hoarded. The typical hoarders of liquidity were financial institutions that were worried about meeting their own obligations. This condition has characterized the global financial system at several junctures since the outbreak of the crisis".[115]

As discussed in Chapter Three, part of the capitalist-social role played by relationship banking is evaluating the creditworthiness of borrowers. This role is similarly played in relation to commercial credit offered to businesses for discounting of bills of exchange. Interest rates are set in the capitalist money market in that regard. They are determined according to "objective" capitalist "rational" criteria of demand and supply of funds. The wider tapping into social sources of idle M by equity markets imported into the capitalist commodity economy a modicum of extra-commodity economic uncertainty. Keynes, in iconic words, saw equity markets akin to a "beauty contest" where the winner determines which of the contestants is most beautiful in the eyes of the judges. Yet, equity valuations in the capitalist production-centered economy are bounded by capitalistically "rational" interest rates set in the money market and expectations of real economy profit rates (though of course these "expectations" lend themselves to exuberance).[116]

But securitization has effectively undermined the capitalist-social relationship role played by banks. Part of this, we have seen, is impelled by the "distributing" of loan obligations off-balance sheet. The other part, as Costas Lapavitsas explains, derives from the fashion by which relational or "soft" qualitative techniques utilized by banks in assessing creditworthiness of borrowers has been eclipsed by financial system reliance upon "hard" or "computationally intensive techniques". The evidence shows the "homogenizing" systemic adopting of "hard" techniques contributes to price swings. And "hard" techniques prove increasingly ineffective under conditions where price movements become frenetic as occurred during the unfolding of the recent meltdown. Lapavitsas thus queries: "if banks have lost capacity reliably to collect information and assess risk, what is their social and economic function"?[117]

Our second point here turns on an important recent intervention by Simon Mohun into the way forces driving financial activities in current society toward securitization of debt and access to funding through the repo market are self-reinforcing. When credit transactions occur in relationship banking, whether the borrowing is for business investment directly, or indirectly for short term discounting bills of exchange, the collateral is always real goods. In the casino economy of securitization it is the repo that constitutes the "asset" which predominates, "and it is undertaken for purely financial reasons", Mohun emphasizes. Repos produce cash funding. Securitized products are the collateral. Investment bank broker-dealers intermediate risk and profit therefrom.[118] Pure snake oil!

Streaming of financial activities toward casino operations of repos occurs due to all the forces misallocating social resources in the current excrescent "surrogate" economy we have identified. The dearth of production-centered investment opportunity. An ocean of idle M swelling in the hands of institutional investors of various sorts. Flow from surplus value toward rents, technological and otherwise. The outcome, highlighted by Mohun, is exorbitant incomes skewing to the über rich. These incomes flood into so-called "institutional cash pools". The pools are run by "cash portfolio managers" whose mission is to increase yield. In this way a perverse "demand" is engendered for interest-bearing securitized credit instruments intermediated in repos.[119] The sheer size of these institutional cash pools, approximately $6 trillion in 2013, and the fact that their access to the safest assets is constrained (demand deposit amounts are capped and marketable Treasuries at any one time are limited), saddles the financial system in perpetuity with tendencies toward the liability-asset mismatches that brought on the meltdown. This is the case notwithstanding recent efforts by the FED to transform itself from lender of last resort to "broker-dealer of last resort".[120] That is, where the FED makes its intentions crisply clear to support the casino surrogate "economy" of Wall Street at all costs.

We can add here that the FED would do well not to avert its eyes from the Big TNBs for too long. The "Big Six" generating of 93 percent of total trading revenues of all banks in the US, cited by Prins above, includes our now $1 quadrillion plus estimated derivatives contracts (adverted to in Chapter One) for which they are counterparties to each other.[121] And this market also continues to be strictly over-the-counter, an opaque world of risk arbitrage managed by a secretive camarilla of financial executives from the likes of JPMorgan Chase, Goldman Sachs and Morgan Stanley.[122] In fact, even in 2010, when derivatives holdings worldwide had diminished to a small extent, derivatives holdings of JPMorgan Chase, Bank of America and Citigroup of $194.7 trillion dwarfed global GDP of $63 trillion in 2010. Such a discrepancy shows this "market" is *not* about "hedging"![123]

Finally, the industrialization-development-growth-prosperity nexus of the capitalist production-centered commodity economy has worked its way through business cycle oscillations between prosperity and depression phases. During the liberal *laissez faire* era of accumulation, capital alternated between tendencies toward "equilibrium" pricing and "optimal" allocations of social resources *and* periods of radical disequilibrium and misallocation. The latter were resolved by the renewal of fixed capital at a "higher" technological level. Both the "method" and "madness" of capital are integral aspects of its "software" program. The increasing roundaboutness of industry in the imperialist period of heavy steel production and ultimately the consumer durable automobile economy of the "golden age" impelled bigger government and bigger bank into action to support accumulation and commanding heights businesses in business cycle troughs.

With the rapid disintegration of the production-centered economy following the Volcker Coup, the US economy, as Duncan argues, has been sustained by credit. No sooner had the Reagan Big Government debt deluge slowed in 1987, and US neoliberal deregulation and liberalization been enforced upon the major advanced economies in a succession of "Big Bang" global market openings, than markets crashed. When uncertainty over US dollar exchange rates destabilized Wall Street, global contagion followed.[124] The point here, on the one hand, is that the FED leaped to the rescue of major financial institutions with low interest rates in 1989-1992.[125] Big TNBs then effectively got their money for nothing. Yet Big TNBs and PFIs turned the rescue into an orgy of securitization beginning with credit card ABS. These were built upon gouging borrowers with usurious rates. The low-interest-money-for-nothing fest animated the run up to the global meltdown of 2008-2009. Big Government was joined by the finance sector and households in the ratcheting up of debt levels. The bailout story is legendary. As is the way Big Government, Big Bank, Big TNBs and Big TNCs fed on the mass public flesh to recoup the credit fueled gambling "losses".[126]

Again, interest rates were dropped to historically low levels. And there they have stayed. In the end, this is really déjà vu. What is most striking in all this, is the way business cycles of the capitalist production-centered economy, through which resource allocations ensuring the viability of capitalism as a human society, no longer operate. They have been displaced by oscillations of financial bubbles and bursts. These engulf society in the "madness" of abstract mercantile wealth augmentation without the corresponding "method" of capitalist material economic reproduction. This is what turns Duncan's "Creditism" into a Merchant of Venice economy. Though evidence continues to mount that even for our Merchants of Venice on Wall Street, neoliberal Big Central Banks, as Duncan forecasted earlier, may no longer have the firepower for a last bubble hurrah.[127]

Endnotes

1   Sekine, *An Outline of the Dialectic of Capital*, Volume 2, p.203.
2   See, for example, John Bell and Thomas T. Sekine, "The Disintegration of Capitalism: A Phase of Ex-Capitalist Transition" in Albritton, Itoh, Westra and Zuege (eds.) *Phases of Capitalist Development*, Chapter Three.
3   Duménil and Lévy, *Capital Resurgent*, p. 192.
4   Benn Steil, *The Battle of Bretton Woods: John Maynard Keynes, Harry Dexter White, and the Making of a New World Order* (Princeton: Princeton University Press, 2013) pp. 142ff.
5   Osenton, *The Death of Demand*, pp. 27, 31.
6   Duménil and Lévy, *Capital Resurgent*, p. 69.
7   Altvater and Hubner, "The End of The U.S. American Empire'?" pp. 58-60, 62, 64.
8   Geisst, *Beggar Thy Neighbor*, pp. 242-3.
9   Westra, *The Evil Axis of Finance*, pp. 79, 84-5.
10 Feinstein, "Structural Change in the Developed Countries During the Twentieth Century", p. 39.
11 See, for example, Suzanne Berger, "Forum: How Finance Gutted Manufacturing", *Boston Review*, April 1 2014, http://www.bostonreview.net/forum/suzanne-berger-how-finance-gutted-manufacturing.
12 Victor Tan Chen, "Manufacturing Employment (G8 Countries)", accessed January 17 2016, http://victortanchen.com/manufacturing-employment-g8-countries/.
13 William Milberg and Deborah Winkler, *Outsourcing Economics:*

	Global Value Chains in Capitalist Development (Cambridge: Cambridge University Press, 2013) pp. 130-1.
14	Martin Hart-Landsberg, "From the Claw to the Lion: A Critical Look at Capitalist Globalization", *Critical Asian Studies* 47, 1 (2015) p. 3.
15	Osenton, *The Death of Demand*, pp. 7ff.
16	To this day such "beggar thy neighbor" export policies are being pursued in the vain attempt to ward off further disintegration and disarticulation of "national" production systems. See Steve Johnson, "Capital gobbles labour's share, but victory is empty", *Financial Times*, October 13 2013, http://www.ft.com/intl/cms/s/0/63f14896-2f6c-11e3-8cb2-00144feab7de.html.
17	Milberg and Winkler, *Outsourcing Economics*, p. 162.
18	See Westra, *The Evil Axis of Finance*, Chapter 2.
19	Robert D. Atkinson, Luke A. Stewart, Scott M. Andes and Stephen J. Ezell, "Worse Than the Great Depression: What Experts Are Missing About American Manufacturing Decline", *The Information Technology & Innovation Foundation*, March 2012, http://www2.itif.org/2012-american-manufacturing-decline.pdf p. 46.
20	Milberg and Winkler, *Outsourcing Economics*, pp. 35-9.
21	Westra, *The Evil Axis of Finance*, pp. 90-3.
22	Westra, *The Evil Axis of Finance*, p. 84.
23	Milberg and Winkler, *Outsourcing Economics*, pp. 33, 42, 53.
24	Milberg and Winkler, *Outsourcing Economics*, p. 130.
25	Martin Hart-Landsberg, *Capitalist Globalization: Consequences, Resistance and Alternatives* (New York: Monthly Review, 2013) pp. 18-9.
26	Hart-Landsberg, "From the Claw to the Lion", pp. 3-4.
27	Leo Panitch and Sam Gindin, *The Making Of Global Capitalism: The Political Economy Of American Empire* (London: Verso, 2013) pp. 288-9.
28	Hart-Landsberg, *Capitalist Globalization*, pp. 24-5.
29	See Nick Mathiason, "Finance: Out of Control? Apple and Microsoft among US tech giants reaping interest payments on offshore cash", Bureau of Investigative Journalism, https://www.thebureauinvestigates.com/2014/03/12/apple-and-microsoft-among-us-tech-giants-reaping-interest-payments-on-offshore-cash/?
30	Milberg and Winkler, *Outsourcing Economics*, pp. 34-5.
31	Will Kimball and Robert E. Scott, "China Trade, Outsourcing and Jobs", Economic Policy Institute Briefing Paper #385, December 11 2014, http://www.epi.org/publication/china-trade-outsourcing-and-jobs/.
32	Atkinson, Stewart, Andes and Ezell, "Worse Than the Great Depression: What Experts Are Missing About American Manufacturing Decline",

p. 47.
33 Michael Burke, "The Cash Hoard of Western Companies", *Irish Left Review*, October 23 2013, http://www.irishleftreview.org/2013/10/23/cash-hoard-western-companies/.
34 Doug Henwood, *Wall Street* (London: Verso, 1998) p. 74.
35 Hart-Landsberg, *Capitalist Globalization*, pp. 59-60.
36 Atkinson, Stewart, Andes and Ezell, "Worse Than the Great Depression: What Experts Are Missing About American Manufacturing Decline", p. 3.
37 Leonard Seabrooke and Duncan Wigan, "Global wealth chains in the international political economy", *Review of International Political Economy*, 21, 1 (2014) p. 259.
38 Lynn Stuart Parramor, "Joseph Stiglitz: Thomas Piketty gets income inequality wrong", *Salon*, January 2 2015, http://www.salon.com/2015/01/02/joseph_stiglitz_thomas_piketty_gets_income_inequality_wrong_partner/
39 Joseph Stiglitz, *The Price of Inequality: How Today's Divided Society Endangers Our Future* (New York: W.W. Norton, 2013) pp. 48ff.
40 *The Economist*, "Slicing an Apple".
41 Karina Fernandez-Stark, Stacey Frederick and Gary Gereffi, *The Apparel Global Value Chain*, Duke Center on Globalization, Governance and Competitiveness, November 2011, http://www.cggc.duke.edu/pdfs/2011-11-11_CGGC_Apparel-Global-Value-Chain.pdf.
42 See, for example, *Moongate Associates*, "Analyzing the Value Chain for Apparel Designed in the United States and Manufactured Overseas", http://tppapparelcoalition.org/uploads/021313_Moongate_Assoc_Global_Value_Chain_Report.pdf.
43 Thomas Schulz, "Man vs. Machine: Are Any Jobs Safe from Innovation?" *Spiegel Online International*, May 3 2013, http://www.spiegel.de/international/business/speed-of-innovation-and-automation-threatens-global-labor-market-a-897412.html.
44 And, we want to make this crisply clear: Singapore and Hong Kong do not count. One, they are simply trading entrepôts. Two, as city states, they never had to confront the daunting challenge of modernity which entails shifting mass populations out of peasant agriculture into industry and the management of social class tensions which derive from that.
45 Westra, *Political Economy and Globalization*, pp. 176ff.
46 See Guy Standing, *The Precariat: The New Dangerous Class* (New York: Bloomsbury Academic, 2011) pp. 106-7.
47 Westra, *The Evil Axis of Finance*, p. 160.
48 Alexander Day, *The Peasant in Postsocialist China* (Cambridge UK:

	Cambridge University Press, 2013) p. 190.
49	Michael Aglietta and Guo Bai, *China's Development: Capitalism and Empire* (London: Routledge, 2013) pp. 224-6
50	United States Department of Labor, accessed January 17 2016, http://data.bls.gov/timeseries/LNS15000000.
51	John Williams' Shadow Government Statistics, accessed January 17 2016, http://www.shadowstats.com/alternate_data/unemployment-charts
52	Ali Meyer, "Food Stamp Beneficiaries Exceed 46,000,000 for 38 Straight Months", CNS News, January 13 2015, http://www.cnsnews.com/news/article/ali-meyer/food-stamp-beneficiaries-exceed-46000000-38-straight-months.
53	Westra, *The Evil Axis of Finance*, pp. 167-8.
54	Lapavitsas, *Profiting Without Production*, p. 134.
55	Lapavitsas, *Profiting Without Production*, p. 135.
56	Richard Duncan, *The New Depression: The Breakdown of the Paper Money Economy* (Singapore: John Wiley & Sons, 2012) pp.87-8.
57	Duncan, *The New Depression*, pp. 133-4.
58	Prins, *All the Presidents' Bankers*, p. 333.
59	Eric F. Gerding, *Law, Bubbles and Financial Regulation* (London: Routledge, 2014) pp. 253-9.
60	Geisst, *Beggar Thy Neighbor*, pp. 250-1, 256.
61	Prins, *All the Presidents' Bankers*, p. 349.
62	Westra, *The Evil Axis of Finance*, p. 88.
63	Westra, *The Evil Axis of Finance*, p. 100.
64	Damien Millet and Eric Toussaint, "Figures relating to the debt for 2009", CADTM, February 27 2009, http://cadtm.org/IMG/pdf/DEF_Figures_relating_to_the_Debt_Vademecum_2009_FEB_2009-2.pdf.
65	Prins, *All the Presidents' Bankers*, pp. 349-50.
66	John Eatwell and Lance Taylor, *Global Finance at Risk: The Case for International Regulation* (New York: The New Press, 2000) p. 36-7.
67	Prins, *All the Presidents' Bankers*, pp. 351-2.
68	Geisst, *Beggar Thy Neighbor*, p. 250.
69	Calomiris and Haber, *Fragile By Design*, pp. 196-7.
70	Eatwell and Taylor, *Global Finance at Risk*, pp. 39-40
71	Eatwell and Taylor, *Global Finance at Risk*, pp. 183ff.
72	Gerding, *Law, Bubbles and Financial Regulation*, pp. 430-1.
73	Geisst, *Beggar Thy Neighbor*, pp. 256-7.
74	Calomiris and Haber, *Fragile By Design*, p. 200.
75	Calomiris and Haber, *Fragile By Design*, pp. 198, 201, note 101.
76	Prins, *All the Presidents' Bankers*, pp. 353-4.
77	Kevin Phillips, *Bad Money: Reckless Finance, Failed Politics, and*

	the *Global Crisis of American Capitalism* (New York: Penguin Books, 2009) p. 42.
78	Prins, *All the Presidents' Bankers*, p. 365
79	Phillips, *Bad Money*, p. xix.
80	Calomiris and Haber, *Fragile By Design*, pp. 201-3.
81	Prins, *All the Presidents' Bankers*, p.395.
82	Luc Laeven, Lev Ratnovski, and Hui Tong, "Bank Size and Systemic Risk", IMF Staff Discussion Note SDN 14/4, https://www.imf.org/external/pubs/ft/sdn/2014/sdn1404.pdf.
83	Gerding, *Law, Bubbles and Financial Regulation*, pp. 147ff. 221-2.
84	Henwood, *Wall Street*, p. 82.
85	Gerding, *Law, Bubbles and Financial Regulation*, p. 435.
86	Calomiris and Haber, *Fragile By Design*, p. 203.
87	Minsky, *Stabilizing an Unstable Economy*, pp. 207-8.
88	Henwood, *Wall Street*, p. 59.
89	Phillips, *Bad Money*, p. xviii.
90	Altvater and Hubner, "The End of The U.S. American Empire?" pp. 62-3.
91	Henwood, *Wall Street*, pp. 63-5.
92	Geisst, *Beggar Thy Neighbor*, pp. 225-6.
93	Geisst, *Beggar Thy Neighbor*, pp. 227-8.
94	Phillips, *Bad Money*, p. xviii.
95	Geisst, *Beggar Thy Neighbor*, pp. 319-22.
96	Geisst, *Beggar Thy Neighbor*, pp. 208, 300, 312.
97	Raghuram Rajan quoted in Calomiris and Haber, *Fragile By Design*, p. 214.
98	Calomiris and Haber, *Fragile By Design*, pp. 208 and passim, 236.
99	Calomiris and Haber, *Fragile By Design*, pp. 251-3, 259. For the question of GSE guarantees, see also Gerding, *Law, Bubbles and Financial Regulation*, pp. 294-5.
100	Geisst, *Beggar Thy Neighbor*, p. 314.
101	Prins, *All the Presidents' Bankers*, pp. 401-2.
102	Calomiris and Haber, *Fragile By Design*, pp. 259-62.
103	Gerding, *Law, Bubbles and Financial Regulation*, pp. 375-6.
104	Gerding, *Law, Bubbles and Financial Regulation*, pp. 405-8.
105	Prins, *All the Presidents' Bankers*, p. 403.
106	Westra, *Evil Axis of Finance*, p. 144.
107	Geisst, *Beggar Thy Neighbor*, p. 313.
108	Geisst, *Beggar Thy Neighbor*, pp. 309, 318.
109	Gerding, *Law, Bubbles and Financial Regulation*, pp. 429-31.
110	Gerding, *Law, Bubbles and Financial Regulation*, p. 410.
111	Gerding, *Law, Bubbles and Financial Regulation*, p. 409.

112	Manmohan Singh and James Aitken, "The (sizeable) Role of Rehypothecation in the Shadow Banking System", IMF Working Paper WP/10/172 July 2010, http://www.imf.org/external/pubs/ft/wp/2010/wp10172.pdf.
113	Geisst, *Beggar Thy Neighbor*, pp. 324-5.
114	Geisst, *Beggar Thy Neighbor*, pp. 325ff.
115	Lapavitsas, *Profiting Without Production*, p. 279.
116	Lapavitsas, *Profiting Without Production*, p. 58.
117	Lapavitsas, *Profiting Without Production*, pp. 319-21.
118	Simon Mohun, "Inequality, Money Markets and Crisis" September 16 2015 version), paper presented at 63 Annual Conference of the Japan Society of Political Economy (JSPE)", Hitotsubashi University, Tokyo.
119	Mohun, "Inequality, Money Markets and Crisis".
120	Cardiff Garcia, "Cash pools, Fed rev-repos, and the stagnationist, future part 1", *Financial Times*, July 3 2014, http://ftalphaville.ft.com/2014/07/03/1890002/cash-pools-fed-rev-repos-and-the-stagnationist-future-part-1/
121	See Robert Lenzner, "Banking Concentration Still A Systemic Risk", *Forbes*, April 7 2011, http://www.forbes.com/sites/robertlenzner/2011/04/07/banking-concentration-still-a-systemic-risk/#4348f509218c.
122	Louise Story, "A Secretive Banking Elite Rules Trading in Derivatives", *New York Times*, December 11 2010, http://www.nytimes.com/2010/12/12/business/12advantage.html?
123	Duncan, *The New Depression*, p. 99.
124	Eatwell and Taylor, *Global Finance at Risk*, p. 98.
125	Phillips, *Bad Money*, p. xxi.
126	See, for example, Hudson, *Killing the Host*, chapters 13 to 17.
127	Michael Sauga and Anne Seith, "Out of Ammo? The Eroding Power of Central Banks", *Spiegel Online*, April 16 2014, http://www.spiegel.de/international/business/central-banks-ability-to-influence-markets-waning-a-964757.html.

| Chapter Six |

THE FINAL "POUND OF FLESH"

At times of great social dislocation, when a once dominant social order is well into its process of disintegration, the ideological apparatuses of society are revved into high gear. Ruling classes shrilly call out, *après nous le déluge*!

When capitalism came into being it did so with the promise of raising human beings up an important rung in the historical ladder toward human freedom. That is, it liberated human beings from the webs of interpersonal social relations of domination and subordination within which they were entrapped in past historical societies. In doing this it opened up a "public sphere" of political and civil society to the world. But capitalism harbors one remaining human non-freedom; that is, it subjects human beings to blind economic forces. As human beings "freely" go about their self-seeking proclivities these are wielded by capital for its own self-aggrandizement. This is the augmentation of value or profit making.

Marx's belief was that socialism would finally liberate human beings from capitalist non-freedom. That human economic life would be pried from the abstract workings of the capitalist market and organized by freely associated human beings according to their concrete freely chosen purposes. Socialism, he claimed, would consummate "humanity's leap from the kingdom of necessity to the kingdom of freedom".[1] The "kingdom of necessity", of course, is what neoclassical economics preaches –

that the best human beings can ever hope for is to learn how to better conform to "the market" and devise economic "policies" for that purpose.

Marx's critique of capital differed from his "utopian socialist" contemporaries. For him capitalism was not *just* an asymmetric wealth distributive, anarchically operating, crisis ridden, exploitative, alienating and so forth, society. Capitalism is an "upside down" society that wields human material existence for its abstract, "extra-human" purpose.

Marx's grasp of capitalism as an historically delimited society also differs from much of the self-styled Marxist profession. Their reveling in radical chic wavers between claims that capitalism persists until overthrown by heroic working class revolution, or that it will be superseded through "reforms". For Marx, however, capitalism like all human societies is destined to be outpaced by history as the conditions of its existence decompose and become a drag on the human future. And history waits for no one. Not neoliberals. Not Marxist gurus. In his economic theory of *Capital* Marx captures the historical delimitations of capital in terms of the "contradiction" use value life poses for value augmentation.

As we argue in Chapter Four, the demise of the "golden age" economy signals the exhaustion of capitalism as an historical society. There simply exists no use value complex on the horizon as the basis for the emergence of a new leading economic sector such as cotton textiles, steel or automobiles, able to spin capital into a period of sustained accumulation and value augmentation.

As Marx hypothesized in his theory of historical materialism, "At a certain stage of development, the material productive forces of society come into conflict with the existing relations of production... From forms of development of the productive forces these relations turn into their fetters". He then added, as quoted in Chapter Two, that "an era of social revolution" follows.

Marx's view of periods of "social revolution" intervening in transitions from one mode of production or historical epoch of economy to another was never intended as a deterministic dictum. Rather, the notion of social revolution captures the fact that monumental social convulsions punctuate intervening periods between historical epochs of economy. Human life, which is managed according to a particular economic principle under one mode of production, hangs in the balance during the intervening period prior to the institution of a new mode of production. Only when other economic principles are brought to bear and a new central principle or "software program" is activated is the material viability of society guaranteed. If this does not occur, human society will descend into barbarism and perish.

Humanity has now reached such an historical juncture. It is a particularly precarious time for human existence because the residues of capitalism that remain are largely those which embody its "madness" as we put it earlier. The "method" of that madness, or the specific way that capital managed to satisfy the general norms of human economic life to guarantee the viability of capitalism as an historical society, no longer operate.

And make no mistake about this. The economic conditions surrounding the demise of the "golden age" are, in the strongest qualitative sense, worlds apart from those of the Great Depression which followed the 1929 stock market collapse. Then, the world economy was pregnant with a new dynamic use value sector potentially manageable by capital, which was struggling to be born. Yet, notwithstanding that, if we look at the intervening period separating the decline of the imperialist phase of capitalism and onset of the "golden age", it was punctuated not only by the Great Depression, but by two world wars and the Soviet Revolution.

If such is even imaginable, the current era of putrefying capitalism is certain to be fraught with ever greater peril for humanity. After all, the intervening period between the demise of the feudal economy and rise of capitalism in Western Europe lasted centuries. As was the case with the Dark Ages which gave birth to it, disintegrating feudalism plumbed new depths of human deprivation. Again, there is no guarantee that humanity and civilization will be remade under current trends: that a descent into global barbarism will be forestalled, or that a new civilization will emerge

The ideological chants of neoliberalism are dangerous. Their one line, as we note, is the spurious claim that "the market" (read capitalism) is in the process of being reloaded. The truth of the matter, as Robert Albritton puts it, is that neoliberalism is less "a new phase of capitalist development than…a desperate attempt to legitimize a dying capitalism by trying to enact ideals of its confident youth, ideals that were always filled with serious contradictions even at the height of nineteenth-century liberalism, and that are totally inappropriate to the current state of the global economy".[2]

The pontificating by today's crop of self-styled Marxist illuminati over this thing they refer to as "global capitalism" is possibly even more dangerous. In itself the notion is as hollow as the reference to 15th century global economic relations as a "capitalist world system". More confoundingly, it offers a generation of radicals a false sense of comfort. This is the case because while progressive segments of society have no illusions about the litany of ills with which capitalism plagues humanity, the reproduction of human material existence continuing under capital, as impoverished as economic life for the many may now be, is still an implicit expectation. But this is rarely critically problematized. People simply assume that they will eke out their lives. On that basis Marxist gurus urge their followers to suffer the austerity mandated by blind economic forces of the "kingdom of necessity". This is what the "no means yes" Syriza Greek tragedy showed. Such false comfort is peddled rather than exhorting people to commence the difficult, but ultimately rewarding, journey to the "kingdom of freedom" and control over their economic lives in the here and now.

As we emphasize across the pages of this book, how capital touches the necessary "bases" to viably reproduce the economic life of a human society as a byproduct of value augmentation is the most under-theorized component of Marx's economic research agenda. Yet it is one of the more crucial elements. During the *laissez faire* period of liberal capitalism it was the market principle of capital that was tasked with meeting the general norms of economic life. It operated even during the prosperity-to-depression business cycle oscillations. By the "golden age" era, both value augmentation and touching the necessary "bases" to ensure workers received the product of their necessary labor and resources were allocated "optimally", demanded herculean extra-capitalist, extra-economic exertions of the capitalist state. The exigencies of accumulation around the consumer durable, automobile society brought the economic principle of *redistribution* to bear upon economic reproduction in a major way. This cushioned the descent into depression. But it did not prevent it.

Each stop on the neoliberal magical mystery tour, beginning with the Volcker Coup itself, leeches what capitalist, market "rationality" remains from the advanced economies in its thrall. As interest rates jumped astronomically at a time of diminishing TNC profit rates, investment in production-centered activities was increasingly discouraged. The disintegration of full-scale industrial production systems and their disarticulation across the globe contributed to the decommodifying of labor power. Outsourcing of production to low wage proto-capitalist relations of production in the third world only accelerated decommodification on a world scale. Without commodification of labor power the capitalist metric for reproducing the livelihood of all workers in society is disrupted.

Much to the chagrin of neoliberals the task of guaranteeing that workers of all stripes receive, at minimum, the product of their necessary labor (those goods necessary to reproduce their economic lives, in common parlance), falls alone to the state. While we will return to the question of the role of the state below, we may point out now that according to the OECD, even with its vicious austerity, the US only managed to chop government spending as a percent of GDP from near 43 percent in 2009 to 38.1 percent by 2013. The UK slashed it from near 50 percent in 2009 to around 45 percent by 2013. Where austerity has not taken hold with much fervor, as in Denmark and Sweden, state spending in 2014 as a percent of GDP is "stratospheric" at 56.3 percent and 51.8 percent respectively.[3] But do not expect the neoliberal state to "wither away" any time soon as more and more hungry homeless masses litter the streets. It remains the last bulwark against the rapidly fraying social fabric.

Further, as production was disarticulated across the globe, the simultaneous investment in ICTs which endowed "branded" TNCs with the logistical wherewithal to create and master global value chains (GVCs), saddled what remained of the production-centered economy with an enlarged proportion of indirect costs. Subsequent haphazard pricing not only contributed to greater misallocation of social resources but saw profits diverted away from production-centered investment toward rents, technological and otherwise.

Finally, idle M began bloating aimlessly in money markets as opportunities for its conversion into capital receded in the wake of the "golden age" demise. Concurrent with the rampant inflation enveloping the US economy, early stirrings of the shadow banking system in the form of money market mutual funds drew savings away from commercial banks where interest rates were capped. The neoliberal response as we discuss was bouts of deregulation and liberalization of the financial system as a whole. These policies were undertaken in the ideologically exciting but erroneous belief that "freeing" of "capital" would resurrect lost "golden age" prosperity. What neoliberals "freed", however, was not real capital but idle M. And once "freed", idle M embarked upon an orgy of "casino capitalist" money games on its own account. Securitization only rendered the casino surrogate "economy" ever more orgiastic.

As giddy prospects of bubble induced "wealth" siphoned idle M from across society into the burgeoning shadow banking system, neoliberals fired their final deregulatory barrage. This destroyed much of what remained of commercial banking, particularly among commanding heights TNBs. Commercial TNBs, shadow bank PFIs and investment banks then merged into an unholy speculative concoction which persists to this day. And the more arcane the securitization instruments became, the more idle M flooded into the speculation economy and the greater the oceans of idle M swelled. In turn, what is left of the commodity economy in small local businesses and relationship banks is starved of funds. As the major holders of idle M, commercial TNBs entwined in shadow banking effectively hold economies hostage. As economist Michael Hudson belabors in his writings, TNBs have become attuned to casino play amongst themselves and their finance, insurance and real-estate (FIRE) sector. And as holders of idle M they can simply bide their time with these funds waiting for opportunities to provide leveraged "asset inflationary credit".[4]

Before we look closer at what the future portends let us revisit one of the earlier points made in this book. Neither merchant capital nor antediluvian usurious "loan capital", we argue in Chapter Three, could constitute a socioeconomic system on their own. They were destined in precapitalist economies to remain parasitic on the predominating modes of material reproduction. We further note that as sophisticated as the banking and finance operations we touched on in Chapter Two were – the Templars, followed by the Florentine financial oligarchs, the Bardi and Peruzzi, and later the Medici bank which collapsed in the 15th century – the wealth that accrued to them was always fleeting, because any augmenting of mercantile wealth which occurred under feudalism was constrained by the limits of wealth production in a predominately agricultural society. It is this dynamic, according to Le Goff, whom we cite above, which "doomed Christendom to a state of almost perpetual crisis".

Lapavitsas is worth quoting at length on this:

> The components of finance do not produce monetary value but merely intervene in its advance and repayment. Thus, a prerequisite for a system of finance to emerge is that social relations must exist such that the deployment,

expansion and accrual of monetary value across the economy could be taken for granted by participants in financial transactions...

In short, a system of finance could emerge only if capitalist relations already permeated economic life. The components of finance would then have a social basis on which to become an integral whole – a system – mobilizing and advancing monetary value systematically... A financial system is a specifically capitalist phenomenon...[5]

As maintained in Chapter Three, the resetting of finance on the material foundations of capitalist social relations of production engendered commercial or relationship banking. Financial intermediation by relationship banking plays a capitalist-social role in mobilizing idle M. It does this by placing the idle M it holds in the money market at the disposal of businesses that require investment funds beyond their own resources to meet profit making opportunities. Commercial or relationship banking, in this fashion, contributes at a macroeconomic level to increased production of goods by businesses along with greater employment incomes. This nexus established in capitalist production-centered societies between enhancing the efficiency of value augmentation and its social wealth effects is precisely what is referred to as the socially redeeming purpose of relationship finance. The hugely important point Thomas Sekine makes here is that without this vital operation of relationship banking at the macroeconomic level to activate idle M in determinate uses, the economy is certain to turn deflationary.[6]

It is against this backdrop of innate deflationary tendencies in advanced economies driven by the simultaneous erosion of capitalist social relations of production and the dismantling of commercial banking that the neoliberal policy-induced cycles of bubbles and bursts is to be understood. The phantasmagoria in all of this, if not its perversity, is TNC business, finance and Big

Government sectors' continued pursuit of financial machinations as a solution to recover a prosperity now long lost and out of sight. The truth of the matter is: this only reinforces the tendency for oceans of idle M to swell. The residues of the capitalist commodity economy are starved for funds, because money games and rent extractions provide a swifter, more lucrative, if not the only means of abstract wealth agglomeration *for those with money.* We should note here, however, that according to a McKinsey Global report of 2015, the most egregious OBS casino leveraging by SIVs shrank by $3 trillion since 2007 and repos decreased by 19 percent.[7] Still, shadow banking continues to grow absolutely in the US. A recent estimate has the financial sector in the US expanding to almost 500 percent of US GDP by 2010 (from less than 200 percent of GDP in 1980). And it is shadow banking activities that account for much of the increase, and credit provision, with no end in sight.[8]

To conclude this book let us explore three further facets of the "Merchant of Venice" economy. One is the intimate integration of financial activities of erstwhile production-centered TNCs into the casino play. The second is the mechanics of wealth expropriation in lieu of specifically capitalist profit making. The third is how Big Government with its Big Central Bank, in thrall to bankrupt neoliberal ideology, has passed control of its sovereign fiat money creating capacity, in the midst of an ongoing storm, to capitalists without capitalism.

Money Making Money, Corporate Style

As we note, following Minsky and Sekine, a tendency toward "financializing" of non-financial production-centered TNCs existed in the "golden age" economy. Part and parcel of this was the evolving by TNCs of financial arms like GM's GMAC to provide credit for accelerated purchase of consumer durables. But, in the aftermath of the Volcker Coup interest hike, a new species of "financialization" is spawned as financial claims expand on TNCs already saddled by diminished profit rates.[9] TNCs responded in part by the disintegration and disarticulation of their production-centered activities to low wage, often proto-capitalist arrangements in the third world. However, the zapping of the high wage commodified labor force, outsourcing their jobs to apartheid SEZs in the third world, concatenates with what emerges as the new casino propensity of TNCs.

Tom Osenton frames this in terms of dual business strategies to realize growth in profits. One is the strategy of lowering the "bottom line" in a competitive race to the basement. But there are limits to that. TNCs thus turned to their second strategy. That is raising the "top line". But how is it possible to raise the "top line" under diminution of advanced economy investment ratios of the scale we revealed in Chapter Five? The immediate answer was mergers and acquisitions (M&A). Not M&A as it played out in the formation of steel and heavy chemical oligopolies of the imperialist era. Or in multiplying competencies as did vertically integrated TNCs of the "golden age". Now we witness M&A as a lucrative short cut to generate the appearance of growth[10] which, as Osenton explains, is nothing but a vehicle for increasing the price of TNC stocks which is the actual endgame of raising the "top line" in the neoliberal era.[11]

MM theory, touched on in Chapter Four, lent respectability to "portfolio" views of the firm. This was imbibed by TNCs as they packed on debt during the early wave of post Volcker Coup M&A. But, as the returns of divesting themselves of their commodified labor forces and advanced economy production-centered accouterment streamed in, lowering the "bottom line", TNCs had cash in hand to play the M&A game (though they continued to take on debt for this, too).

Between 1980 and 1997 US TNCs alone shelled out over $3 trillion buying each other. TNBs, PFIs and their lawyers snatched $20 to $40 billion in fees out of these transactions. Two new phenomena marked this process. On the one hand TNCs hungrily bought their *own* stock, spending $864 billion on this between 1984 and 1997 (far more than money market mutual funds spent on stocks then). On the other hand TNCs paid out ever greater proportions of the earnings from the M&A game in the form of dividends to outside creditors. What Henwood dubs the "rentier share" of TNC surpluses jumped to 60 percent in the 1990s from the 20 to 30 percent it constituted during the "golden age". TNCs, in short, "have been stuffing Wall Street's pockets with money".[12]

Beyond MM theory another ivy-league intellectual veneer termed "agency theory" was applied to the morphing of erstwhile production-centered TNCs into arch casino arbitragers in their own right. Quite simply it claims the TNC management stratum which had navigated TNCs through nearly three decades of "golden age" high profits, business growth and generalized economic prosperity, is now subject to greater "discipline" by shareholders to yield "shareholder value". Agency theory captures the new mode of evaluating TNC business success according to market capitalization (calculated by multiplying the total number of shares by their price as a ratio of the net worth of a business) and the return on corporate stock.[13] Agency theory is itself backed up by the "efficient markets hypothesis" (EMH). EMH maintains how financial market operations ultimately price securities correctly according to so-called "fundamentals" (this in turn intimates that somewhere beneath financial market machinations there exists a functioning "real" economy from which soundings can be taken).[14]

From what we have said in Chapter Five on the leeching of capitalist "rational" (read market) substance from current economic life, the surrealism of the foregoing must be evident. However, let us look at some of the figures. In the period 1982 to 1999 Kindleberger and Aliber declare, "US stock prices increased by a factor of thirteen – the most remarkable run of annual increases in stock prices in the two hundred years of the American republic". And, this period saw the market value of US stocks jump from but 60 percent of US GDP in 1982 to 300 percent of GDP by 1999.[15]

Yet, in relation to the "real", production-centered economy, if what is purportedly being referred to is the contribution of stock markets to capital expenditure, between 1980 and 1997 figures show stock markets were "a negative source of funds". More stocks were retired than issued: *Minus* 11 percent to be precise! We can only contrast this with "golden age" stock market investment where between 1946 and 1979 equities financed up to 5 percent of "real investment" in the US: a pattern similar to that existing in other advanced economies of that era.[16] Thus, by 2000, estimates have it that equities in the US were valued at approximately 45 times the underlying corporate earnings, exceeding the figure preceding the Great Depression where equity values were *only* 30 times corporate earnings![17]

Remember, all this takes place against the backdrop of bloating pools of idle M in the hands of so-called institutional investors. Institutional investor assets – originated, ironically, in "golden age" social savings – amount to 140.8 percent of US GDP in 1995, growing to 185 percent of US GDP by 2000. At that point institutional investors own 46 percent of all publicly trade equities. And they were responsible for 75 percent of all trading activities.[18]

We need to add something else into the mix here. The mid 1990s to the close of the century initially presented themselves as halcyon years. The unemployment wave of the 1970s and 1980s ebbed. There was an uptick in the rate of US GDP growth. The "new economy" of "brain work" around widespread adoption of ICTs exploded. Productivity, in the doldrums from the demise of the "golden age", was now rising, so arguments went. In addition to the development of actual ICT industries, ICT impacted the sales and marketing capacities of a wide gamut of businesses. And it fostered a new business genre, the dot com. A coterie of "venture capitalists" with access to Wall Street funds built portfolios around entrepreneurial start ups which attracted investors eager to get in on the action when a success story went public. Investment banks gleefully collected fees on the Initial Public Offerings (IPOs). The US appeared to have conjured up "its own perpetual motion machine" as Kindleberger and Aliber have it, "one designed to enrich the fortunes of hundreds of thousands of families". Yet, by 1996 FED Chairman Alan Greenspan was already muttering about "irrational exuberance".[19]

When the bubble crashed it crashed hard. In early 2000, the National Association of Securities Dealers Automated Quotations (NASDAQ) went into a free fall of 80 percent, while US stock markets as a whole lost 40 percent of their value.[20] As the 2000s proceeded, a preponderance of evidence showed there had not really been much of a "productivity miracle". Overall, those productivity gains that did occur revolved around the massive but brief investment spurt in ICTs which fuelled the stock market bubble. But these had no long lasting impact beyond those measures which lowered TNC "bottom lines", discussed above.[21]

Rather, a mutually reinforcing relationship crystallized between the disarticulation of TNC production-centered activities into GVCs and TNC "financialization" or casino gamesmanship. M&A was but a part of this. Outsourcing of production-centered activities started the process of TNC cost reduction. Non-equity modes (NEM) of control type contract arrangements which passed off production-centered activities to supplier firms reduced TNC spending. During the 2000s US TNC profits increased as did their profits' share of GDP. This in turn enabled TNCs to expand dividend payouts to stockholders. TNCs also found themselves awash with mounting cash holdings, much of which they stashed offshore. Businesses then could repurchase more of their own stock, which drove up prices, enabling more "value" to be dispersed to shareholders. And, the more shareholder value that was returned in this fashion, all the more were TNCs induced to focus on core competencies. Hence, a "downsize and distribute" model was imposed upon an erstwhile production-centered TNCs as the dysfunctional twin of "originate-to-distribute" (OTD) banking.[22] And this "downsize and distribute" model which originated in the US during the early neoliberal period following the Volcker Coup, has since been spreading across other advanced economies.[23]

The rising trend of stock buybacks and dividend payments as a share of TNC internal funds was briefly put to a halt by the 2008-2009 meltdown. But it soon revved up again. Figures confirm both for the 2000 to 2007 period and 2010 that those companies with the most extensive global supply chains or GVC production networks were simultaneously the TNCs which applied the greatest percentage of business net income to share repurchases and dividend payments. Wal-Mart, notorious for its ruthless cost cutting pressure on global suppliers, undertook share buybacks and dividend payments amounting to 57 percent of its net income in 2000-2007. In 2010 the figure rose to 125.1 percent.[24]

A recent calculation of TNC financial gamesmanship finds, in the decade 2003-2012, 449 TNCs listed in the S&P 500 index utilized $2.4 trillion or 54 percent of their earnings on stock buybacks while paying out 37 percent as dividends – this leaving but 9 percent of earnings for investment. Hudson emphasizes that it is corporate executives, key shareholders with stock options as a significant percent of their compensation, who immediately benefit from such "financialization" strategies augmenting shareholder value. Over 80 percent of the compensation for the 500 highest paid executives in 2012, averaging out to $30.3 million for each, came from such share price machinations.[25]

In 2013, the value of publicly traded companies worldwide had reached $51 trillion, an increase of 524 percent from the 1990 level. Yet global GDP only grew 228 percent during that period.[26] And by 2014, M&A fever was back again with the value of announced transactions amounting to $1.5 trillion, an increase of $500 billion from 2013.[27] Of course, this game mandates further indebtedness. By 2015 major global TNCs had racked up $29 trillion in debt with debt at businesses rated by S&P, for example, amounting to three times their earnings before deductions. As *Bloomberg Business* put it: "Much of the cheap credit accumulated by companies was spent on a $3.8 trillion M&A binge, and to fund share buybacks and dividend payments".[28] And so the casino turns.

Usury Without Limit

In our brief comments on Piketty above we make the point that Marx was not interested in the issue of social inequality *per se*. Marx, rather, was intent on explaining how capital managed to reproduce the economic life of human beings in capitalist society as a byproduct of value augmentation, and under the constraints of capitalist social class relations. To recapitulate, with the decommodifying of labor power, capital relinquishes the mechanism which both ensured workers of all stripes could access the product of their necessary labor as well as ensured an allocation of resources adequate to materially reproduce an historical society. But what about the augmentation of value? The extraction of surplus value constitutes the internal fount of capitalist mercantile wealth expansion. While capital has abdicated its mass commodified labor forces it nevertheless continues to pump surplus labor from the remaining workers across its production-centered activities. This surplus labor is materialized in surplus value and value augmentation. It is from surplus value that profits, rent (including technological rents and fees for use of "intangible assets"), interest and dividends flow.

As explained in Chapter Three, in the rarefied world of bourgeois classical and ultimately neoclassical economics, indications of surplus value production and value augmentation in capitalist wielding of the labor and production process of society are expunged. Capital in all its cunning, we point out, undergoes a "reconceptualization" as an "asset", the ownership of which mysteriously commands an income. Again, while we have occasionally used the term "profit" interchangeably with surplus value in our interfacing with statistical sources based upon neoclassical categories, strictly speaking that is not correct. It also profoundly obfuscates current economic goings on where commanding heights TNCs have *actually* shed much of their surplus value producing production-centered accouterment as they reduced their businesses to core competencies, but continue to register "profit".

Remember, in its "reconceptualizing" of itself capital takes "profit" as reward for wily entrepreneurial acumen. But return on capital invested is now termed monies accruing as "interest" to the owner of "capital". The reality, of course, from the perspective of Marxian economics, is that money emerging from the sale of commodities at the end of the capitalist production-centered circuit represents value transferred to the product from production inputs plus surplus value. Profit is that portion of surplus value not claimed as interest for funds borrowed or rents owed (we have bracketed questions of tax claims for reasons of brevity) that is to then be reinvested in production-centered activities. Reinvestment of profits as such spurs accumulation and economic growth.

In Marxian economic theory there are two key means of increasing surplus value and, ultimately, the rate of profit. The first, important in Marx's day, is the increase in "absolute surplus value" achieved by lengthening the working day. The second is increase in "relative surplus value". This is achieved through technological revolutionizing of the forces of production to raise labor productivity and/or intensification of labor. Relative surplus value may also be increased by reducing wages below that sufficient for workers to obtain the product of their necessary labor.[29]

The disarticulating of production to proto-capitalist forms in the third world deploys the debilitating Trifecta of wage reduction below that necessary and sufficient to reproduce the livelihood of the direct producing class, the intensification of labor, and prolongation of the working day. Recent baleful documenting of a day in the life of a worker at iPhone supplier Foxconn is testament to this.[30] Under such conditions the amount of surplus value produced is colossal. Measuring the sheer extent of it is approximated in our example of the iPhone where the so-called value added accruing to third world supply is in the single digits as a percentage of the iPhone sales price. This Trifecta is reproducible only in the third world socioeconomic milieu (most often requiring an authoritarian polity). Its feasibility is based upon the existence of a rural subsistence agriculture fallback option for workers to ensure or supplement their access to the means of their survival, insofar as their wage is insufficient. Otherwise the direct producing class and hence the society would perish. A huge surplus population is also obligatory, as such working conditions are sure to exhaust the life capacities of the individual workers in extremely short order.

But the process by which capital cements the virtuous nexus of value augmentation, economic growth, and expanding social prosperity is through technologically revolutionizing the forces of production to raise the productive powers of labor. Labor productivity is increased incrementally in the course of business cycles. Major, qualitative transformation, which revolutionizes the forces of production substantively, occurs in capitalist economies in the context of phases of capitalist development. The change in use value complexes managed by capital from cotton factory production, through heavy steel and chemicals, and finally to the automobile consumer durable economy exemplifies these seismic shifts. In each, labor productivity is dramatically expanded. The fruit of this for workers is a cheapening of goods factoring into their wage basket which can also mean access to "new" products such as the automobile that betters living standards. For capital the benefit is higher throughput that, as per Postone's "treadmill effect" touched on in Chapter Three, facilitates greater augmentation of value per unit of time, hence the increase in relative surplus value.

What figures assembled by Lapavitsas on major advanced economies show, however, is that from the demise of the "golden age" and into the neoliberal decades no productivity enhancing revolutionizing of the forces of production, through which relative surplus value production is dynamically increased, has occurred. That fact is manifested in GDP growth becoming ever more anemic. It is also confirmed by actual diminution in the rates of productivity growth. This is the case for the US notwithstanding its brief productivity uptick during the ICT bubble. In the end there were no long lasting productivity gains from this and the US rate of productivity decline fell in line with that of Germany, Japan and the UK after 2003.[31] Calculations by Atkinson, Stewart, Andes and Ezell for the period 2000 to 2010 display a plummeting of US labor productivity in manufacturing by a full 11 percent. Manufacturing profits as a share of pre tax total corporate profits, already falling through the 1980s, accelerated their decline in the 2000s. In 2010 they amounted to 15 percent of the total (after dropping to 10 percent at the time of the meltdown).[32] By contrast pre tax financial profits rose to 40 percent of total US profits in 2005. In 2010 they had climbed back to 35 percent after their precipitous meltdown.[33]

Drawing together threads from material presented above in this chapter and Chapter Five yields a disconcerting picture. Specifically capitalist value augmentation through production-centered activity which produces *new* value, the ownership of which falls to the capitalist who then plies it in capital accumulation and value augmentation on an expanded scale, has stalled. Our backing for this claim is robust. Capital accumulation spurring investment is scant as our figures adduced from various perspectives and sources demonstrate. With no relative surplus value producing labor productivity and output enhancing investment, surplus value in manufacturing is increasingly extracted by what Osenton refers to as lowering the "bottom line". And, from that surplus value produced, much is siphoned off toward rents, interest and dividends. Precious little in the way of profits in the Marxist sense is making its way back into investment in new value and surplus value creating productive capacity.

Yet our prognosis on the dearth of new value accumulation is belied by the way obscene amounts of wealth are being amassed in ruling class hands. A quick look at a recent "wealth report" shows the global species of so-called ultra-high net worth individuals (UHNWIs), those with $30 million plus of investable wealth, growing! Their wealth, along with lesser cousins HNWIs, is estimated to top out globally at over $70 trillion by 2017. In North America the HNWI cohort as a whole, including the "millionaires next door" with $1 million plus in investable wealth, held $16.2 trillion in their hands in 2014.[34]

Oxfam has recently come forward with a startling report which shows that in 2015 "62 individuals had the same wealth as 3.6 billion people" (50 percent of the world's population!). And the wealth of the 62 "has risen by 44% in the five years since 2010", representing "an increase of more than half a trillion dollars…to $1.76 trillion". Not only that, 46 percent of all global income flowed into the clutches of the top 10 percent cohort during the neoliberal years 1988 to 2011. And not to be outdone, from 1978 to 2014 US CEO pay rose 997.2 percent.[35]

From the perspective of neoclassical economics and neoliberal ideological mouthpieces of the cohort of über rich – neoliberal mouthpieces abound in mainstream media and "ivy league" academia from where they spout their neoclassical banalities – this is all about capitalism or "the market". However, what we make crisply clear in this book is that the current plague of asymmetric wealth distribution has virtually nothing to do with capitalism (we have dealt with the decommodification of labor power aspect of this above). *Capitalist* profits derive from production. What has characterized the neoliberal era, however, is the vast enlargement of profits from financial gamesmanship which originate in "circulation" as monetary flows become detached from the production-centered economy and move into financial assets and speculation. Hence the phenomenon of "profiting without production" as Lapavitsas has it. And, at the most fundamental level, it is such financial profits diverted from circulation which are akin to ancient usury where money made money simply by loaning it with no socially redeeming purpose.[36]

Michael Hudson, as touched on above, stresses asset inflation and the credit/leverage gambits which animate the FIRE sector, so prominent in advanced economies. Hudson adopts the term "Asset-Price Gains" to capture flows of wealth accruing to property and financial asset ownership around which he sees the drawing of "a cloak of invisibility" preventing national accounting statistics from truly measuring the extent of wealth accrual. Hudson differentiates between "Asset-Price" and *capital* gains given how the rise in asset prices are accounted for by the latter only when property is sold and taxes paid. The transfer of asset titles through inheritance or the rise in asset values which underpin further asset purchases and the leverage deployed in these do not properly enter the calculus of FIRE sector profits.[37] Yet it was such asset-inflation and "asset inflationary credit" which contributed to both the housing and stock market bubble.

The roots of the distortion reside in the national income and product accounts (NIPA) which Hudson notes were created following the Great Depression and WWII to measure real production-centered categories of wages and profits in relation to real output. FIRE sector activities at the time were fit into this calculus as producers of imaginary output. This might have made some macroeconomic policy sense (despite its wrongheaded neoclassical ideological slant) when the FIRE sector played a minor economic role. However, under current conditions where both rents (monopoly and otherwise), asset prices, and financial casino arbitrage figure mountainously in wealth flows, NIPA convolutes economic assessments skewing both tax and regulatory policy in favor of FIRE as opposed to the real economy where most people earn their living, according to Hudson.[38]

Duncan Foley in the same vein examines the way NIPA corrupts analysis of the impact the meltdown of 2008-2009 continues to have upon GDP growth and employment. His work builds on Marx's distinction between "productive" and "unproductive labor". Quite simply, productive labor is the commodified labor power which produces value and surplus value (where wages are paid out of the value created). Unproductive labor (and we are bracketing here questions of the import to capitalism of variegated "unproductive" services, for example) does not directly produce value or surplus value but is remunerated out of surplus value and hence constitutes a "leakage" from the capitalist circuit of value augmentation.[39]

The "imputing" of an imaginary output or value added to FIRE activity, emphatically finance, for Foley, thus constitutes "double-counting". "Interest payments are a transfer of a part of surplus value appropriated in production, not the purchase of a good or service", he declares.[40] Ditto for the exorbitant salaries and bonuses paid to financial executives and functionaries, the raison d'être for which is purportedly the vast contribution of FIRE to national "output" and hence, GDP. Not only is Big Government and Big Bank policy support for the financial casino misdirected and a misallocation of social resources, but for Foley the NIPA calculus disguises both the depth of the meltdown fall and the true limpness of the so-called recovery. Nevertheless, Foley is still left with "the question of just how these remarkable financial incomes are generated economically".[41]

Part of the answer has already been given by Hudson. We will revisit it in the final section of this chapter in discussion of current Big Government and Big Bank action. The other part returns us to the point of Lapavitsas' quote at the beginning of the chapter. The "systemic" nature of finance resides in the existence of capitalist social relations of production such that the financial transactions always presuppose the viability of the generalized conditions of production and augmentation of value. The resurrection of usury in finance begins when profits made through circulation in the trading of idle M in money markets or trading of securities in capital markets no longer reflect claims that are "validated" by the production of surplus value and value augmentation itself.[42] They now depend on beggaring thy neighbor. This is what we describe in Chapter One as *expropriation* where money or incomes are stripped from the hand of one and dropped into the hand of another through financial gamesmanship with no socially redeeming purpose and a potentially socially ruinous "measurelessness".

The scourge of ancient usury reincarnated as "casino capital" is compounded when the expropriation of wealth predatorily feeds upon the household incomes of workers of various sorts under conditions of widespread expansion of mortgage and consumption lending in society. Casino play also generates a flow of financial profits from handling the pension and insurance funds which represent the savings of ordinary workers and households. Notwithstanding the complex architecture of securitization and the streaming of fees to sundry categories of financial intermediaries, it remains the case that it is the future wages of workers that will supposedly cover those liabilities that financial play swirls around and exorbitant financial profit is made. The trillions of dollars of arcane derivative instruments that featured in the bubbles of the 2000s and unceremonious meltdown of 2008-2009 were, despite all other factors fomenting the bubble, ultimately based upon worker debts. Bubble and burst cycles, we point to in Chapter Five, foment a deepening of the usurious expropriation dynamic by transferring significant value from one part of society (the "99 percent") to another (the "1 percent").[43]

Remember, the dissolution of relationship banking and morphing of erstwhile relationship commercial banks into active OTD shadow banking participants is both a manifestation of the putrefying capitalist production-centered economy and an instrument of its further disintegration. What increasingly remains is our aforementioned surrogate "economy" of faux wealth creation and Merchant of Venice expropriation. Idle M from all corners of the economy whether agglomerated in the hands of so-called institutional investors or the institutional cash pools we met in Chapter Five are increasingly drawn into the vortex of the Wall Street-based global casino. The central Wall Street casino mechanism of securitization and repo based liquidity manufacturing however must be perpetually replenished. And it must find more remnants of real production-centered economic life and real incomes upon which to feed..

Continued mortgage securitization under conditions of renewed inflation of global housing prices constitutes one avenue.[44] As Hudson notes, "about 80 percent of asset-price gains are for real estate".[45] Another path is to cultivate new candidates for the securitization orgy such as student loan asset-backed securitization (SLABS). By 2015 this had racked up around $1 trillion in outstanding liabilities.[46] SLABS entail similar predatory expropriation of incomes as mortgage and consumption loans where financial profits accruing to owners of the security are carved from the flesh of students as their ability to pay loans down diminishes with their shrinking income potentialities. Then there is what has been dubbed the "granddaddy" of all securitizations and finance bubbles – "the global government finance Bubble".[47] Let us turn to this.

"Gilded Tombs do Worms Enfold"

Inching toward an explanation of the current, unprecedented global malaise, a remarkable feat for an institution steeped in mainstream neoclassical economic thinking, the BIS in its last report of 2015 begins with the following words:

> Globally, interest rates have been extraordinarily low for an exceptionally long time, in nominal and inflation-adjusted terms, against any benchmark. Such low rates are the most remarkable symptom of a broader malaise in the global economy... The unthinkable risks becoming routine and being perceived as the new normal.
>
> This malaise has proved exceedingly difficult to understand... [I]t reflects to a considerable extent the failure to come to grips with financial booms and busts that leave deep and enduring economic scars.[48]

The IMF has embarrassingly been revising its global growth estimates down with its heady 2011 estimate for 2016 now proven to be a full 5 percent off the mark.[49] The most recent UN report on the global economy, *World Economic Situation and Prospects 2016*, has also weighed in, claiming the 2015 figures on growth of global GDP show a "stumbling" to "a mere 2.4 per cent". The report displays a global employment gap from the pre meltdown period to be 63.2 million in 2015 and projected to leap to 80.2 million by 2019. Currently total global unemployment is 203 million human beings with 44 million in OECD economies alone, a hike of 12 million from 2007.[50]

This doom and gloom scenario emanating from the usual neoliberal cheerleading suspects must at first glance seem to run counter to what neoliberal ideologues at the controls of Big Government and Big Bank have been telling us. Former FED Chair Ben Bernanke in his role as Princeton University economics professor had lectured Japan during its "lost decades" on the supposedly vital role of the money supply. Bernanke opined: "monetary authorities can issue as much money as they like... money issuance must ultimately raise the price level, even if nominal interest rates are bounded at zero".[51] Bernanke, Sekine notes, in thrall to his guru Milton Friedman, believed that if drastically reducing the money supply, strangling credit to the real economy, managed to slay the 1970s inflation dragon, taking the opposite course would fire it back up. But Friedman and Bernanke never grasped the distinction between idle M and active money, the specific means by which the former is converted into the latter for socially redeeming capitalist production-centered activity, and the effective demand that incomes so produced generate.[52]

Through QE machinations of varying dimensions the FED, EU central bank, Bank of England and Bank of Japan expanded their collective monetary base by $6 trillion between mid 2008 and early 2014.[53] The US monetary base alone exploded from around $874 billion in September 2008 to over $4 trillion in October 2015, only settling at $3.9 trillion in mid-February 2016.[54] Added together, the central bank assets in early 2016 of the US, EU, UK, Japan, plus Switzerland, Sweden and Denmark equal nearly 35 percent of global GDP. And even then major states have ratcheted down interest rates from ZIRP (zero interest rate policy) to NIRP (negative interest rate policy). In fact, the share of world GDP at NIRP is around 25 percent.[55] Not only is capital no longer scarce, but it stands ready to be lent for less than nothing!

Yet all this frenetic QE "money printing" created only Himalayan idle balances adding to global idle M which, across the neoliberal decades, flows increasingly one way – into the surrogate casino "economy". While global debt securities have expanded in total from over $35 trillion in 2001 to around $100 trillion in 2014, Big Government debt securities make up the greatest single part of the increase, more than that of the financial sector.[56] Respected financial analyst Doug Noland, updating his earlier prognosis on the "granddaddy" of all bubbles, "the global government finance Bubble", now is talking about a "Global Government Finance Quasi-Capitalism" bubble. His thinking runs along a similar tangent as our Chapter Five allusion to the FED playing the part not only of lender of last resort to bolster commercial TNBs but "broker-dealer of last resort" to backstop repo mechanisms and ongoing diverse gambits by investment banks and other PFIs. Noland, therefore, puts things in the starkest terms: "governments globally have now overtly commandeered...

[s]ecurities markets... Trillions of securities have been monetized. Prices and risk perceptions throughout global securities and derivatives markets have been perverted like never before... Never have such enormous quantities of global securities and financial instruments been perceived as safe or low-risk ('money-like')".[57]

Notwithstanding the trillions and possibly quadrillions (accounting for derivatives) of dollars in securitization and asset play which would surely seem to shout out warnings of impending inflation, advanced economies actually teeter on the edge of *deflation*. This is the endgame of economies managed by capitalists without capitalism where wealth can only be agglomerated by expropriation which inevitably gets more ferocious. Chief economist at Nomura Research Institute, Richard Koo, shows that if August 2008 is set as the baseline at 100 points, the spiking of the monetary base through QE in the US reached 479 points by July 2015. Yet credit and loans to real economic activity languish at 115 points at that point. This is the case as well despite M2 money supply (M1 cash and checking accounts plus time deposits and money market mutual funds) much of the time deposits held by commercial banks, rising to 157 points. In other words, precious little funding currently makes its way into remnants of the capitalist production-centered economy. All the trillions of dollars in collective central bank QE huffing and puffing predictably generates only "wealth effects" of luxury consumption, as Koo puts it.[58]

The so-called wealth effect is itself a product of the asset-inflation and asset-inflationary credit that is the focus of Hudson's writing. In this game the TNBs and PFIs essentially get their money for nothing (or less than nothing) as per our discussion of the surrogate economy of bubble and burst cycles. Again, deflationary tendencies lurked in the earliest corrupting of the capitalist-social macroeconomic role of relationship banking and the aimless pooling of idle M. Such tendencies are only exacerbated when idle M commences its own operations in speculative orgies. Deflationary trends are even further bolstered as major shares of enduring surplus value production flow toward rent and interest.

Even "classical" economist David Ricardo well knew that if rents ate away at investible profits (that portion of surplus value destined for production-centered investment in Marx's terms) the economy would drift into a "stationary state".[59] QE does nothing to change this.

Duncan puts the current policy conundrum in terms of "fire and ice".[60] To pull the plug risks a frightening deflationary spiral. Continuing QE type liquidity creation, even if funds are not readily converted into active money and funneled into remnants of the real production-centered income generating economy, still risks the possibility of hyperinflation and select currency collapses spreading havoc through the global economy. On the one hand, as government debt machinations are ultimately liabilities of citizens, the exploding of these liabilities never to be covered by real economic income generation mandates policies of *austerity* across advanced economies. For Duncan, austerity already means economic collapse.[61] On the other hand, the continued building of securitization and casino asset gambits on mortgage and credit debt of workers and students deepens the dynamic of expropriation. Both of the above are carving the "final pounds of flesh" from the bones of humanity.

In my previous work, *The Evil Axis of Finance*, I argued that so-called globalization and its cousin "financialization" were simply sexed up terms for the US morphing into a *global economy* with the world's largest debt – Mariana-Trench-sized current, capital account and trade deficits, near zero savings rate – yet managing to ride high in the global economic saddle through the fact of the dollar as the global hub currency. The full spectrum of pathologies infecting the global economy which the present book has covered had their origins in the US economy in the neoliberal decades following the Volcker coup. By ramming policies of "liberalization" and "deregulation" down the throats of governments around the world the US empowered Wall Street to act as a global command center for managing the world's idle M in surrogate economy casino operations. Wall Street therefore distributed the cycles of bubbles and bursts originated in the US economy to the world. Rotating meltdowns from Latin America to East Asia, Russia, to the US itself, and back around again, are evidence of this.

While abdicating its production-centered economy the US intended itself to be the primary beneficiary of this excrescence. Of course we are not talking about US "Main Street", or its real economy, which, along with the world Wall Street shapes, is trapped on the road to serfdom. We can thus be assured that the US über rich and their political lap dogs will fight tooth and nail to maintain the current course, whatever the ultimate cost to humanity.

The two domestic economy remedies being bandied about in Left (including Left liberal and Keynesian Marxist) circles are therefore extremely quixotic. One, the most ubiquitously called for, is a return to fiscal policy making as key to managing the economy.[62] The other, more of a niche view, entails variations on a theme of shrinking banks, breaking up banks, fostering responsible "public banking" or straight out nationalizing banking.[63] Democratic Party presidential challenger in 2016, Bernie Sanders, has even been touted as throwing his weight behind the latter.[64]

Though the aforementioned writings are ambivalent on the *kind* of economy they are talking about, which brings to bear all the important questions addressed in this book about how different economies, including capitalism, ensure the viable material reproduction of a human society in the first place, we may infer that they are still talking about a capitalist economy of some sort, when the time for that has already passed. Capitalist economies already had "public" banks in the capitalist-social role of commercial, relationship banks under 19th century laissez faire conditions, where gold constituted the monetary reserve, as discussed in Chapter Three. Then, commercial banks performed their "public" service role as market forces determined an "optimal" supply of money; the relationship banks accordingly lent funds "socialized" in their hands for determinate income and social wealth generating purposes.

Problems flowed not from the specific institutions but

from the contradictions of capitalism itself as a mode of organizing human economic affairs. The rise of Big Government and Big Bank with its fiat money regime, reserves of government securities, and dependence upon monetary policy levers to manage the money supply, was part and parcel of the transformation of capitalism as it struggled to manage new "heavier" more "roundabout" forms of use value production for its abstract purpose of value augmentation. Capitalism, hence, as accumulation shifted to the "golden age" automobile society became "less capitalist" to put this in the simplest terms. But even that could not forestall the inevitable. That capitalism was destined to be outpaced by history. The early bloating pools of idle M with no possibility of ever being converted into real capital were a symptom of this.

Hence, resurrecting fiscal policy in any meaningful way will require a substantive transformation in social infrastructure, forms of energy deliverance, types of transportation, geospatial reorganizations of communities, and the list goes on and on. It will also necessitate new forms of fiat money such as pioneered by community currencies, local exchange and employment systems, around the world. These will be needed to cushion the impact for human communities of the unwinding of pathologies currently fomented by reckless state fiat money issuance. This in turn demands significant restructuring of democratic political systems and renewed popular empowerment to have any hope of being achieved. Of course, the foregoing is the topic of another book.[65] The present book has made the case in as clear a fashion as possible, why the time has long passed for band-aid "policy" solutions. Humanity faces a choice between reinventing human economic life around new modes of socialism or the descent into chaos and barbarism.

Endnotes

1   Frederick Engels, *Anti-Dühring* Part II, 1877, http://www.marxists.org/archive/marx/works/1877/anti-duhring/ch24.htm.

2   Robert Albritton, "A phase of transition away from capitalism", in Westra, Badeen and Albritton (eds.) *The Future of Capitalism After the Financial Crisis*, p. 152.
3   OECD Data, Central Government, accessed February 10 2016, https://data.oecd.org/gga/general-government-spending.htm
4   Michael Hudson, "Banking Wasn't Meant to Be Like This", January 27 2012, http://michael-hudson.com/2012/01/banking-wasnt-meant-to-be-like-this/.
5   Lapavitsas, *Profiting Without Production*, pp. 108-9.
6   Sekine, "Fiat Money and how to combat debt deflation".
7   McKinsey Global Institute, *Debt and (not much) deleveraging*, p.8.
8   Ratna Sahay et al. "Rethinking Financial Deepening: Stability and Growth in Emerging Markets", IMF Staff Discussion Note, May 2015, https://www.imf.org/external/pubs/ft/sdn/2015/sdn1508.pdf.
9   Altvater and Hubner, "The End of The U.S. American Empire?" pp. 62-3.
10 Osenton, *The Death of Demand*, pp. 90ff.
11 Osenton, *The Death of Demand*, pp. 234-6.
12 Henwood, *Wall Street*, pp. 73-4.
13 William Lazonick and Mary O'Sullivan, "Maximizing shareholder value: a new ideology for corporate governance", *Economy and Society*, 29, 1 (2000).
14 Thomas T. Sekine, "Towards a Critique of Bourgeois Economics", in Bell (ed.) *Towards a Critique of Bourgeois Economics*, p. 265.
15 Kindleberger and Aliber, *Manias, Panics and Crashes*, p. 137.
16 Henwood, *Wall Street*, pp. 72-3.
17 Andrew Glyn, *Capitalism Unleashed: Finance, Globalization, and Welfare* (Oxford: Oxford University Press, 2006) pp. 56-7.
18 Westra, *The Evil Axis of Finance*, p. 112.
19 Kindleberger and Aliber, *Manias, Panics and Crashes*, pp. 137-9.
20 Kindleberger and Aliber, *Manias, Panics and Crashes*, pp. 141-2.
21 Lapavitsas, *Profiting Without Production*, pp. 181-4.
22 Milberg and Winkler, *Outsourcing Economics*, pp. 210-3.
23 Milberg and Winkler, *Outsourcing Economics*, pp. 233-4.
24 Milberg and Winkler, *Outsourcing Economics*, pp. 220-2.
25 Hudson, *Killing the Host*, p. 124.
26 Martin Hesse and Anne Seith, "Feeding the Bubble: Is the Next Crash Brewing?" *Spiegel Online*, December 03 2013, http://www.spiegel.de/international/business/cheap-central-bank-money-contributes-to-dangerous-bubbles-a-936823.html.
27 Deloitte, M&A Trends Report 2015, http://www2.deloitte.com/content/dam/Deloitte/us/Documents/mergers-acqisitions/us-ma-

trends-report15-042115.pdf.
28   Sally Bakewell, "The $29 Trillion Corporate Debt Hangover That Could Spark a Recession", *Bloomberg Business*, January 27 2016, http://www.bloomberg.com/news/articles/2016-01-28/some-29-trillion-later-the-corporate-debt-boom-looks-exhausted.
29   See Marx, Marx, Part 3 and 4, *Capital*, Volume 1.
30   Libcom Blog, "The poetry and brief life of a Foxconn worker: Xu Lizhi (1990-2014)", https://libcom.org/blog/xulizhi-foxconn-suicide-poetry.
31   Lapavitsas, *Profiting Without Production*, pp. 174ff.
32   Atkinson, Stewart, Andes and Ezell, "Worse Than the Great Depression: What Experts Are Missing About American Manufacturing Decline", pp. 44, 58.
33   Lapavitsas, *Profiting Without Production*, p. 214.
34   Capgemini & RBC Wealth Management, 2015 World Wealth Report, https://www.worldwealthreport.com/.
35   Oxfam, "An Economy for the 1%", 210 Oxfam Briefing Paper, January 18 2016, https://www.oxfam.org/sites/www.oxfam.org/files/file_attachments/bp210-economy-one-percent-tax-havens-180116-en_0.pdf.
36   See Lapavitsas, *Profiting Without Production*, p. 145.
37   Hudson, *Killing the Host*, pp. 161-2.
38   Hudson, *Killing the Host*, pp. 88-97.
39   Duncan K. Foley, "The Political Economy of U.S. Output and Employment 2001-2010", Schwartz Center for Economic Policy Analysis, The New School for Social Research, Working Paper 2011-5, http://www.economicpolicyresearch.org/images/docs/research/political_economy/Foley%20revised%20WP%202011_5.pdf, pp. 7-8.
40   Foley, "The Political Economy of U.S. Output and Employment 2001-2010", p. 9.
41   Foley, "The Political Economy of U.S. Output and Employment 2001-2010", p. 11.
42   Lapavitsas, *Profiting Without Production*, pp. 145-6.
43   Lapavitsas, *Profiting Without Production*, pp. 144-5, 166-8.
44   Robin Harding, "IMF sounds global housing alarm", *Financial Times*, June 11 2014, http://www.ft.com/intl/cms/s/0/91bf83de-f17f-11e3-a2da-00144feabdc0.html.
45   Hudson, *Killing the Host*, p. 162.
46   Susanne Soederberg, "The Student Loan Crisis and the Debtfare State", *Dollars & Sense*, May/June 2015, http://www.dollarsandsense.org/archives/2015/0515soederberg.html.
47   Doug Noland, "Uninsurable Risks", *SafeHaven*, June 28 2013, http://

www.safehaven.com/article/30320/uninsurable-risks.

48 BIS, 85th Annual Report, June 28 2015, http://www.bis.org/publ/arpdf/ar2015_ec.pdf.

49 Myles Udland, "This is the most depressing chart in the world", *Business Insider*, February 24 2016, http://www.businessinsider.com/imf-global-economic-revisions-2016-2.

50 UN, *World Economic Situation and Prospects 2016*, New York 2016, http://www.un.org/en/development/desa/policy/wesp/wesp_current/2016wesp_ch1_en.pdf, pp. vi, 6-7.

51 Ben Bernanke, "Japanese Monetary Policy: A Case of Self-Induced Paralysis?" in Ryoichi Mikitani and Adam S. Posen (eds.), *Japan's Financial Crisis and Its Parallels to the U.S. Experience* (Washington, DC: Institute for International Economics, 2000), p. 158.

52 Sekine, "Fiat Money and how to combat debt deflation".

53 *Economist Intelligence Unit*, "The end isn't nigh: Central bank challenges as the era of cheap money enters a new phase", 2013, http://www.eiuresources.com/EndOfCheapMoney/ p. 4.

54 Federal Reserve Bank of St Louis, Economic Research, accessed on February 27 2016, https://research.stlouisfed.org/fred2/series/BASE.

55 Martin Wolf, "Helicopter drops might not be far away", *Financial Times*, February 23 2016, http://www.ft.com/cms/s/0/9b3c71f8-d97f-11e5-a72f-1e7744c66818.html.

56 UN, *World Economic Situation and Prospects 2016*, p. 100.

57 Doug Noland, "Out of Thin Air, *Credit Bubble Bulletin*, May 29 2015, http://creditbubblebulletin.blogspot.ca/2015/05/my-weekly-commentary-out-of-thin-air.html.

58 David Scutt, "RICHARD KOO: 'Struggle between markets and central banks has only just begun'", *Business Insider UK*, September 16 2015, http://uk.businessinsider.com/richard-koo-struggle-between-markets-and-central-banks-has-only-just-begun-2015-9.

59 Thomas Sekine, "A Thought on Recent Trends in the World Economy", The Uno Newsletter: Rejuvenating Marxian Economics through Uno Theory, Vol. II, No. 9, November 2012, http://www.unotheory.org/en/news_II_9.

60 Duncan, *The New Depression*, pp. 149ff.

61 Duncan, *The New Depression*, p. 170.

62 See for example Mike Whitney, "Seven Years of Monetary Quackery; Can the Fed Admit it Was Wrong Yet?" *Information Clearing House*, January 28 2016, http://www.informationclearinghouse.info/article44073.htm.

63 Ellen Brown, "The Populist Revolution: Bernie and Beyond", *Information Clearing House*, January 27, 2016, http://www.

informationclearinghouse.info/article44063.htm.
64 Zach Cartwright, "Bernie Sanders SLAMS Wall Street in Major Speech That Has Bankers and Hillary Panicking", *Portside*, January 5 2016, http://portside.org/2016-01-09/bernie-sanders-slams-wall-street-major-speech-has-bankers-and-hillary-panicking.
65 See Richard Westra, *Exit from Globalization* (London: Routledge, 2015).

INDEX

A

asset backed security (ABS) 186, 187, 189, 190, 192, 195
adjustable rate mortgage (ARM) 188, 190

B

banking
    commercial/relationship 102, 103, 104, 105, 107, 108, 120, 143, 144, 156, 175, 178, 181, 182, 183, 184, 186, 187, 191, 192, 207, 209, 223, 226, 228
    investment 143, 144, 176, 181, 184, 186, 189, 190, 191, 192, 193, 207, 213, 225
    originate-to-distribute (OTD) 187, 191, 214, 223
Bank for International Settlements (BIS) 149, 179, 223, 232
Bretton Woods International Monetary System (BWIMS) 144-146, 148-150, 159, 177, 180

C

capital (equity/stock) market 107, 129, 130, 132, 135, 137, 138, 148, 157, 175, 176, 181, 184, 192, 204, 212, 213, 214, 220, 222
capitalism 13, 14, 16, 19, 20, 23, 24, 30, 31, 32, 33, 35, 37, 41, 42, 43, 47, 52, 64, 65, 68, 71-4,78, 82, 83, 86, 88, 89, 91, 95, 99, 103, 107, 114-7, 123, 130, 136, 143, 146, 147, 158, 160, 171, 174, 178, 187, 196, 202-6, 210, 220, 221, 228, 229
capitalist bases (*see also* general norms of economic life) 82-96
capitalists without capitalism 25, 26, 210, 226
collateralized debt obligation (CDO) 189, 190, 192
commercial capital 105-6, 108, 109, 118, 128, 156
Community Reinvestment Act (CRA) 188
collateralized debt obligation (CDO) 189-90
corporate capital (see also TNCs) 136-140, 142
credit default swaps (CDS) 189-90
Creditism 178, 196
crisis (economic) 19, 27, 63, 74, 94, 109, 122, 123, 125, 150, 161, 162, 181, 183, 190, 192, 203, 208

D

Depository Institutions Deregulation and Monetary Control Act (DIDMCA) 182
downsize and distribute 214
Drucker, Peter 22-3, 27
Duménil, Gérard 134, 135, 159, 161

Duncan, Richard 177-8, 184-5, 195-6, 227

E

economic bases (see also general norms of economic life) 47, 64, 88
economic viability of human society (see also general norms of economic life) 18, 21,24, 32, 43, 47, 51, 52, 82, 83, 91, 92, 95, 102, 128, 157, 168, 171, 172, 196, 204
efficient markets hypothesis (EMH) 212
entrepreneurial profit 106, 107
European Union (EU) 19, 167, 170, 190

F

Federal Deposit Insurance Corporation (FDIC) 143, 149, 183
Federal Reserve System (FED) 131, 133, 143, 149, 182, 186, 194, 195, 213, 224, 225
feudal bases (see also general norms of economic life) 46-53
finance capital 130, 137, 175, 176
finance, insurance and real estate (FIRE) 208, 220, 221
Foley, Duncan 221
foreign direct investment (FDI) 147, 148, 162, 163, 165

G

Geisst, Charles 62, 179
general norms of economic life (see also economic bases) 47, 56, 69, 74, 82, 85, 86, 88, 89, 90, 96, 139, 160, 168, 169, 178, 204, 206
Gerding, Eric 179
global value chain (GVC) 164-167, 173, 174, 180, 207, 214
Graeber, David 28-9, 50, 52
gross domestic product (GDP) 22, 25, 26, 126, 128, 134, 144, 149, 165, 166, 170, 177, 178, 180, 183, 185, 190, 194, 206, 207, 210, 212-215, 218, 221, 224, 225
General Motors Acceptance Corporation (GMAC) 137, 210
government sponsored enterprise (GSE) 186, 188-190, 192, 200
Great Depression 131, 133, 134, 135, 137, 139, 141, 142, 148, 170, 187, 204, 213, 220

H

Hegel, G.W. F. 25
high net worth individuals (HNWIs) 219
Hudson, Michael 101, 131, 208, 215, 220, 221, 222, 223, 226

I

idle money (idle M) 23, 24, 25, 27, 35, 103, 104, 105, 106, 107, 108, 118, 126, 128, 144, 145, 147, 157, 161, 170, 175, 176, 180, 181, 184, 187, 192, 194, 207, 208, 209, 210, 213, 222, 223, 225, 226, 227, 229
imperialism 126, 131, 140
information and computer technology (ICT) 20-22, 160, 161, 165, 166, 170-173, 207, 213, 214, 218
International Monetary Fund (IMF) 146, 150, 159, 162, 165, 178-181, 200, 201, 224, 230, 231
import substitution industrialization (ISI) 161, 162
industrial capital 42, 85, 86, 88, 93, 97, 100, 101, 102, 103, 104, 105, 106, 107, 108, 109, 110, 158

interest 25, 26, 60, 61, 63, 64, 65, 94, 97, 98, 99, 101, 103, 104, 105, 106, 107, 108, 109, 126, 129-30, 143-4, 149, 157, 161, 162, 172, 175-6, 179, 180, 182, 185, 187, 189, 192-3, 194-5, 206, 207, 216-7, 219, 221, 224, 225, 226

L

Lapavitsas, Costas 119, 130, 176, 193, 208, 218, 220, 222
Lévy, Dominique 134, 135, 159, 161
loan capital (see also usury) 11, 25, 41, 47, 61, 67, 82, 88, 104, 156, 158, 175, 208
  global meltdown (of 2008-2009) 22, 26, 35, 174, 178, 183, 190, 191, 193, 194, 195, 214, 218, 219, 221, 222, 224, 228

M

Marx, Karl 14-8, 20, 21, 25, 27, 28, 29, 30, 33, 35, 41-2, 68, 71, 72, 73, 74, 78, 82, 83, 86, 88, 89, 90, 92, 93, 94, 96, 97, 98, 101, 105, 110, 115, 116, 117, 121, 122, 126, 139, 158, 192, 202-3, 205, 215, 221, 227
merchant capital 78, 79, 81, 86, 88, 156, 208
mergers and acquisitions (M&A) 183, 211, 214, 215, 230
Minsky, Hyman 147-8, 150, 163, 177, 185, 210
MM theory 147, 211, 212
Mohun, Simon 193-4
money market 104, , 105, 106, 129, 130, 157, 175, 176, 181, 182, 186, 192, 193, 207, 209, 211, 222, 226
monopoly capital 137, 141
mortgage backed security (MBS) 189, 190

N

necessary labor 48-51, 85, 89-90, 92, 98, 126, 168, 171, 173, 174, 206, 216, 217
negative interest rate policies (NIRP) 26, 225
Noland, Doug 225-6
non-equity mode (NEM) 165, 166, 214

O

off-balance sheet (OBS) 179, 184, 210
Organization for Economic Cooperation and Development (OECD) 22, 38, 139, 144, 152, 162, 169, 180, 187, 206, 224, 230
Organization of Petroleum Exporting Countries (OPEC) 148, 161, 180
Osenton, Tom 160, 211, 219

P

Piketty, Thomas 13-4, 17, 18, 107, 172, 215
Polanyi, Karl 15, 29, 47, 50, 51, 52, 59
Postone, Moishe 98, 99, 218
private financial intermediary (PFI) 24, 25, 182, 186, 190, 195, 207, 211, 225, 226
productive labor 50, 221
profit (see also value augmentation) 11, 16, 17, 22, 23, 24, 25, 26, 30, 32, 33, 35, 60, 62, 63, 74, 75, 80, 81, 83, 86, 87, 90, 91, 92, 93, 94, 96, 97, 99, 102, 103, 105, 106, 108, 109, 115, 118, 125, 129, 130, 135, 138, 142, 146, 147, 156, 167, 168, 170, 171, 172, 175, 176, 180, 185, 193, 202, 207, 209, 211, 212,

Index | 237

216, 217, 219, 220, 222, 227

Q

quantitative easing (QE) 26, 225-227
Queen Elizabeth II 26

R

reciprocity 51-2, 53, 87, 88
redistribution 50-3, 87, 88, 155, 158, 206
rent 22, 56, 57, 58, 59, 97, 98, 107, 172, 194, 207, 216, 217, 219
repurchase agreement (REPO) 191-193, 223, 225
Ricardo, David 27, 28, 100, 227

S

Savings & Loan (S&L) 182, 183
Securities and Exchange Commission (SEC) 182, 189
Sekine, Thomas T. 34, 94, 108, 147, 158, 163, 209, 210, 224
shareholder value 212, 214, 215
socially necessary labor 90-2, 168, 171
special economic zone (SEZs) 165, 166, 173, 211
special investment vehicle (SIV) 191, 210
Smith, Adam 27, 28, 33, 40, 100, 114, 116, 133
Stiglitz, Joseph 13, 172
Strange, Susan 24
student loan asset-backed securitization (SLABS) 223
surplus labor 45, 46, 48, 50, 52, 56, 89, 90, 98, 216
surplus value 89, 90, 97, 98, 101, 102, 106, 107, 109, 156, 158, 169, 171, 172, 173, 194, 216, 217, 218, 219, 221, 222, 226, 227
Syriza 205

T

there is no alternative (TINA) 23, 32
transnational bank (TNB) 23, 25, 144, 150, 161, 162, 178, 179, 181, 182, 184, 186, 188, 189, 190, 191, 192, 194, 195, 207, 208, 211, 225, 226
transnational corporation (TNC) 21-23, 25, 117, 137-142, 144, 146-150, 157, 159, 162-167, 169, 172, 180, 182, 185, 195, 206, 207, 209-212, 214-216

U

ultra-high net worth individuals (UHNWI) 219
United States (US) 18-20, 22, 27, 38, 119, 122-126, 128, 131-140, 143-150, 159, 161, 162, 164, 166-171, 174, 177, 178, 180-191, 194, 195, 197, 206, 207, 210-214, 218, 219, 225-228
Uno, Kōzō 7
unproductive labor 221
use value 29, 30, 32, 33, 34, 59, 66, 67, 72, 86, 87, 95, 96, 105, 114, 115, 116, 117, 118, 121, 122, 124, 125, 129, 133, 136, 141, 147, 155, 158, 160, 168, 169, 171, 175, 203, 204, 218
usury (see also loan capital) 11, 23, 24, 25, 35, 36, 58, 60-3, 64-7, 74, 77, 99-100, 104, 115, 156, 175, 182, 215, 220, 222

V

value 29, 30, 33, 66, 74, 86, 89, 90, 91, 92, 96, 97, 98, 99, 114, 115, 116, 117, 158, 192, 208-9, 217, 219, 221
value augmentation (see also profit) 73, 80, 86, 87, 91, 96, 97, 98, 99, 102, 103, 104, 105, 106,

108, 110, 115, 116, 117, 122,
129, 135, 138, 156, 157, 158,
160, 169, 171, 175, 176, 181,
203, 205, 206, 209, 216, 218,
219, 221, 222, 229

W

Wall Street 132, 150, 162, 174, 176,
183, 186, 191, 194, 195, 196,
212, 213, 223, 227, 228
World Bank (WB) 146, 159, 162,
165, 178-181
World War I (WWI) 123, 127, 131,
133, 134
World War II (WWII) 136, 137, 139,
140, 142-144, 147, 173, 176,
187, 220

Z

zero interest rate policies (ZIRP) 26,
225